Data Analysis: The Key to Data Base Design

ALSO FROM QED®

MANAGEMENT
Strategic Planning for Information Systems
Applying Business Planning Techniques to Information Systems
Managing for Productivity in Data Processing
Effective Methods of EDP Quality Assurance
Managing Systems Maintenance
A Guide to EDP Performance Management
The Handbook for Data Center Management
The Data Center Disaster Consultant
Handbook for Data Processing Educators

TECHNICAL
Computer Control and Audit
Humanizing Office Automation: The Impact of Ergonomics on Productivity
Handbook of Screen Format Design
Architecture and Implementation of Large Scale IBM Computer Systems
1001 Questions and Answers to Help You Prepare for the CDP® Exam
Handbook of COBOL Techniques
High Level COBOL Programming
Humanized Input: Techniques for Reliable Keyed Input
CICS/VS Command Level Reference Guide for COBOL Programmers
EDP System Development Guidelines
Time Is of the Essence: The DP Professional's Guide to Getting the Right Things Done
Managing Data Base: Four Critical Factors
Data Base Analysis: The Key to Data Base Design

DATA BASE
Data Base Management Systems in the Eighties
Creating and Planning the Corporate Data Base System Project
Data Base Techniques
IMS Design and Implementation Techniques
Design Guide for CODASYL Data Base Management Systems
The Data Base Monograph Series
Data Base Systems: A Practical Reference
Information Resource/Data Dictionary Systems

TELECOMM/DATA COMM
Transnational Data Regulation: The Realities
Distributed Processing: Current Practice and Future Developments

THE QED® PERSONAL COMPUTING SERIES
The IBM Personal Computer: What You Should Know
Learning to Use the IBM Personal Computer
How to Buy Software for Personal Computers
Peachtree Software for Personal Computers: Introduction & Description

QED® LEADING EDGE LEARNING SOFTWARE
PC PLUS: Learn The IBM PC . . . Plus Computing Fundamentals
DOS PLUS: Learn to Use IBM PC DOS

FOR INFORMATION, CONTACT:
QED® Information Sciences, Inc.
QED Plaza • P.O. Box 181
Wellesley, Massachusetts 02181

Data Analysis: The Key to Data Base Design

Richard C. Perkinson

QED® Information Sciences, Inc.
Wellesley, Massachusetts

I would like to thank several publishers for permitting me to use material from their publications. Figure 1.2 is reprinted from the December 8, 1980, issue of COMPU-TERWORLD, copyright 1980 by CW Communications/Inc. Figure 1.8 was adapted with the permission of Nolan & Norton Company, Lexington, Mass., and based on Richard L. Nolan, "Managing the Crisis in Data Processing," *Harvard Business Review*, March-April 1979. Specified brief excerpts in Chapter 2 of this book are from *Management: Tasks, Responsibilities, Practices*, by Peter F. Drucker (copyright 1973, 1974, Peter F. Drucker) and are reprinted by permission of Harper & Row, Publishers, Inc. Figure 8.8 was adapted with the permission of Cullinet Software, Inc., Westwood, Mass.

Library of Congress Catalog Card Number 83-63212
ISBN 0-89435-105-2

Printed in the United States of America.

Acknowledgments

I wish to thank several people at QED Information Sciences, Inc., without whom this book would never have come to such a successful fruition.

First, let me thank Peters P. Jones, my colleague at QED, who reviewed every word of this text. The "how to" list found in Appendix E is almost entirely his creation. It synthesizes beautifully all the steps in data analysis. I know the readers of this text will appreciate that contribution when they do their first data analysis. I would like to acknowledge another colleague, Parker Shannon, who did the original planning on which the banking case study in Appendix F is based.

Second, I wish to acknowledge the many contributions and hard work of QED's art department, in particular, Donna St. Martin and Sybil Norwood, whose artistic and timely contributions are greatly appreciated by this author.

Last, to the many students in my classes who have made countless suggestions and improvements in this manuscript, I say thank you.

PREFACE

The inability of most data base designers to articulate to their user community the steps necessary to design a data base successfully, or even, in a basic sense, to group data together, is the reason for this book. This inability to articulate is for the most part unintentional on the part of the designers. The designers themselves have never really been asked to describe how they do it. They offer excuses, saying the task is "intuitively obvious," or that their techniques are "based on my eleven years experience," or some other such remark and never really analyze for anyone how they do what they do.

Implementation of the data base designs have gotten bogged down in the syntax and technology of the data base management system (DBMS) chosen. Lost in the shuffle are the user and the application—the raison d'être for the whole thing. Unnecessary constraints are applied to the design by the data base administrator (DBA) or designer based solely on the methodology of the DBMS, not the restrictions of the data.

This book is an effort to relieve some of this user discomfort with data base. Through the technique of *data analysis*, users will be able to understand data and communicate to the designer their needs more accurately. For the designer, data analysis provides a simple means to a desired end. It allows reliable prognostication of the performance and reliability of a design while it is still in the paper and pencil stage. The products of the handbook can easily be mapped to any commercially available

DBMS. The entire technique is a five-step process from initial data analysis to final physical data base design.

In addition to espousing data analysis and data base design techniques, this text will cover what the role of data is in an organization; when and how to use data dictionaries; and why and how to use data administration and the data base administration function.

In short, this book is an attempt to bridge the gap between structured analysis and design and management disciplines, such as business systems planning (BSP) or long-range systems planning (LRSP), by providing a simple method of going from one to the other in either direction by following a few simple rules.

CONTENTS

12 Designing for the Inverted List Structure 193

ADABAS Schema (Inverted List Structure)
System 2000 Schema—Fully Inverted List Structures
ADABAS Subschema
System 2000 Subschema
Inverted List Data Integrity
ADABAS Operations and Performance Design
System 2000's Operation and Performance
Review

Appendixes

FIGURES

Part One

DATA ANALYSIS

1 Introduction to Data Analysis

Given for one instant an intelligence which could comprehend all the forces by which nature is animated and the respective positions of the beings which compose it, if moreover this intelligence were vast enough to submit this data to analysis, it would embrace in the same formula both the movements of the largest bodies in the universe and those of the lightest atom; to it nothing would be uncertain, and the future as the past would be present to its eyes.

Pierre Simon de Laplace
Théorie Analytique des Probabilités, 1812

WHAT PART I IS ALL ABOUT

This chapter will introduce *data analysis,* a practical methodology for gathering information and converting it into a logical data model. The stress of this methodology is on its practical aspects. Not only can the results of data analysis be applied to the design of standard file systems and data base systems, but also the products of the methodology fill information gaps in system and program documentation.

Data analysis is a bottom-up process that works with and analyzes the products of the application system for which the data files are being designed. Being bottom-up implies it is opposite of functional or structured analysis, which is "top-down." Data analysis and functional analysis do, however, work hand in hand. Data analysis requires top-down analysis first. How else would the products of a system be analyzed unless functional analysis has revealed what those products are and what they look like? (Chapter 2 describes the methodology behind top-down design.)

Products of a system is intended to mean the physical output of an application. As an example, if the application being designed were to accomplish the order-processing function, then sample products might be invoices, orders, bills of lading, and inventory reports. If there are on-line systems components, then the various screen report formats would be considered products also.

It is the goal of data analysis to examine these products and, through a step-by-step process, convert the data into a detailed model of how the data in the system

3

interact. The process to be followed in the text is really quite mechanical, yet the results of the process can be quite astounding as to the implications upon file design.

DATA IDENTIFICATION PROCESSES

The data-oriented approach to data base design, utilizing a relational conceptual data model, is the heart and soul of the data analysis methodology. In the past few years substantial numbers of authors have been writing on data analysis and the relational data model. Of particular note are the works of S. Atre, C. W. Bachman, P. Chen, T. DeMarco, C. Finkelstein, C. Gane and T. Sarson, J. Yanko, J. King and W. J. Waghorn. Their works are documented in the bibliography. A comparative analysis of their contributions to the data analysis methodology is offered here. This methodology consists of the following four stages:

Stage 1 *Data Collection and Normalization*
Gather and break data up into small logical groups called entities, using normalization, thus making each entity as independent as possible.

Stage 2 *Entity-relationship (E-R) Mapping*
Associate the entities that are identified with each other (i.e., related) using E-R mapping techniques.

Stage 3 *Transaction Analysis*
Determine the path of usage, the types of usage (read or update), and the entry point of each transaction for the various entities.

Stage 4 *Data modeling*
Draw a logical structure (schema) and/or structure (subschema) using logical synthesis. Then utilize a load matrix to prejudice entity placement within the data model.

To begin collecting and normalizing data, first group data into relations by examining the paperwork of the organization being analyzed. These documents and reports may be produced manually or by computer. Form the relations on the basis of the document being examined rather than on any internal grouping of data you may find within the application producing the document. More often than not, the output report reflects a better understanding of the data relationships. Discuss the user's data with the user. Keep in mind that although users may have a limited understanding of data processing, their fresh outlook on the data may open new vistas for you as the analyst.

You can then normalize the data into *third normal form*. This aspect of data analysis is the key to creating the small logical groups necessary to complete stage 1 of data analysis. (This topic will be covered fully in Chapter 3.)

Stage 2 is to build relational maps from the rules by which an organization operates. Resolve the one-to-one, one-to-many, and many-to-many relationships that exist within the groups. (Relational mapping is extensively covered in Chapter 4.)

Next, perform a transaction-by-transaction analysis, stage 3, in order to define the usage paths that operate across the relationships that were established in the pervious step. Thus the third stage is really a subjective, *qualitative analysis*. Each transaction is reviewed individually as to the activity along its path in the system. From this activity along the path, keep a count of the total number of relations that you have identified. Then overlay all the separate usage paths into a composite map of relations for the entire application being analyzed. This produces an effective logical structure of the entire application. Usage paths and transaction analysis techniques are also described in detail in Chapter 5.

The fourth and final stage in the analysis process is described in Chapter 6: constructing the data model. Data modeling is really a *quantitative analysis* of the transactions reviewed in stage 3. In this stage the designer is introduced to some tools to help play a numbers games that will answer questions about response time, system stress, and individual transaction cost relative to the other transactions in the system. These steps involve utilizing the structure derived from the relational map and totaling all the counts obtained from the transaction plotting. The total load for each usage path in the logical path can be calculated from the figures. This information is compiled into a device called a load matrix.

Each stage has at least one product, or deliverable, which when combined with previous products creates a new and more useful piece of information. At the end of the process you the designer will not only have an excellent first-cut logical data base,

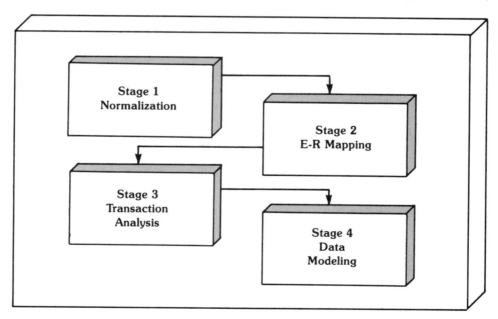

FIGURE 1.1   Stages of Data Analysis

but also a very good idea of first-cut physical design and individual transaction response time! What is especially convenient is that this kind of information is provided early enough in the design analysis for you to do something about it. These results come in when the design is still in the paper-and-pencil stage. There are no programs written or a data base structure to alter yet.

The key to the entire process is putting the data being gathered into a form that maximizes data independence and minimizes redundancy. This form is the third normal form. The normalization process is not as difficult to understand as some of the current literature on the subject seems to portend. The language of normalization—a language whose vocabulary is filled with tuples, domains, projections, joins, and transitory dependencies—is the roadblock to the understanding of the process by the average designer. It is my fervent hope that I can shed some light on the truly useful tool and remove it from the context of an impractical ideal understood only by mathematicians or data base theoreticians.

The Products of Data Analysis

In stage 1 the data collection and normalization stage, each output document of the system being worked on is normalized. Each document is "functionally decomposed" into the data entities of which it is made up. These entities are said to be in third normal form—that is, all the attributes (fields) within the entity are functionally dependent upon a key composed of one or more attributes. This process results in the first deliverable product.

1. *A third-normal-form entity list.*

The entity list contains all the logical data entities in the system as revealed in the normalization process. The next task is to determine the volume of each of these entities within the proposed system. As an example, in a sample system we might have customer, order, vendor, and product entities; the task is to determine how many of each will exist in the system. How many customers? How many products? How many different vendors? And soon. Where direct volumes cannot be found, perhaps the average frequency of occurrence can be found. Say the number of customers is known, but the number of orders is not. However, the average frequency of occurrence of customer to order, five orders per customer, is derived by multiplying the two, producing a close approximation of the order volume. Thus the second deliverable is

2. *A volume table.*

When these two deliverables are completed, so is the first stage of data analysis. The second stage, entity-relationship mapping, takes these two items and uses them to build the third deliverable,

3.   *A relationship map.*

The relationship map graphically represents the entities, their volumes, and the relationships between the entities. It is the first inkling of what is to come in the design process. It provides the first clues as to which data entities "talk to" each other and which entities do not. The relationship map in the sole product of the E-R mapping stage.

Rather than stop here and make your assumptions about the physical design, the data analysis methodology requires you as designer to consider the actual use of the data in question. Stage 3, the transaction analysis phase, requires the designer to examine each process or transaction the system is going to undertake. Thus the fourth deliverable is

4.   *A usage map of each transaction.*

In constructing the usage map the designer considers only the data needs of the transaction and how they could be accomplished with a minimum of effort. It is like the song, "If I had my druthers," from the musical "Li'l Abner." The designer at this point says, "If I had my druthers how would I like the data to be?" The only requirements of this stage of the analysis game is to determine: What data do I want? Where do I start? What is the flow from entity to entity? And last, what kind of access am I doing to each entity: read, update, delete, or insert? Thus each transaction in turn has a usage map created for it.

The next step is to combine all these usage maps together in order to compare the duplicate uses of data along the corresponding data paths. The composite picture is done on top of the relationship map. The process is done twice in order to produce two more deliverables.

5.   *The initial composite map.*

6.   *The revised composite map.*

The reason for doing it twice is to resolve the "transportation" conflicts that arise from the idealized "druthers" to actual paths and relationships using known keys. This finishes the qualitative analysis phase.

The first deliverable in quantitative analysis is to take the revised composite map and reexamine each transaction volume and system peak loading to produce

7.   *The transaction path analysis form.*

One form is created for each transaction. The numbers generated in this process allow the designer to grade each transaction as to cost and impact on the system and even to estimate roughly the actual transaction response time.

The designer must compare the result of each transaction. In order to construct

FIGURE 1.2 Price Performance

the data model, the numbers obtained in output 7 must be combined onto an eighth deliverable.

   8. *The load matrix.*

It is in the load matrix that the designer discovers the activity along the paths between the entities. This activity is expressed in terms of total numbers of accesses. The numbers are then plotted back onto the relationship map again to create the final deliverable,

   9. *The loaded data model.*

Each relationship or path is assigned a number approximating the input output activity along that path. The natural correlation to make is to arrange the data entities physically according to the numbers. Where the number is high, the I/O activity is high, and therefore to minimize expensive physical I/O, the entities should be placed physically close together. Smaller numbers indicated less of a need to do so.

This final step in the analysis is to review the load matrix within the constraints of a particular DBMS. For the sake of convenience, you can compromise and combine or split relations. Redo the logical structure with these revisions, and from it construct the physical schema that can be efficiently supported by your chosen DBMS. This method has forms, documents, and illustrations that provide a complete picture of how the data should be organized and the data model implemented in a finalized data base design.

Part II of this text will deal data base management systems, their architecture, history, and development. The outputs of the data analysis process will be utilized to provide a sample design solution for a variety of different data base management systems (DBMS).

The intent is to provide a standard of the data analysis process and provide readers with the skills to accomplish the analysis task on their own. The Part II material on data base design will be informational and given from the perspective of an analyst looking over the designer's shoulder.

RELEVANCE OF DATA ANALYSIS AND DESIGN

Many of us in the industry are familiar with the Computerworld advertisement reprinted in Figure 1.2. This classic quote, though somewhat astounding, is nevertheless quite true.

From the advent of the computer age, circa 1950, to the present day, there has been a dramatic shift in the cost of computing. The costs divide into two components: hardware costs and people costs. To put it simply, people costs are dramatically increasing in proportion to a corporation's total EDP budget, while hardware costs are just as dramatically being reduced.

When these costs are viewed as percentages of the total EDP budget, hardware costs have declined from 75% 20 years ago to 10% today, and corresponding people costs have increased from 25% 20 years ago to 90% today (see Figure 1.3).

The problem now confronting us is where do these increased people costs come from? Analysis of early data processing applications of the 1950s and 1960s indicates a heavy reliance on large, batch-oriented systems. The people costs were largely low-paid data entry clerks and keypunch operators. With the advent of on-line systems in the seventies, there was a dramatic reduction in this clerical work force, which was reflected in EDP budgets. The application end-users were using terminals in their respective departments to accomplish the bulk of the data entry task.

However, with increased reliance upon on-line systems, the complexity and cost factor of development rose sharply. No longer was the work delegated to low-paid clerks. As a result, the demand for highly skilled and consequently highly paid analysts and programmers increased. The cost factor was further increased by the ever upward spiraling wage scale of the 1960s, and 1970s. Consequently in the 1980s the cost of using a computer is up to nine times the cost of the computer itself!

With the ever-increasing use of computers in an organization comes an ever-increasing demand by departments within an organization to be computerized. Hardware costs that precluded development of new applications in the past are no longer a restricting factor today. Thus two extremes are created: on one hand a

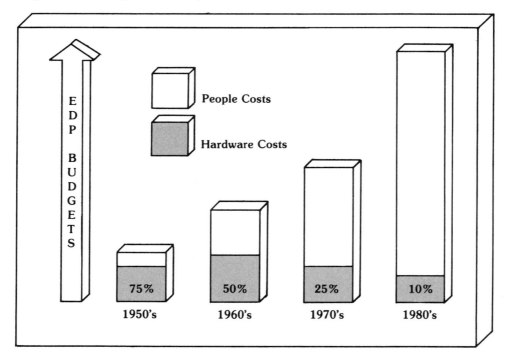

FIGURE 1.3 People Costs versus Hardware Costs

tremendous demand for services, and on the other an increased hardware capability to service that demand.

In between these extremes is a bottleneck: the current methodology of developing and maintaining application systems. The development of software methodology has not kept pace. Each application is meticulously and laboriously custom designed and hand built.

Application programming is the next candidate for automation. Already some attempts to accomplish this are on the market such as IBM's Application Development Facility (ADF) or ADMIN's INC, Development Management System (DMS) and ADMINS/11. There are also the "user-friendly" systems like SAS, RAMIS, and FOCUS. These early products will naturally lead to more sophisticated and more automated application development systems or code generators.

The input to these systems will be from the end-user of the application and will bypass not only the programmer but eventually even the analyst. With these types of processes comes a need to understand the fundamentals of an organization and how information is used in these organizations.

Data analysis and data base design together constitute a methodology, a step-by-step process, by which to analyze and utilize the information about an organization and translate it into a form comprehensible to both top management and data processing departments. That form is the essential input to a process translating directly into application systems by the EDP staff.

Though computers are new, information processing is not. It can even be argued that programming is not new. Programming is merely an extension of instruction sets or processing manuals that have been around for hundreds of years. The big difference is the speed and slavelike obedience to instruction brought about by electronic data processing. The tasks asked for a computer system are not new tasks either, but the same tasks as found in manual systems. Just as errors in a manual system cause errors in the end objective, the same holds true for computers. Only the scale of error increases because of the scope and magnitude of electronic data processing.

CHARACTERISTICS OF AN ORGANIZATION

Business organizations start small and grow larger. Consider the information needs of a small organization such as a one-man chair factory. Typically, all the information that organization needs in order to function is in the head of one person. All the data resources of the organization can be contained in one small set of books—one data base.

As the business grows, the need to manage the company's assets and accounts interferes with the selling ability of the individuals. Demand for the product, more chairs, increases; clients accumulate; staff is added. In short, the business is expanding at such a rate that one individual can no longer keep the pulse of the entire organization.

The natural tendency is to separate the organization into smaller, more manageable functional units. Soon a single individual is no longer able to completely manage every aspect of even a moderately sized organization.

Hence, with organizational growth, different people must be assigned to manage different areas of functional responsibility. Each individual then operates on a subset of the total organization's data, relevant to a particular functional area.

The one-man chair company now has a purchasing department, a sales department, a manufacturing department, and so on. It now employs 50 people and has plans for diversification and expansion. The owner and founder, Elmo Zitt, realizes the need of the sales department to report to the manufacturing department, which in turn reports to the purchasing department for raw materials. The whole area of management needs, which encompasses decision making, payroll, personnel, and marketing, must also be handled.

Each functional area in our sample organization operates with a subset of the total data resources of the corporation. No longer can a single set of books adequately function as the sole repository of data. Versions of the same data are required for different departments. As an example, information regarding each customer order may be required by the sales department, the manufacturing department, and the accounts department. While each department requires specific information relating to that order, other order information may be universally required by all departments. Data redundancy results when the same data exists in different functional versions, which are in turn used by different departments.

Consider the following typical questions as represented by the different departments from the sample organization of the mythical E-Z Chair Company:

Manufacturing Department: How do I build a chair?
Sales Department: Who buys our chairs?
Accounts Department: How much does a chair cost?
Purchasing Department: How much raw material do I need for 100 chairs?

Each department has a different file to answer its questions (see Figure 1.4).

Now the problem becomes one of synchronization. For instance, if the manufacturing department changes the design of a chair, this information would be of interest to all the other departments. What are the changes in materials? What are the costs? How will the change affect sales? Each department's subset of information must be updated in order for the impact of a change to be reflected throughout the organization. Not keeping the files synchronized could result in inaccurate files. The potential for chaos or corporate disaster multiplies.

The necessity to communicate between departments breeds paperwork. When the item being updated resides in one place, the paperwork had informational value only. When the data being changed resides in many places, the paperwork is essential to the existence of the organization. Memos, reports, and requests for change must flow from department to department in order to ensure that data changes in one place are reflected throughout the organization.

Paperwork serves to communicate the change from department to department, serving as a data transport mechanism. When analyzing the procedures of an organization, one examines the data flow as represented by the paperwork of that organization. An example of this paper flow would be the following: A sales order generates a picking slip for the warehouse, which picks the chairs. This process generates a packing slip, which is sent to accounting to create a bill and to manufacturing to replace inventory. This process in turn generates a work order and a raw materials request, which goes to purchasing. (see Figure 1.5).

Another aspect of functional separation within an organization and working with subsets of data is the problem faced by management when trying to satisfy an inquiry or get some information. While it is fine for the individual departments to function with subsets of information, it is imperative that management have access to a broader spectrum of data by which to make decisions. Operationally, an organization may handle the data flow problem well. However, data is not information. Information is data combined in logically arranged groups. Birthdates, names, addresses, and employee numbers are data, but a matched set of birthdate, name, address, and employee number is information. Thus if data resides in separate files, it cannot become useful until it is combined into an information set.

In general, management requires information summaries of activity in order to make decisions. While the order department may be concerned with a particular

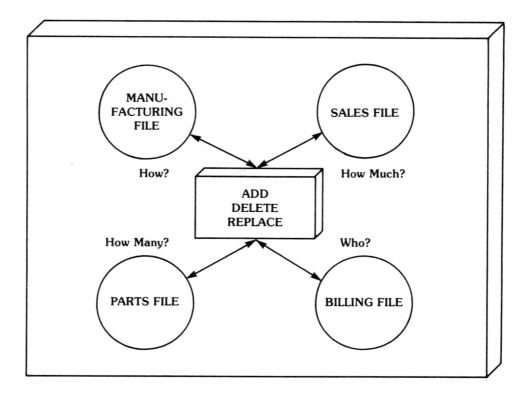

FIGURE 1.4 Files Answer Questions

FIGURE 1.5 Typical Data Flow at E-Z Chair Corporation

14

order's status, management most probably is concerned with the status of orders for a week, a month, or an entire year.

Although subsets of data work well in the functional departments, this separation of data can prevent top management from gaining an overall appreciation of the status of the entire organization. Computer applications of the 1960s and 1970s focused their processing upon the functional departments of an organization. Any number of separate payroll, accounting, general ledger, open order, and inventory applications can be found among a typical organization computer system. Systems of the 1980s and beyond, however, will be expected to aid management more directly in the decision-making process. A single person's capacity to function diminishes as the amount of data increases. On the other hand, massive amounts of data and the digestion thereof are the bread and butter of the computer. The computer is able to gather data within an organization, consolidate, organize, summarize, and generally make it available to top management to aid in the decision-making process.

It is data base technology that will make it possible for management to tap the total data resource of an organization. Data base can effectively manage, and therefore avoid, the pitfalls of functional subsets of data. However, the problem in general is that data base has not lived up to its potential!

If for instance, the E-Z Chair Company now uses a consolidated data base instead of separate subsets of files, the communication problems vastly improve. Now no data redundancy is in evidence. Each functional department has its own view of the data (subschema) just as before. However, the management information problem is now a simple task of defining a subschema for a particular management requirement. We are back to that one set of books, the one data base that Elmo Zitt had when he founded E-Z Chair Company.

Data base consolidates data used by all departments into a single repository of data (see Figure 1.6).

TRADITIONAL DATA PROCESSING APPROACHES

The case of E-Z Chair illustrates the potential of data base, but in reality few organizations utilize such a consolidated system. "Why not?" you may ask. The problem lies with the traditional approaches companies have used when they automated the function or department. When told to automate payroll, general ledger, or production control, the EDP people dispatched analysts to the user department, found their needs, drew up specifications, and handed over to them a system complete with its own files and interfaces to existing systems. They analyzed and designed, and built a specific system for each department. These specific systems were departmentalized, procedure-oriented. In some cases, they required inter-system file communication in order to accomplish their mission (see Figure 1.7).

Now comes the need for an inventory control system. Again the troops descend upon the inventory control department. Right away they recognize the amount of paperwork that flows between inventory control and the production control depart-

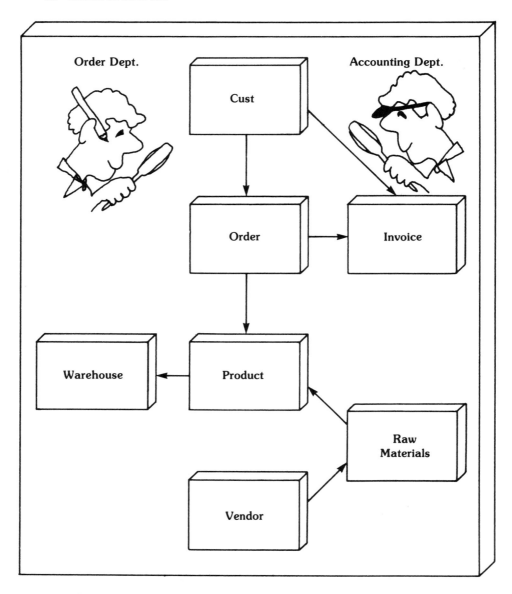

FIGURE 1.6 **Departmental View of the Data Base**

ment (which is already automated). At this point someone recommends a consolidated production-inventory control data base. It would solve the communication problem when changes have to be reflected in both departments.

However, when the analysts attempt to match the requirements of the new inventory system with those of the up-and-running production control system, they

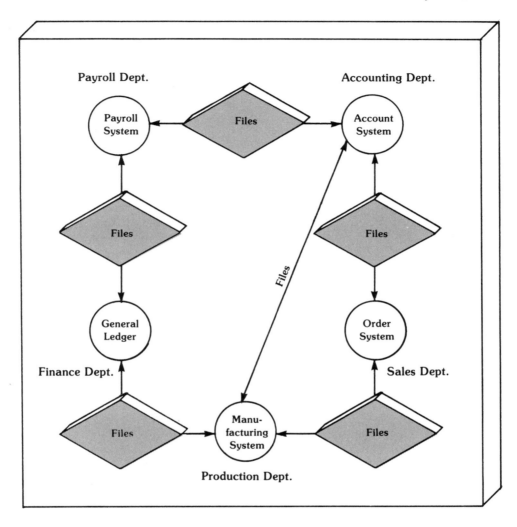

FIGURE 1.7 Traditional Departmentalized Files and Application Intercommunication

find both functions' requirements cannot be met without substantial changes to an already existing system. In fact the restructuring effort might in effect result in an entire rewrite of the production control system!

Thus they abandon the attempt to start to design an integrated data base, and instead tailor another data base for the inventory control system. The intercommunication problems are handled by multiple update runs or transaction-driven files. The result is they not only succeed in automating the department, but they also succeed in automating that department's communication problems! Operationally, the new system is a success; however, top management's information requirements are up the proverbial creek without a paddle.

In most organizations, unfortunately, data base is used to automate existing systems, incurring all the overhead without deriving 100% of the benefits. Basically data base is being used as nothing more than a glorified access method! Some attempts have been made via query languages to supply management with the information it requires. For the most part, the English-like control text of these systems was something that nontechnical user could not understand or program well.

The underutilization of data base is not a result of the DBMS, however. The data base failures and seeming inflexibility of some data base systems are not a technological problem at all. The problem is the analysis and design approach(es) used to implement data base systems.

One would never consider designing a railroad without a plan. One would not haphazardly lay some track here, some track there, or build a station over there without first determining the paths from place to place and the natural population centers and locations for terminals and stations. One would consider several different railroad system designs in order to weigh cost benefits of the various alternatives. Railroad architects would be remiss in their duty if they did not provide for system expansion in the initial design.

Now relate this example to the traditional development of computer systems. Professionals in data processing have been laying track all over the landscape. When we require communication from one track to another (system to system), we must hope we do not encounter a river gorge or mountain range requiring elaborate building or extensive tunnel blasting! In other words, with a little planning and foresight, we can reduce future problems by anticipating possible directions for future change and incorporating them in the current design.

PROCEDURE-ORIENTED VERSUS DATA-ORIENTED DESIGN

Systems designers dash around laying track by examining a specific department or functional area. When another system is required they lay a different stretch of track, not necessarily connected to the earlier section of track.

When examining a department, function, or application, system designers analyze the operational aspects of that area. They identify the data flows via the paperwork generated, determining the input and output requirements, and thereby identifying the data items to be placed on a data base for input and in reports or inquiries for output. They follow the procedure-oriented approach that examines only a limited existing environment. In some instances, managers even *prevent* designers and system analysts from venturing outside their departments or areas for more information!

What is created is an application system that exists as if it were a lonely stretch of track as in the analogy above. And the next system, which is developed in much the same manner, is another isolated organizational subset to be automated. When people try to connect the tracks together, they may find many obstacles in the way.

They may have to reprogram, rip up track, in order to accomplish this. Redundant data is needed because the cost of modifying the older system is prohibitive. What procedure-oriented development lacks is an overall architect's plan.

Functional separation in an organization results in fragmented subsets of an organization's data. Procedure-oriented development utilizes these subsets to analyze a particular area's system needs. Each subset reflects only a fraction of the total amount of data utilized throughout an organization; thus the data tends to be redundantly represented throughout the organization. Data base technology will allow us to minimize this redundancy if we can identify where the redundancies are.

This data identification process is by no means an easy task. It is like a scavenger hunt, with each new clue leading willy-nilly from one place to another. Data-oriented analysis and design techniques concentrate on completing a map of the hunt before you run off to assemble clues. Data-oriented analysis and design techniques provide the architect's plan. The plan in the railroad analogy identifies the best locations for stations, bridges, tunnels and roadbeds in order to reduce redundant contruction, address the needs of the railroad's customers, and provide for future change or expansion.

Similarly the data-oriented approach provides a framework for organizing the data in a department, or across departments. As in the example in Figure 1.6, an integrated data base allows for a departmentalized view of the total data entity. An integrated data base meets management's informational requirements and at the same time eliminates data redundancy. In the E-Z Chair example, each department is represented by an eye with a narrow view of the whole. This one-eyed approach to systems, while allowing operational management to do its thing, presents a confusing and disoriented picture to top management.

Data-oriented techniques provide a binocular view of an organization's data. With an additional data-oriented eye, top management can judge distances and have a true perspective of just what the organization is doing. This does not mean abandoning the procedure-oriented approach to problem solving, but rather adding a broader perspective via the data-oriented eye. To close the procedure-oriented eye would lead us back to a less desirable one-eyed approach. The impact and thrust of this text will be to show you how to get that other eye working so that you realize the full potential of data base.

CORPORATE DATA PROCESSING GROWTH

What strategies can be used to merge the procedure-oriented and data-oriented analysis techniques? Let us examine the steps in overall corporate data processing growth. Richard F. Nolan, of Nolan and Norton Company, Lexington, Massachusetts, has developed a theory on corporate data processing growth. Nolan's article entitled "Managing the Crises in Data Processing", outlines his theory on the stages of data processing (DP) growth within an organization.[1] Nolan developed this theory over a decade of examining a hundred or so large corporations and many large IBM accounts. His stages are as follows:

Stage I   Initiation
Stage II   Contagion
Stage III   Control
Stage IV   Integration
Stage V   Data administration
Stage VI   Maturity

The six stages of development are best illustrated in Figure 1.8, which is based on Nolan's article. In the illustration, the six stages are plotted against growth processes identified as the applications portfolio, DP organization, DP planning and control, and user awareness. Superimposed over this grid is the level of DP expenditures at each stage.

Stage I: Initiation.   A computer is introduced in order to run applications that would bring about functional cost reduction. DP planning and control are lax or nonexistent. Users have a "hands off" approach to the new computer. As systems are successfully implemented, the user departments become more enthusiastic about converting more systems.

Stage II: Contagion.   Applications proliferate; the DP organization develops a large user-oriented programmer base; cost escalate. The demand for newer applications places such stress on the DP department that controls become even more lax than they were in stage I. Often new applications are implemented; these are supposedly based solely on the specific user's needs rather than on the actual needs of the organization as a whole.

Stage III: Control.   The often chaotic situation in Stage II leads to the third stage. During stage III attempts are made to clean up the application portfolio by upgrading the documentation and restructuring some of the existing applications. The DP organization adds a new layer of middle management whose function is to formalize and control planning. The user community is arbitrarily being held accountable for new systems development.

Stage IV: Integration.   The restructuring and redesign of existing applications eventually leads to the integration stage. In this stage the applications portfolio is retrofitted to utilize data base technology. The DP organization establishes computer utility and user account teams. Tailored planning and control systems are developed. The user is going through a process of learning accountability. Just when users are resigned to being charged for expenses without themselves having any control over the costs of DP, they get interactive terminals and the support and assistance they need for using and profiting from data base technology. The users' enthusiasm builds; they literally demand more support and more function; and they are now very willing to pay for it. However, late in state IV the exclusive reliance on computer controls proves to be ineffective. The new demands of rapid growth create a new wave of

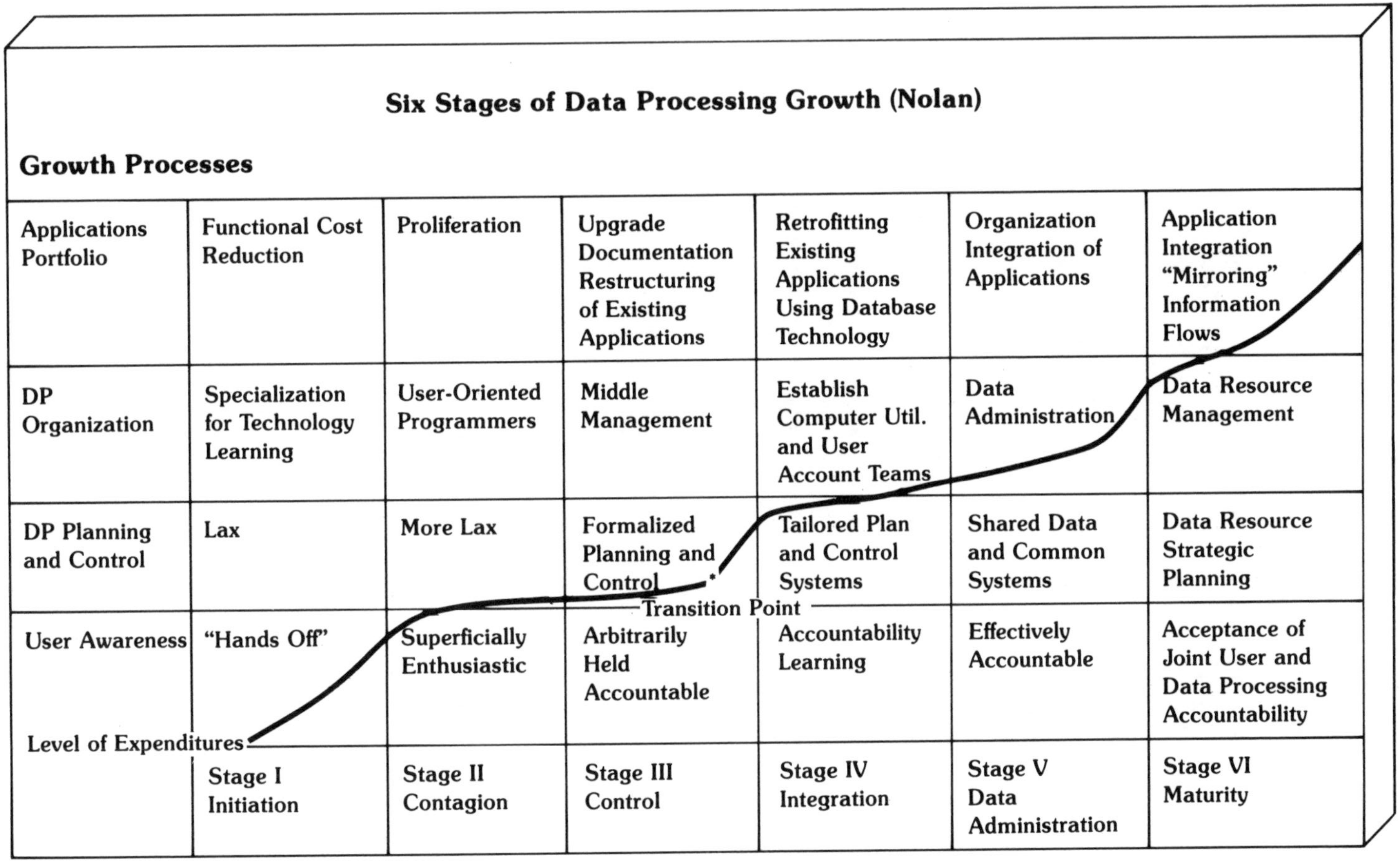

Six Stages of Data Processing Growth (Nolan)

Growth Processes

	Stage I Initiation	Stage II Contagion	Stage III Control	Stage IV Integration	Stage V Data Administration	Stage VI Maturity
Applications Portfolio	Functional Cost Reduction	Proliferation	Upgrade Documentation Restructuring of Existing Applications	Retrofitting Existing Applications Using Database Technology	Organization Integration of Applications	Application Integration "Mirroring" Information Flows
DP Organization	Specialization for Technology Learning	User-Oriented Programmers	Middle Management	Establish Computer Util. and User Account Teams	Data Administration	Data Resource Management
DP Planning and Control	Lax	More Lax	Formalized Planning and Control	Tailored Plan and Control Systems	Shared Data and Common Systems	Data Resource Strategic Planning
User Awareness	"Hands Off"	Superficially Enthusiastic	Arbitrarily Held Accountable	Accountability Learning	Effectively Accountable	Acceptance of Joint User and Data Processing Accountability

Level of Expenditures

Transition Point

FIGURE 1.8   Nolan's Six Stages of EDP Growth

21

problems. The redundancy of data complicates control and planning systems. Demand for more efficiency and for better controls increases.

Stage V: Data Administration.   Thus we come to the stage of data administration. There is organization and integration of the organization's applications portfolio. The DP organization has a formalized data administration department. There is a great deal of stored data and many common systems. Users are effectively held accountable for DP costs.

Stage VI: Maturity.   The applications portfolio is now complete. Their structure effectively mirrors the organization and the information flow in the company. Data Administration matures into Corporate Data Resource Management. Control and planning center around data resource strategic planning. There is joint acceptance of accountability by the user and the data processing department.

Another important point recognized by Nolan and depicted in the chart is the transition, somewhere between stages III and IV; a shift in emphasis occurs from the organization's managing the computer to the organization's managing the corporate data resource. Nolan also mentions that he knows of no organization that has reached stage VI. The key point to recognize from this is the inevitability of having to cope with the data and not the computer. The data-oriented approach to analysis will provide a mechanism for achieving this eventual end.

Nolan points out the inevitability of having to cope with data base if the organization is to grow. Data analysis is a methodology one can use to implement the data-oriented approach to system problem solving. Data analysis works in concert with functional analysis, and therefore any in-depth pursuit of data analysis without first understanding functional analysis would be incomplete.

A system cannot be designed without knowing what you want to deliver as an end product. The process to identify these products is functional analysis.

NOTES

1.   Richard F. Nolan, "Managing the Crisis in Data Processing," *Harvard Business Review*, March–April 1979, p. 115.

2 Functional Analysis

Form ever follows function.

Louis Henri Sullivan, 1896

DETERMINING WHAT TO DO

"Analysis is the study of a problem prior to taking some action."[1] Before starting data analysis you must study the problem. Indeed you must know what the problem is. The specification document is the most important product of the functional or system's analysis project. Without a plan with specific goals and objectives a system will never come to fruition. Consider the plight of poor Alice in Wonderland:

Alice: I'm lost and I don't know which path to take.
Cheshire Cat: Where do you want to be?
Alice: I don't know.
Cheshire Cat: Then any path will do.

Alice is like so many of us when confronted with a problem and myriad choices. Which path do we take? The question should be, "What do we want to do?" The process of functional analysis is to provide these answers. There are also some new tools available to the system designer to aid in this process.

These new tools evolve around building a model of the system. If you can't build a model, then you can't build a system. The new modeling tools arose because of two major problems, communication and size.

The communication problems arise because a narrative text is not a particularly effective way to describe a procedure. The reader gets lost in the words. The other problem with words is that the user knows what is going on but cannot describe it. The analyst cannot design what is not understood. There is demonstrated a need for a model that both the end-user and the analyst can use to understand the problem.

By their very nature, large systems change. These changes do not go away because we "freeze the specifications." Specifications must be maintained. Likewise, the model should be maintainable. If you cannot maintain the model, how can you maintain the system?

The size problem is the corollary to the communication problem. How big is big? When working with large, complex systems, there is a need for an intelligent way to deal with size. A model helps to define where to effectively modularize or partition the design.

It is important to realize that systems analysis and data structure analysis move forward together. The systems analysis project identifies the data needed to suppport the application, while the data structure analysis defines the dependencies that influence how the data can be manipulated by the system. This chapter first deals with how to identify the problem and then with the modeling tools available to describe the results of the identification process.

In his article "Managing the Crisis in Data Processing," Richard Nolan points out that organizations are gradually coming to grips with the problems of decision making. The growth trends within an organization all point to ways of managing data, and not of managing the computer, as discussed in Chapter 1.

How is it done? What technique can designers use to identify the total informational needs of an organization? What type of analysis can designers perform to satisfy operating, management, and top management? One good way of gathering information is to use a top-down approach, or *functional analysis*.

STAGES OF FUNCTIONAL ANALYSIS

Peter F. Drucker developed the stages of functional analysis. His functional analysis method is broken into three stages:

Stage I   Determine the mission and purpose of the organization.
Stage II   Examine the products, markets, channels, and services of the organization.
Stage III Determine the corporate objectives and problems of the organization.

Drucker, in his landmark text, *Management: Tasks, Responsibilities , Practices*, identified the questions to ask in order to determine the purpose and mission of an organization.

"What is our business?"
"What will it be?"
"What should it be?"[2]

By understanding the purpose and mission of the organization, one can gain a broad view of what the organization is now and what it will be in the future. Alternatives for future directions can also be considered. An organization does not stand still; it must change in response to the business climate—competition, marketing, economics. Drucker calls this "the need for planned abandonment."[3] An organization that does not change with time dies in time.

A statement is composed containing the answer to an organization's purpose and mission, and it should be scrutinized to extract the implicit or explicit entities. Use this entity list as a basis for building up a list of attributes for each entity. The succeeding stages of functional analysis add to the entity list and provide further attribute examples. The lists are then put into third normal form and compared with those entities developed through data analysis.

To see how this process works, examine the documents produced by a functional analysis of E-Z Chair Corporation. First examine the purpose and mission of the organization. Drucker stated, "There is only one definition of business purpose: to create a customer."[4] Business organizations do not create a product and then see if it sells; they find out the climate—the market, the needs of the customer—then they develop the product.

Thus, the market and the customer define the purpose and mission of an organization and the customer. According to Drucker, top management must reply to several questions:

"Who is our customer?"
"Where is the customer?"
"What does he buy?"
"What is value to the customer?"[5]

SAMPLE FUNCTIONAL ANALYSIS PROBLEM

The organization's existence depends on its customers. In the answers to the above questions lie an organization's purpose and mission. A good place to start with "E-Z Chair" might be the annual report to its stockholders (see Figure 2.1) and the opening letter from the president.

Notice the underlined words. From them, the following entities can be implicitly or explicitly derived:

STOCKHOLDER
EMPLOYEE
CUSTOMER
PRODUCT
INVOICE
WAREHOUSING
ORDER
PARTS
VENDOR
SERVICE

E-Z Chair Corporation

Armrest, MA 02909

1985
Annual Report

Dear <u>Stockholders</u>,

Welcome to the 20th annual meeting of E-Z Chair Corporation. E-Z Chair is a public corporation founded in 1930 by Elmo Zitt. In the past fifty-two years the company has grown from a one man hobby to a national corporation <u>employing</u> over 6,000 persons and serving <u>customers</u> in all the fifty states and Canada.

E-Z Chair manufactures a wide variety of finished and unfinished furniture <u>products</u> which are <u>sold</u> through our own regional <u>warehouse</u> outlets or distributed to fine furniture stores throughout North America. Individuals also <u>order</u> our products through our ever expanding do-it-yourself mail order catalogue.

<u>Raw materials</u> for our products are purchased from a variety of national and international <u>vendors</u>, providing a selection and quality unavailable in similar products.

Above all E-Z Chair takes pride in the outstanding quality of its products and its <u>service</u> to customers which have made E-Z Chair one of the largest manufacturers and distributors of home and office furnishings in the United States.

Sincerely,

Elmo Zitt, III
President and Chairman of the Board

FIGURE 2.1   Annual Report of the E-Z Chair Corporation

Through a simple analysis of a single short letter, you can identify 10 entities. Notice also that you can identify major entities of our order entry system, CUSTO-MER, ORDER, PRODUCT, INVOICE, even at this very early stage. This should be a substantial clue as to importance of these items in the running of E-Z Chair.

In the E-Z Chair example, the system being analyzed is order processing. What is the business of ordering? What are the functions being performed in the order processing department? Order taking, order status, invoicing, inventory control, credit adjustment, and customer verification are just a few of the department's possible functions or tasks. Now the question is which, or more accurately, how many of the department's functions are to be included in the new system? Once recorded, then these tasks should be scrutinized in light of Drucker's third question, "What *should* the system be doing?"

Through careful and complete interviewing of the system sponsors and end-users, an accurate picture of the system's tasks and major documentation flows can be ascertained. We are going to pay particular attention later to these documentation flows, because it is the documents that contain the data and it is data from which data bases are made.

The second stage of functional analysis consists of resolving more entities and adding attributes to those entities by examining the products, services, markets, and channels of distribution of an organization. This stage of the analysis involves a greater level of detail.

In order to garner this information, interview middle management in both the operating and innovative managment areas. Then prepare a statement outlining the current and future products markets and channels. This stage is just an outgrowth of Drucker's prime questions—"What is our business?", "What will our business be?", "What should our business be?"[6]

Send interviewers into E-Z Chairs' warehouse, ordering, manufacturing, and accounting departments to ascertain the nature of the organization. Interview market research and product development departments to project the future growth of E-Z Chair. Examine the list that should be the result of the interview.

List the products, the output documents, of the E-Z chair order processing system. Every piece of paper produced by the system should be itemized and catalogued for scrutiny later in data analysis. Even "paperless" on line systems have outputs; its screens are outputs full of data elements to be retrieved and stored.

Be very objective in your analysis. If the users do not know exactly what they want, go in with blank worksheets and contract output material one on one. Typically the problem is not that the user does not know what he or she wants, it is just that the user cannot communicate those needs in a language that can be successfully inter-preted by the designer.

Now is the time to "get physical," build real outputs, real screens, and real reports. These are things the user understands, and these are things designers can understand and for which specifications can be developed.

Drucker speaks of "the market"; there is a market for the system. Identify what that market is, and record its objectives and needs. There are "channels" for the system also. The products of the system must get to the market being serviced by the system. What are the characteristics of these available channels? Is the system batch; is it on line; are there remote job entry functions; is it distributed, or is there a need for extensive networking? Developing the products, markets, and channels is not complete without also considering possible future products markets and channels.

Eventually the system has to be designed and implemented. By trying to assess in the beginning what possible changes or enhancements will be made to that system, you may avoid future maintenance problems. The design should be flexible and the data base very data-independent. Data independence insulates the structure from change. But data independence does not come cheaply, for it implies less redundancy and physical separation of data. The converse of this separation is that it will be more expensive to combine the data together into new logical record sets.

Having some idea of the implications of data separation of future data consolidation will greatly enhance the flexibility of the system. It is incumbent upon the functional analyst to provide as much of this type of information as possible. This Drucker methodology is rather a broad survey technique. Top-down analysis, because it is so broad, produces almost unlimited quantities of data. The functional entities grow in size and number. Even the small E-Z chair system is expanding.

Here are the entities obtained thus far with some suggested possible attributes:

CUSTOMER	*Customer number*, name, shipping address, bill-to address, discount rate.
SALESMAN	*Salesman number*, name, salary, commission rate, monthly quota, territory number
PRODUCT	*Product number*, description, sale price, manufacturing cost, quantity on hand, quantity on order, product discount
VENDOR	*Vendor number*, name, address (part number, part name, part price)
ORDER	*Order number*, date, delivery address, customer number, (*product number, name, quantity, price*)
INVOICE	*Invoice number*, date order number, customer number, (*product number, name, quantity shipped, backordered, price, discount*)
PART	*Part number*, name, quantity on hand, quantity on order, vendor number, cost.
WAREHOUSE	*Warehouse number*, address, capacity, (*product number, name, quantity on hand, warehouse location*)
STOCKHOLDER	*Stockholder number*, name, address, shares

The items in parentheses are repeating groups within the entity. The first attribute for each item, printed in italic, is the probable primary key candidate.

The final stage in functional analysis is to determine the corporate objectives of the organization. Drucker, in his book on managment, uses the example of the large English retailing firm, Marks and Spencer, to illustrate how to use objectives.

Marks and Spencer is a retailing chain about the size of Sears & Roebuck. Having started in business before World War I, by the early 1920's it was a very successful variety retailing chain. Simon Marks, one of the partners in Marks and Spencer, then made a trip to the United States to study the Sears operation. Upon his return to England, he completely changed the objectives of the organization. The partners decided the business of Marks and Spencer was "not retailing" but "social revolution."[7]

As Drucker states, "Marks and Spencer redefined its business as the subversion of the class structure of nineteenth-century England by making available to the working and lower middle classes upper-class goods of better than upper-class quality, and yet at prices the working and lower-middle-class customer could afford."[8]

The company reversed its trend to merchandise a large variety of products with nothing more in common than low price and began to concentrate on marketing wearing apparel and household fabrics, such as towels and draperies.

The decision was correct. England after World War I was becoming very fashion conscious, and dress was still the most visible of class distinctions. The timing was also correct because of the state of the textile industry. Cheaper new materials such as rayon and acetate were available for clothing manufacture. Within a few years, Marks and Spencer became the leading clothing and textile distributor in England, a position held to this day. By 1972, 75% of the firm's sales were in clothing.

After World War II the same thought processes were applied to another commodity: food. Innovation in this area accounted for the remaining 25% of Marks and Spencer's sales in 1972.

As Drucker states, "The Marks & Spencer story reaffirms the central importance of thinking through "what our business *is* and what it *should* be." But it also shows that this, by itself, is not enough. The basic definition of the business and of its purpose and mission have to be translated into objectives. Otherwise, they remain insight, good intentions, and brilliant epigrams that never become achievement."[9]

Drucker sets out eight key objectives. First, the organization must create a customer; therefore, a *marketing objective* is necessary. Second, to avoid obsolescence and to keep pace with the competitor an organization must have an *innovation objective*. The third, fourth, and fifth objectives are *human resources, financial resources,* and *physical resources*, which pertain to supply, employment, and development. Sixth, there is need of a *productivity objective* to employ and cultivate those resources effectively if the organization is to survive. Seventh, because organizations exist in the community and in society, they have *social responsibilities*. Organizations are responsible for their impact upon the environment. Finally, there is a *profit objective*, without which the other objectives are unattainable. All the other objectives involve costs and risks; profit is required to pay for them. In summary, Drucker states:

> Objectives in these key areas enable us to do five things: to organize and explain the whole range of business phenomena in a small number of

general statements; to test these statements in actual experience; to predict behavior; to appraise the soundness of decisions while they are still being made; and to let managers on all levels analyze their own experience, and as a result, improve their performance.[10]

He concludes:

Objectives are not fate; they are direction. They are not commands; they are commitments. They do not determine the future; they are the means to mobilize the resources and energies of the business for the making of the future.[11]

We in the data processing industry have studiously avoided the reality of change because we could not predict it with absolute certainty. Thus the useful life of most application systems we design today is restricted at best. We must design systems that are more responsive to change. Analyzing an organization's objectives gives us insights into change. Creating designs that are more data oriented allows programs to be more data-independent and more adaptable to future changes. The only change that can be predicted with absolute certainty is that change will come. The time has come to face change up front in the design phase.

As an example of what is meant by determining the goals of a system, let's review the E-Z Chair Corporation in the light of these eight objectives:

Market Goals
1. The new system must service the needs already provided by the current system. (These needs should be listed and categorized in separate documentation.)
2. The new system must respond faster to market changes regarding pricing and shipping.

Innovation Goals
1. The data availability should supply us with material for a new decisions support system. Items such as daily cost flow, materials management and short-term product demand should be more readily recognized.
2. Enough prior and current data should be available to allow for market forecasting by region.

Resource Assessment
1. Human resources for the new system will be increased, but the increased order activity on the nature of 12% per quarter must offset cost. Itemize these costs.

2. Physical resources for a new on-line system will include new hardware, increased phone costs, and new distribution and warehouse facilities. Itemize and assess these costs.

3. Financial resources for the system will require out-of-pocket expenses and a true measure of what total return an investment will be.

Productivity Goal

1. New system must be able to handle increased daily workload with average transaction response time of 3 seconds.

2. Anticipated growth rate is 15% to 20% per quarter.

3. Shipments must be on time 95% of the time.

Social Objectives

1. The new system must be flexible to interact with current systems.

2. Impact of new information demands must not dictate complete obsolescence of the current design.

3. Categorize and list past problems with system and review the new system in light of these past problems.

Profit Goal

1. The new system must be cost-effective. It must meet the goals but not cost more than the benefit derived.

2. Careful evaluation of the resource assessment will determine the cost versus benefit analysis.

In actual practice the goals assessment would be a very detailed document with appendixes for each catalog.

In the example two new requirements of the organization are recognized: the need to improve customer service by tracing performance and the requirement for tracking sales in order to manage organization profitability. The results are three new entities: VENDOR-PERFORMANCE, PRODUCT-PERFORMANCE, and SALES-RECORDS.

The performance entities develop out of the need to respond to a customer's service demands. Vendors must be monitored as to how well they respond to demands for raw materials, and products must be monitored based on orders placed on them. Delivery times, customer and vendor contracts, and price variances must all be logged into the two entities.

The Sales-Record entity will contain all information about a particular sale, such as order, customer, invoice, and salesman plus year-to-date figures for sales and profit information for the current and previous years.

The entities described might look like this:

VENDOR PERFORMANCE   *Performance record number, vendor number (part number, actual delivery time, actual price), supplier contact name, contact phone number.*

PRODUCT-PERFORMANCE   *Performance record number, product number* (order number, actual delivery time, actual price) shipping contact name, phone extension.

SALES-RECORD   *Sale number, customer number* (order number, invoice number, salesman number), current year-to-date sales, last year's YTD sales, current profit YTD, last year's profit.

By convention, repeating groups items that take on more than one value occurrence per record are in parentheses and candidate keys are in italic.

The sales record would allow for all manner of tracking to enable top management to make inquiries that would aid in the decision-making process. Naturally this example is incomplete. Functional analysis of an entire corporate organization would produce volumes of data. A thorough treatment of the sample problem would require several separate chapters.

Using the information obtained thus far, designers should construct a functional analysis of the example that contains: entities and their attributes; a simple entity-relation map, attributes; and entities detailed thus far (defined in a data dictionary).

An entity-relational map of the sample problem can be found in Figure 2.2. The structure results from connecting those entities that contain each other's key attributes. The sample problem is too limited to address fully the personnel management and the manufacturing portion of the organization. Although exploring these areas is a natural avenue in real-life functional analysis, it is not within the scope of this text.

Next, designers must reduce the entities to third normal form. This process would resolve the sales record entity in the example to several sales record types and otherwise stabilize the data and establish the connecting entities for those entities not in optional third normal form. This normalization task will be discussed in detail in the next chapter.

INTRODUCTION TO THE DATA FLOW DIAGRAM

One of the more popular tools developed in the last few years to aid in handling the functions of the system is the data flow diagram. "A data flow diagram is a network representation of a system . . . (it) portrays the system in terms of its component pieces, with all interfaces among the components indicated."[12] A data flow diagram is *not* a flow chart. The diagram has no decision boxes or hardware symbols. A data flow diagram (DFD) shows motions and processes, the motion of data from one process to another. A process is defined as a place where the data is modified or undergoes change. There are only four components to a DFD. The first component is a symbol to represent a source/destination for data, usually symbolized by a square. The second component is a process symbol usually represented by a rectangle (or in Gane & Sarson methodology, a rectangle with rounded corners).[13] Arrows labeled as to data content connect the first two components together, the arrowheads representing the direction of that data flow. The last component is a symbol to represent a data collection point or data store. The symbol for this data at rest is usually an appropriately labeled open-ended rectangle.

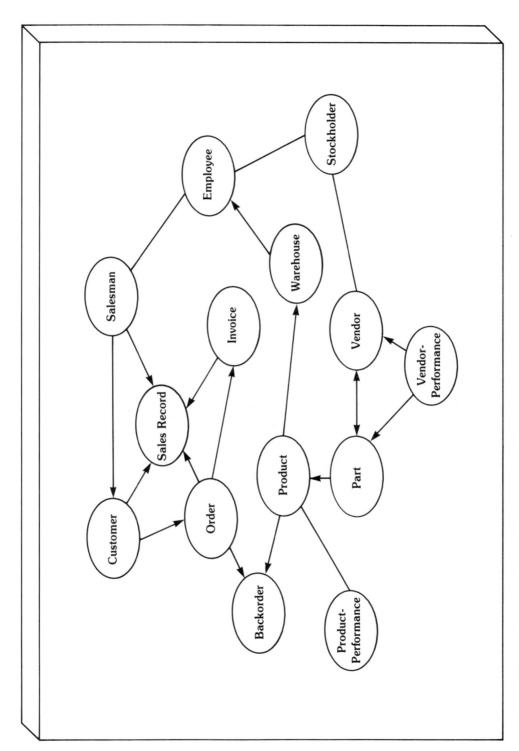

FIGURE 2.2   Sample Relational Map from E-Z Chair Functional Analysis

DFD's come in various levels of detail and complexity, the simplest being level zero. Any system should be able to be completely represented by a level 0 DFD on a single sheet of paper. If the system does not fit, then the diagram is too detailed or the scope of the system is too large. Figure 2.3 illustrates a possible level 0 DFD that might be drawn for a portion of E-Z Chair.

In the illustration four process blocks are identified.

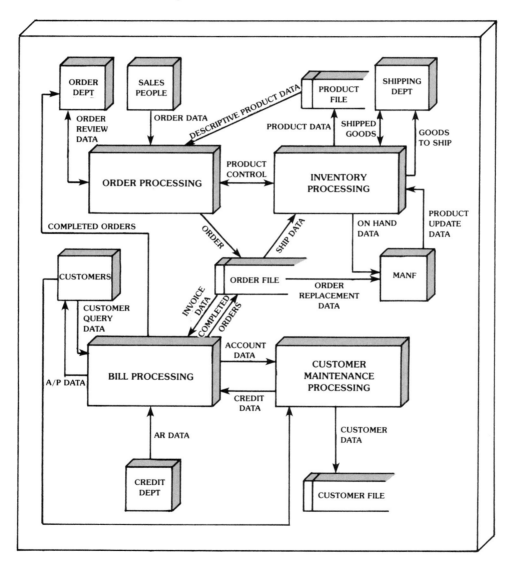

FIGURE 2.3   Sample Data Flow Diagram for E-Z Chair Corporation

Orders
Inventory control
Billing
Customer maintenance

The source destination(s) for data are as follows:

Salespeople
Order Department
Credit-finance Department
Customers
Manufacturing Department
Shipping Department

Three data stores or files are identified.

Customer
Order and backorder
Product

The data flows are clearly labeled. Notice that some flows are unidirectional, while others are bidirectional. The data labels are very general. The chart could indicate a little more detail by identifying which specific vehicles transport the data, such as an invoice, form number, or screen identifier. Any forms or documents thus mentioned would be appendixed to the functional specification documents.

The next step would be to break down each major process into a level 1 diagram, which treats the data and processes in greater detail. Each transaction within the process could then be identified in a separate process block and individual information trails plotted more finely. Successive levels of DFD, if constructed, could further decompose the functions. This kind of effect can successfully identify natural points to modularize the functions performed by the system.

This briefly describes functional analysis, a process that necessarily must precede data analysis. Both types of analysis must precede data base design. The thrust of this book however will be toward data analysis and logical file design. The data analysis project develops a logical model of the data.

The succeeding chapters in Part I will illustrate this data analysis project. It takes the data that was identified in functional analysis and gives the designer a methodology for analyzing and assessing it. The data base designer is concerned with what is in those data stores. The data flow diagram showed the data in motion; data analysis will show what the data will look like at rest.

NOTES

1. T. DeMarco, *Structured Analysis and Systems Specification* (New York: Yourdon, Inc., 1978–79), p. 4.

2. Peter F. Drucker, *Management: Tasks, Responsibilities, Practices* (New York: Harper & Row Publishers, 1974), p. 86.
3. Ibid., p. 93.
4. Ibid., p. 61.
5. Ibid., p. 80.
6. Ibid., p. 96.
7. Ibid.
8. Ibid., p. 99.
9. Ibid.
10. Ibid., p. 100.
11. Ibid., p. 102.
12. T. DeMarco, *Structured Analysis*, p. 47.
13. C. Gane and T. Sarson, *Structured Systems Analyses: Tools and Techniques* (New York: IST Data Books, 1977).

3 Normalization—Creating the Relations

Though this be madness, yet there is method in it.

Shakespeare, *Hamlet*

GROUPING DATA

Grouping data is the initial task in the data-oriented approach to analysis and design. The key to this task is normalization. However, no discussion of data grouping using normalization techniques can proceed without a definition of key terms. The definition merely serves to aid the reader in dealing with the techniques expressed within this text. Appendix B, at the end of the book, is a complete glossary of terms.

Entity
Something requiring identification either through names or description. It can be conceptual or physical. A customer's order is an example of an entity.

Attribute
A characteristic of an entity, a means of describing an entity. Different entities may have common attributes such as color, size and cost. An example of an attribute of a customer's order might be the date the order was placed.

Element, Data-item, Field
A name given the attribute, within the computer system, that represents the attribute. In our example the date the order is placed might be ORD DATE.

File
A set of entities composed of one or more fields for each entity. All the orders placed with a particular company would be the order file.

Identifiers
One or more fields that uniquely define an entity. For example, an identifier would be a number for a purchase order or an order number-part number for a line-item in combination on that order.

Key
An identifier, a field or fields used to access records directly or to sequence records based on the field's contents. Some entities may have more than one key that can still serve as an identifier, such as a class list being keyed by name as well as student number.

Candidate key
Any key that identifies an entity, such as student name or student number used in the previous example.

Primary key
The candidate key chosen to represent the entity.

Secondary key
An alternate candidate key that may or may not be unique, used to represent an entity. A name is one example, for a name may be duplicated.

Foreign key
A field that is an attribute of one entity set while at the same time being a candidate key of a different entity set. An example would be the field customer number that is an attribute in an order entity and a primary key in the customer entity.

Relation
A set of all entities of tuples or a single type arranged in tabular form.

Relationship
A single type of association between two units of data. Examples are the one to many, many to many, and one to one.

Tuple
An ordered collection of one or more data elements that make up a record, such as a row within a relation.

One problem right from the beginning of studies written on data base design and analysis, and in particular relational data base, is the terminology. A basic understanding is possible only by establishing a lexicon of basic terms. Tuples, attributes, relations, candidate keys, and domains are rather abstract notions. Field, file, and record are more concrete. It is easier to visualize a row in a table than the term "tuple in a relation," which, it turns out, means exactly the same thing. The problem arises in trying to develop a common vocabulary that will accommodate any situation in data processing using vocabulary and terminology from the world of mathematics.

The solution to this problem is to ignore it. Draw parallels based on common understanding and relate these relational concepts in terms of those understandings. In Figure 3.1, the E-Z Chair Order Form, the form itself is an *Entity*. "The entity has many attributes"; in order words the form has lots of data elements.

Now the basic tools of the data gathering process have been defined. At this point two steps are necessary to produce normalized relations: first group the relations, then normalize them.

Analysts tackling the task of grouping data into relationships are often faced with many conflicting or confusing statements about the data, depending upon where and how they obtain the data: from reports, from data in the reports, from comments by users about the reports, or from other users using the same data in different ways. Traditionally, attempts were made in this very early stage to refine the data and proceed immediately to schematize it into some sort of physical organization. However, fully refined data relations are not the objective of this step in data analysis. The important thing in step 1 is gaining an understanding of how the user perceives the key entities. Grouping elements around the key fields, gathering attributes, and assigning keys lay the foundation for step 2.

Data analysis identifies the data from a particular functional area by examining

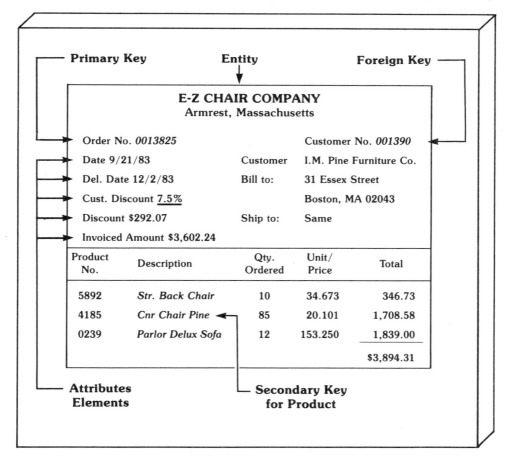

FIGURE 3.1 Sample E-Z Chair Corporation Order Form

the data flow, as represented by paperwork, within that functional area. Examples of such items are reports, file layouts, procedures, documents, inquiries, transactions, and even proposed future reports. Data analysis is a bottom-up approach to design. The specific pieces are examined in order to perceive the whole. Atre describes this process as being "outside-in." She states "It is desirable to examine systematically the purpose, inputs, and the desired outputs of the application."[1]

The task for the designer upon encountering an output document is threefold:

1. Give the document (the entry) a name.
2. Find any candidate keys.
3. Put it in a form that can be readily analyzed.

Giving the document a name means a *unique* name such as ORDER for the piece of paper in Figure 3.1. A different document with similar attributes in different physical locations should be called something else.

Finding the key or candidate key(s) is another matter entirely. Beware of assuming that you know the documents key. ORDER# may look like the key to you but you must verify that with the user. What if ORDER# recycles every January 1. Then ORDER# and DATE become the key or order. The test of a key is that by knowing first the key, you can retrieve only one particular order. If you had a file cabinet full of orders, what would you need to know in order to retrieve a particular order from the file? Could the same ORDER # be used on a different order? Could the same order have more than one ORDER #? Ask the user questions such as this, and you should have no trouble determining the candidate key(s).

As for putting the document into a format that can be more readily analyzed, just list the fields on the document. Put the entity name first, list the candidate key(s) next, then list all the other attributes of the entity. Fields that can take on more than one value occurrence within a single entity, such as PROD# and DESCRIPTION on order can be underlined. The underlined items are thus called *repeating* elements.

This example provides us with a preliminary order entity consisting of the following unnormalized relations:

ORDER (ORDER#, CUSTOMER#, ORDER DATE,

ORDER DEL. DATE, CUSTOMER NAME,

CUSTOMER DISCOUNT, CUSTOMER BILL TO,

CUSTOMER SHIP TO, TOT. ORDER AMT.,

ORDER DISCOUNT AMT., INVOICED AMT.,

<u>PRODUCT#, PROD. DESC., PROD. PRICE,</u>

<u>PROD. QTY ORDERED, TOT. PROD. ORDERED)</u>

The underlined fields are values that recur throughout the order. Thus, through analysis of the physical order form we have produced the unnormalized "Order" entity.

NORMALIZATION: FIRST, SECOND, AND THIRD NORMAL FORMS

The problem remains: how to normalize the data? In fact, what is normalization, and why should data be normalized?

It is generally recognized that the father of normalization is E.F. Codd. He proposed a technique for decomposing data into smaller structures in which each attribute was totally dependent upon the primary key of the entity in which it resides. Codd's contribution was in making the process a human one, and in removing it from the abstract-theoretical mathematics in which normalization theory has its roots.

The process of data normalization is not new; data base administrators (DBAs) have been intuitively doing precisely that for years. What is new is that normalization should not be an exclusive skill of the DBA. Normalization depends upon a knowledge and understanding of data in the functional business unit being examined and the way it relates together. It does not depend upon any particular data base knowledge or skills.

Analysts, users, and even management can produce third-normal-form data structures comparable to those produced by an experienced DBA by following the normalization stages, step by step. There is one key difference between the two, however; when asked to explain why the entities are structured in this manner, most DBA's would say "experience." On the other hand analysts, users, and managers could give definite reasons for the structure, for they understand how the data is used, and they use normalization to express that understanding.

RELEVANCE OF NORMALIZATION

The benefits of reducing data to small stable structures through normalization can be quite substantial. Gane and Sarson refer to the process as "inspired common sense." Consider the following typical file maintenance problem.

Maintenance involves both minor tasks, such as expanding the length of a field and more complex tasks such as adding new fields with increased functional complexity. For the sake of argument, let us say the purchase order described earlier included a product warehouse location for each item orderd so that the order serves as a picking slip. What happens if the location changes? All orders for that product would have to be found and updated. This could be a trivial problem, or it could prove to be a significant one. What if the change also involved several warehouses? The data field for warehouse locations would have to be expanded. This would necessitate locating and updating every program that used the order file, even for programs that do not concern product location.

Certainly the impact of changes like that could be minimized by putting filler in files to accommodate larger record formats. But the point is this: a product location change should affect only those programs that utilize the data in question—not every program that uses the file.

Instead, if product numbers were the only product-related attributes retained on the order file, that key could be used to find product location from another product file or table.

In fact, you may have intuitively decided to do precisely that—separate product information onto a separate file. In so doing, you would have intuitively normalized that order entity.

What has been done in this process is to say "product data, such as description and location, have nothing to do with order," rather that they are dependent on product number. Thus the product "attribute" of an order entity could be the "foreign key" product number. Product number, in all probability, would be the primary key of a product data base or table.

Through normalization we thus minimize the impact of future change on data. In the example a product location change would only affect the product entity. The programs that did not utilize this information remained unaffected by the change. Normalization in this case not only minimizes program maintenance, it also minimizes data maintenance.

What about the normalization process itself? There are three main stages in normalization: first normal form, second normal form, and third normal form.

First normal form requires the identification or repeating groups that exist within an entity. A relation is in first normal form if all its attributes are simple, with no repeating groups. Thus, the first rule of normalization:

Repeating groups are removed into a new entity.

Let us illustrate this by examining our earlier ORDER entity garnered from analysis of the E-Z Chair purchase order.

ORDER   (ORDER#, CUSTOMER#, ORDER DATE,

ORDER DEL. DATE, CUSTOMER NAME,

CUSTOMER DISCOUNT, CUSTOMER BILL TO,

CUSTOMER SHIP TO, TOT. ORDER AMT.,

ORDER DISCOUNT AMT., INVOICED AMT.,

PRODUCT#, PROD. DESC., PROD. PRICE,

PROD. QTY ORDERED, TOT. PROD. ORDERED)

Since the convention we chose for indicating repeating groups within an entity was underlining, we can readily identify the repeating group within this entity. First normal form requires us to remove this product repeating group from the order entity and make a new entity, LINEITEM. Thus we have PRODUCT NUMBER, PROD. DESC.,

PRODUCT QUANTITY, PROD. PRICE, TOT. PROD. ORDERED as a separate entity. We must uniquely define each entity occurrence of LINEITEM. The thing to realize here is that removing repeating group *always* results in a compound key. The first part of the key will be the key of the entity from which you removed the repeating group. What can readily be recognized is that PRODUCT#, in and of itself, is not sufficient to uniquely qualify LINEITEM. There is no way to identify the parent order for each product quantity ordered, that is, to differentiate it from other line items on other orders. In order to uniquely identify LINEITEM, we need a compound key of ORDER# *and* PRODUCT#. Thus our two entities, ORDER and LINEITEM (ORDERED-PRODUCT), can be illustrated as follows:

ORDER   (ORDER#, CUSTOMER#, ORDER DATE,

ORDER DEL. DATE, CUSTOMER NAME,

CUSTOMER DISCOUNT, CUSTOMER BILL TO,

CUSTOMER SHIP TO, TOT. ORDER AMT.,

ORDER DISCOUNT AMT., INVOICED AMT.)

LINEITEM   (ORDER#, PRODUCT#, PRODUCT DESC.,

PROD. PRICE, PROD. QTY ORDERED,

TOT. PROD. ORDERED AMT.)

Finding the key requires understanding what functional dependence is and how it is determined. An attribute Y is said to be functionally dependent on another attribute X if for *every* value of X there can be associated with it only one value of Y. X is thus called the determinant of Y, and Y is functionally dependent on X.

Second Normal Form, the next step in the normalization process, requires the identity of those attributes which are only partially dependent on the primary or compound key of the entity in which they reside. A relation is in second normal form if it is in first form and every nonkey attribute is fully functionally dependent on the whole compound key. Thus the second rule of normalization:

Attributes that are wholly dependent on only part of the primary key or primary compound key are removed into a separate entity.

Let's apply this rule to the two entities we have extracted in first normal form. In the ORDER entity none of the attributes is partially dependent upon the ORDER# key; the thing to examine here in the ORDER # is order number in fact a single field?

Perhaps it is made up of several subfields. An example might be that the first three digits of ORDER# *represent region code*. If this were the case, then any attribute dependent on REGION is partially dependent on the entire ORDER# key and therefore should be removed into a new entity, REGION. In our example this is not the case. When a key cannot be broken into subfields it is said to be *atomic*. Order number is atomic. Second-normal-form analysis is not done on entities with atomic keys.

However, the LINEITEM entity is another matter. This ordered-product entity is a compound key, and certain attributes of this entity are dependent solely on PRODUCT#. Attributes such as unit price and name are describing PRODUCT# and are not dependent on ORDER#. PRODUCT DESC. does not change every time the order changes. Thus, a new entity called PRODUCT results from second-normal-form analysis as follows:

ORDER (ORDER#, CUSTOMER#, ORDER DATE,

     ORDER DEL. DATE, CUSTOMER NAME,

     CUSTOMER DISCOUNT, CUSTOMER BILL TO,

     CUSTOMER SHIP TO, TOT. ORDERED AMT.,

     ORDER DISCOUNT AMT., INVOICED AMT.)

LINEITEM (ORDER#, PRODUCT#, PROD. QTY ORDERED,

     TOT. PROD. ORDERED AMT.)

PRODUCT (PRODUCT#, PROD. DESC., PROD. PRICE)

What you really do is pull off any attributes that do not depend on the entire nonatomic key. *Third normal form*, our last step in normalization identifies those attributes in an entity not dependent upon the primary key of that entity, whether singular or compound, but on some other key within the entity. A relation is in third normal form if it is in second normal form and each nonkey attribute is functionally dependent on the primary key and not dependent on any nonkey attribute. Thus the last rule of normalization:

Attributes wholly dependent upon another key within an entity should be removed into another entity.

Look for groups of attributes seemingly on the "wrong" record.

The terms for attributes not totally dependent on the primary key of the entity in which they reside are called "transitory dependents." Their apparent dependence is only because of their existence within the entity in the first place, not because of a direct relationship established externally. These attributes are there because they start out on the order form due to user needs. They were "in transit" with each other, on the same bus so to speak. Well now it's their stop, and time to kick them off. It is the elimination of such transitive dependence that can have the greatest stabilizing influence upon data structures.

When we return to the example and apply this third rule of normalization, we recognize certain attributes of the ORDER entity as transitory dependents. Customer name, customer address, delivery address and discount rate are totally dependent on the foreign key CUSTOMER#, not the primary key ORDER#. The only dependence on ORDER# is transitive. Therefore, remove them into a separate entity called CUSTOMER. Third-normal-form analysis gives our fully normalized set of entities as follows:

ORDER (ORDER#, CUSTOMER#, ORDER DATE,

ORDER DEL. DATE, ORDER DISCOUNT AMT.,

INVOICED AMT., TOT. ORDER AMT.)

CUSTOMER (CUSTOMER#, CUSTOMER NAME,

CUSTOMER DISCOUNT, CUSTOMER BILL TO,

CUSTOMER SHIP TO.)

LINEITEM (ORDER#, PRODUCT#, PROD. QTY ORDERED,

TOT. PROD. ORDERED AMT.)

PRODUCT (PRODUCT#, PROD. DESC., PROD. PRICE)

The result of this final third-normal-form analysis is to produce relationships whose nonkey attributes are mutually independent yet entirely dependent upon the primary key of the entity in which they reside. As an exercise, examine the copy of an

E-Z CHAIR COMPANY
Armrest, Mass.

Invoice No. 0091833   Shipment 0396   Invoice Date 9/21/83

Order No. 0013825   Customer No. 001390

Order Date 09/21/83   Name I.M. PINE FURNITURE CO.

Del. Date 12/02/83   31 ESSEX STREET
                             BOSTON,MA 02043
Ship To: 31 ESSEX STREET
          BOSTON,MA 02043

Special Inst: Delivery to rear, loading dock #8

Product No.	Description	Qty Ord.	Qty Ship.	Qty Back.	Unit Price	Total Price
5892	Str.Back Chair	10	10		34.673	346.73
4185	Cnr. Chair Pine	85	85		20.101	1708.58
0239	Palor Delx. Sofa	12	9	3	153.250	1379.25

TOTAL AMOUNT   3434.56
___ **DISCOUNT**   257.58
PLEASE PAY   3176.98

FIGURE 3.2 Sample Problem

invoice for E-Z Chair Corporation in Figure 3.2 and normalize the data into third normal form. The answer is outlined in Appendix C.

BUSINESS FUNCTIONS AND RELATIONSHIPS

In the previous explanation of normalization, what also should have been realized is the emphasis placed on relationships. In fact, the next task of data analysis is to formally establish the relationship between data entities.

This process is repetitive, and normalization serves to clarify the relationships. Determining these basic relationships between entities can be called determining "business functions." In other words, what can be specifically stated about a particular relationship? If possible, business functions should be determined prior to normalization. When normalization has been completed, finalize the business functions.

What are examples of business functions? In the previous example, a number of questions could arise regarding orders. Can more than one customer be on an order?

What is the relationship between product and orders and order to products? When these questions are resolved we have our functions.

In our example we have the following relationships:

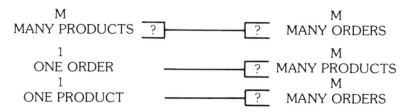

This means that many products can be involved in many orders, and, thus, there are many order-to-product and product-to-order relationships.

implies the relationship

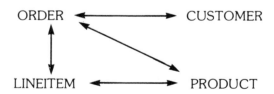

Only one customer corresponds with a particular order. When the many becomes a one, the relationship becomes one to one.

If we map the four entities from the example, the following occurs:

```
ORDER  ◄─────────►  CUSTOMER
   ▲  ╲
   │    ╲
   │      ╲
   ▼        ╲►
LINEITEM ◄─────────► PRODUCT
```

This chart can be a very useful tool to help clarify the relationships. Notice that third normal form does not destroy the intrinsic relationships of the entities. The products involved in an order can be resolved by looking at LINEITEM, and the relation of a particular product to that order is also found in the same relation.

J.J. Yanko describes the need to "check the relations with the user"[3] after performing normalization and list them. The list of business functions indicates volumes and frequency of occurrence of entities. The following is an example of a formal statement of a company's business functions.

Business Functions of E-Z Chair Corporation

E-Z Chair Corporation has 5,000 customers who place orders for 5,000 products. An average of up to 5 orders at any time may be in process for any single customer. Ten percent of the total orders being processed may have backorders to be filled.

The average order has 6 products ordered with a range of anywhere from 1 to 30 products. Because of backorder processing, the average order generates 2 invoices to cover an average of 2 shipments per order. Each product has an average of 60 invoice product lines with an average of 1 backorder for every 2 products.

Analyze these functions for volume and frequency of occurrence. Analysis of these functions shows there are 5,000 customers, each having an average of 5 outstanding orders at any one time, resulting in an average of 25,000 pending orders. The number of line items in process (ordered-products) at 6 per order is 150,000. Continue along in this manner until a volume for each entity and an associative frequency of occurrence between them can be determined. Also, use the entities derived from normalization of the invoice. See Table 3.1 for results of this analysis.

TABLE 3.1 Business Function Table for E-Z Chair Example

Entity	Volume	Frequency
CUSTOMER	5,000	Stated
ORDER	25,000	5/Customer
LINEITEM	150,000	6/order
BACKORDER	2,500	1/2 products; 1/10 orders
INVOICE	50,000	2/order; 10/customer
PRODUCTS	5,000	Stated
INVLINE	300,000	60/product

RELATIONAL CONSIDERATIONS: PROJECTION, JOINING, AND PARTITIONING

Before continuing to relational mapping, and combining the analysis of business functions with fully normalized entities, consider the following review of normalization and the manipulation of relations.

The process of normalization, extracting logical entities from a larger whole, is called projection. (It is a process of removal of fields in a relation that are not required or that are duplicated.) Normalization involves the removal of the superfluous fields in a relation.

Consider the following example of a teacher-course relation.

TEACHER-COURSE

Teacher #	Classroom #	Course #
10	5	1
11	3	2
12	1	3
20	5	1
21	1	3

Project the classroom number and course number from the relation to form a new entity called room-course:

ROOM-COURSE

Classroom #	Course #
5	1
3	2
1	3

Notice that teacher numbers 10 and 20 and 12 and 21 have duplicate values for classroom number and course number. Notice also that the key of the new entity is classroom number. This key is in third normal form as long as there is one and only one value of course for each value of classroom number. This new entity may or may not be useful. It may indicate a room-course dependency that could help reduce the redundancy found in the TEACHER-COURSE entity.

The problem lies in the nature of the relationship of the projected elements to the key. As long as it is one on one everything is fine. If the same classroom is used for another course, the whole projection becomes valueless.

Projection is really just another way of looking at the normalization process. The more you refine the dependencies, the more you reduce individual entity redundancy. This of course results in generating more records or entities. The negative aspect of all this redundancy reduction is the number of new entities being created. In order to create meaningful information from the data one must now collect a number of entities. This is where the concept of *joining* comes into play.

Joining is the reverse of projection. *Joining* combines entities together to reduce the cost of collecting many different entities. However, in order to join two entities together, they must have at least one attribute in common. It is the nature of that common attribute that we must focus on now.

The attribute that is common to both relations has two options. Either the attribute in common is a foreign key, or the attribute in common is not a key. What we need is a rule for determining the key of the joined entity.

Illustrated below is a FACULTY and DEPARTMENT relation which join using the common field Dept # which is the key of the DEPARTMENT entity.

FACULTY

Teacher #	Name	Title	Dept #
100	M. Mouse	Prof	16
210	D. Duck	Ass't Prof	10
220	P. Dog	Ass't Prof	10
300	I.M. Goofy	Inst	17
410	P. Pan	T.A.	12

DEPARTMENT

Dept. #	Name	Location
10	History	Toad Hall
16	Math	Wonderland
17	Psychology	Nutt House

Results of the merger:

Teacher	Name	Title	Dept #	Dept Name	Location
100	M. Mouse	Prof	16	Math	Wonderland
210	D. Duck	Ass't Prof	10	History	Toad Hall
220	P. Dog	Ass't Prof	10	History	Toad Hall
300	I.M. Goofy	Inst	17	Psychology	Nutt House
410	P. Pan	T.A.	12	Physics	Never Land

The key of the resultant entity is teacher number. Notice the result is only in second normal form.

Project a new relation over a field which is *not* a key field of either entity and observe the results. Combine the new entity STATUS with the old entity FACULTY, using the name key field TITLE.

STATUS

Status	Title	Tenure
A	Prof	10
B	Ass't. Prof	7
C	Inst	5
D	T.A.	1

Result of merger:

Teacher #	Status	Title	Dept #	Names	Tenure
100	A	Prof	16	M. Mouse	10
210	B	Ass't. Prof	10	D. Duck	7
220	B	Ass't. Prof	10	P. Dog	7
300	C	Inst	17	I.M. Goofy	5
410	D	T.A.	12	P. Pan	1

The key of the resultant entity is TEACHER # and STATUS. Note that from the example one can derive the following rules of key formation:

When two entities are joined over a common field and that field:

1. is not a key field in either entity, then the key of the combined entity is the compound key resulting from both original keys; or

2. is a key of one of them, then the key of the combined entity is the key of the other entity.

The logic seems circular here. First I say normalize everything and reduce redundancy. Then I say join it all back together again because retrieving all those extra entities is too expensive. Well you can't have your cake and eat it too.

Normalization will give your design flexibility. Normalization will reduce redundancy and decrease your duplicate data maintenance problems. But combining records gives you better performance. What are you supposed to do?

I am attempting to teach you an ideal set of rules for developing entities. Then you break those rules when you practice joining. All I am really saying is that you must know the rules before you break the rules. The designer must realize the implications of sacrificing data independence for performance. The rest of this book will try and aid you in this decision.

Another form of projection of fully normalized relationship is through a technique called *partitioning*. Partitioning of data results from some external factor introducing a reason for further restructuring or separation of data. The partitioning is of two types: vertical and horizontal. (This process is sometimes referred to as fourth normal form.)

Suppose for ease of processing, the FACULTY entity would work better if all the personal data were in one entity and all the departmental data were in another. One could *vertically* partition the entity. Literally draw a vertical line through the entity and group data items on either side of that line accordingly.
The result might look like this:

FACULTY-DEPT	TEACHER #,	DEPT #	
FACULTY-PERSON	TEACHER #,	NAME,	TITLE

The structure is developed by weighting the entity's individual attribute characteristics. The relationship is externally imposed and is therefore artifical and not intrinsic to the data. Horizontal partitioning is similar to vertical partitioning in that the new relation formed results from external manipulation and not from the data itself. Using the FACULTY entity, group by title all the full professors together, all the associates, all the instructors, and so forth. The entity structure remains unchanged as follows:

FAC-PROF	TEACHER #,	NAME,	TITLE,	DEPT #
FAC-ASS'T	TEACHER #,	NAME,	TITLE,	DEPT #
FAC-INST	TEACHER #,	NAME,	TITLE,	DEPT #

Another method of partitioning is to assign ranges of values to teacher number to indicate their title. Notice, however, that the first digit of each teacher number could be used to group the teachers by title. The horizontal partitioning of a data base by teacher number would in reality group by title. Those teachers having numbers below 200 are professors. Those teachers having numbers between 199 and 300 are assistant professors. In this example the entity structures are developed from externally imposed value considerations based upon the entity's key. Notice that the entity and the fields from which it is made remain constant, but the values of the fields are important in the partitioning process. This is horizontal partitioning of data.

The key point to remember is that vertical partitioning makes entities physically smaller by dividing them into two or more separate entities. Horizontal partitioning does not physically alter the entity content, but it makes the volume of data in each entity smaller and tends to organize the different-valued entities of the same type into distinct groupings. This tends to clump the relations into subrelations on mini-data bases within a single larger data base.

Partitioning can be a very useful technique to learn. In the data base environment, anything the designer can do to reduce the cost of locating the right record is good.

Vertical partitioning might enable you to put the most frequently accessed attributes in a different record from the less frequently accessed attributes. This size reduction would enable you to put more records on a block; thus more "good" data could be accessed with less physical input and output. Maybe grouping data on records by security requirements through vertical partitioning might expedite a security problem.

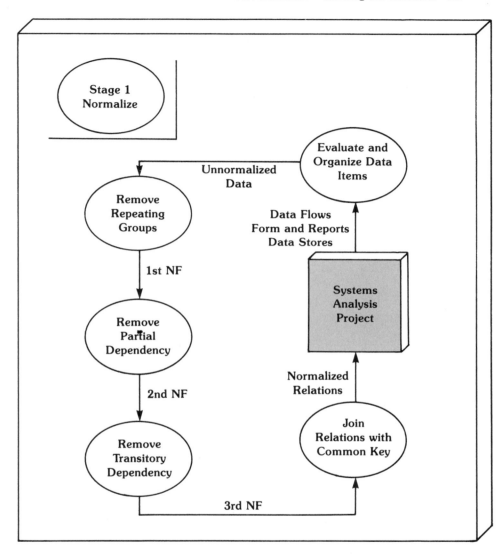

FIGURE 3.3   Stage 1—Normalization of Data Flow

Horizontal partitioning—grouping entities with the same attributes by some external characterization type—can be a powerful tool also. Identify those customers on your file who placed the bulk of your orders and assign them a special type code. If you then sort on that code, all your "good" customers are grouped physically near each other. If they could be positioned properly you could reduce the I/O expense in locating those customers at the expense of those customers you do not access as often. The performance gains can be significant.

If all of this sounds like it should be a physical design consideration, you are right. The reason for dicussing it here is that most partitioning involves special attributes or "intelligent keys," and this is too important not to discuss at the earliest possible time. Overall, however, the normalization process can best be summarized in Figure 3.3. Partitioning is a secondary consideration at this point in the analysis.

4 Relational Mapping

A picture shows me at a glance what it takes dozens of pages of a book to expound.

Ivan Sergeyevich Turgenev,
Fathers and Sons

RELATIONAL MAPS: TYPES AND NATURE

In the previous chapter we derived two constructs that are essential in the next step in data analysis, relational mapping. Those two constructs, third-normal-form entities and the business function analysis, are combined graphically to indicate the links between relations. Relationship mapping is a process to graphically represent the relationships defined by the structure of records. There are only three linkage relation types: one to one, one to many, and many to many.

Relationship mapping or E-R modeling has its roots in the early data structure diagrams developed by C.W. Bachman. The "Bachman diagram" represented data records with the use of an appropriately labeled rectangle. Relationships between records were expressed in one-to-many "sets" consisting of owner records and member records indicated by the use of arrows. The arrowhead being at the many or "member" end of the records. The notation has evolved from Bachman's arrow to IBM's double arrow, to Geoffrey Baker's crow's feet to my use of a box, which best represents the diagrammatic needs of data analysis. Data relationships are nondirectional, whereas arrowheads by their very nature are directional. (See Figure 4.1).

Of all the relational linkage types, the most common by far is the one-to-many relationship. A typical example of this linkage type used earlier is the ORDER:LINE-ITEM relation. There is one ORDER, and there are many LINEITEMS. The most

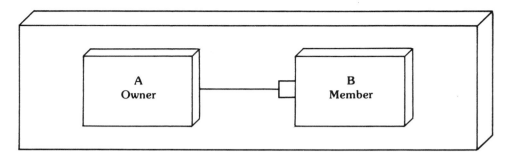

FIGURE 4.1   Example of One-to-Many Set

common way to structure a one-to-many (1:M) relation is through the use of the tree or hierarchical architecture (see Figure 4.2).

The one-to-one (1:1) relationship is less common than the 1:M relationship since most organizations have a hierarchical structure. The relationship can be graphically symbolized as a hierarchy, (a special case of the 1:M relation) or as a simple lateral connection between two entity relations, (see Figure 4.3) as exemplified by the ORDER to CUSTOMER relation.

The many-to-many relationship (M:M) is the most complex relationship. In the example the relation of ORDER to PRODUCT is a M:M relationship: many orders can have many products. This relational linkage type can be more easily handled by dividing the relationship into two 1:M relations; this can be accomplished by constructing a third intermediary entity with the combined key of the two relations involved in the M:M relationship. The ORDER to PRODUCT relation, (many to many), developed the ORDERED-PRODUCT (LINEITEM) entity (see Figure 4.4).

Notice that normalization resolved the problem in first-normal-form analysis of the data. If the M:M relationship is significant to understanding an integral function of the data, normalization will resolve the bridging entity. If the M:M relationship exists, and it is not significant to the problem, such as PRODUCT to CUSTOMER, normalization does not resolve the problem.

The resultant entity created from two entities involved in a many-to-many relationship is called a junction entity. The name comes to us from the practitioners of set theory. (IMS people would call this *intersection data*). Junction data is always dependent. Junction data always has at least two owners or parents. The key of the junction entity is always created by combining the keys of all the owners of that data.

Every data base management system handles the M:M relationship by creating a junction entity. By breaking the M:M into two one:M relationships, you have reduced the mechanics of pointer implementation considerably. Also the data that is contained on the junction record can be seen as belonging to many other records with the advantage of only having to be stored once.

In Chapter 3, boxes around an entity and arrows pointing from entity to entity

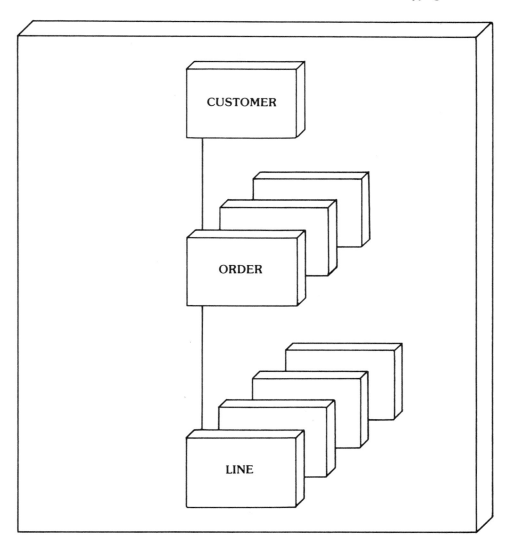

FIGURE 4.2   Example of Tree or Hierarchical Data Base Architecture

indicate the relationship between them as indicated in the business rules. This is an example of a relational map. Let us now formalize that structure by going through all the entities provided in the E-Z Chair example, and map the relations between them.

The diagramming rules are as follows:

Enclose entities in circles.

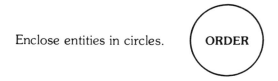

Indicate linkage types by using lines to connect circles. Boxes on lines indicate the type of relation as shown in Figure 4.5

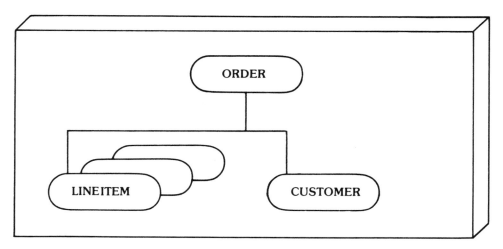

FIGURE 4.3   Sample Hierarchy

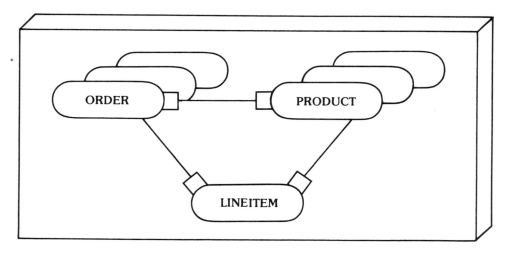

FIGURE 4.4   Many-to-Many Relationship

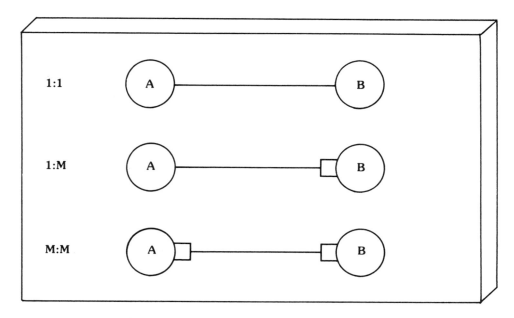

FIGURE 4.5 Sample Relationship Types

Other diagramming techniques using arrowheads (single and double) to indicate the one and the many end of a relationship are currently used by IBM and are documented in works by S. Atre and M.L. Gillenson (see Bibliography). However, because arrows indicate direction and flow, they can be confused, with usage paths, which are to be discussed later. Hence the box is used instead here to indicate "many." Note the M:M relationship is usually normalized to two one:M relations.

The relationship map is developed from relations in third normal form. The lines are drawn based upon foreign key to candidate key principals. As stated earlier a *foreign key* is an attribute or group of attributes in one relation that is a candidate key in another relation. Thus any relation with a foreign key attribute is the many end of a one-to-many relationship. A *candidate key* is an attribute or group of attributes that can serve to identify each tuple in a relation (row in a table). This is the one end of the one-to-many relationship. Now proceed to the entities in the following example:

An order can have one and only one CUSTOMER, but a CUSTOMER can have many ORDERs. Order number is the key; it is found embedded as a foreign key in LINEITEM (see Figure 4.6).

An ORDER can have many LINEITEM entities, but that LINEITEM exists on only one ORDER (as in Figure 4.7).

Orders can have many PRODUCTS and vice versa. (Figure 4.8).

PRODUCT can have many LINEITEM entities in different orders, but a particular LINEITEM specifies only one PRODUCT. Again, the foreign key to candidate key relationship determines the one and the many. (See Figure 4.9.) Notice there are two

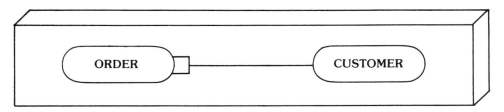

FIGURE 4.6   Many-to-One Relationship of ORDERS to CUSTOMER

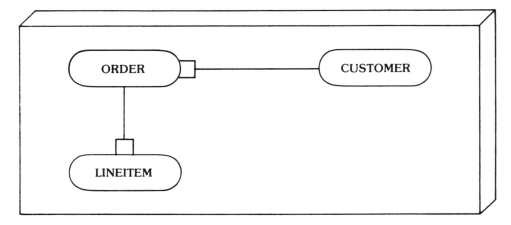

FIGURE 4.7   Additional One-to-Many Relationship between ORDER and LINEITEM

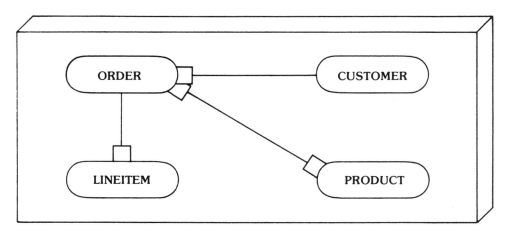

FIGURE 4.8   The Many-to-Many PRODUCT to ORDER Relationship

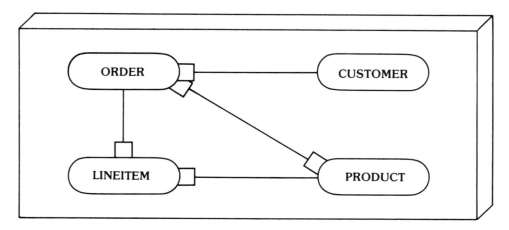

FIGURE 4.9   The One-to-Many PRODUCT to LINEITEM Relationship

links to get from PRODUCT to ORDER—a direct M:M link and two 1:M links through LINEITEM. The normalization into the LINEITEM entity requires the compound key of order number and product number. Since this path also provides a direct way to get from PRODUCT to ORDER or ORDER to PRODUCT, the M:M relation becomes superfluous. Redrawn, the structure looks like Figure 4.10.

The INVOICE has three relational paths—a 1:M from ORDER to INVOICE, a 1:M from CUSTOMER to INVOICE, and a M:M from INVOICE to PRODUCT. INVOICE has customer number and order number in it as foreign key attributes. (See Figure 4.11.)

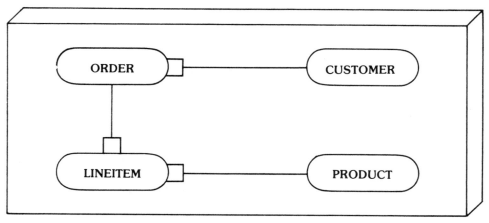

FIGURE 4.10   The LINEITEM Junction Allows Removal of the ORDER to PRODUCT Many-to-Many Relationship

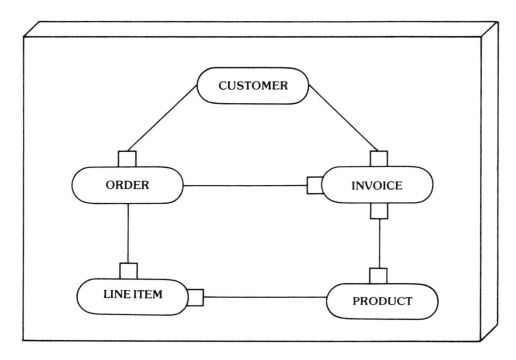

FIGURE 4.11   Relational Map After Introducing the INVOICE Entity

INVLINE is a product of normalizing the INVOICE data and projecting out the invoice line repeating group. PRODUCT can have many INVLINES, and INVOICE can have many INVOICE-LINES. Mapping these new paths negates the need for the M:M from PRODUCT to INVOICE. The compound key of INVLINE is really two foreign keys, invoice number and product number, as shown in Figure 4.12.
The last entity to map is BACKORDER. This entity is related to ORDER and PRODUCT in two one-to-many linkages. The final structure, the completed relational map, is shown in Figure 4.13.

RELATIONSHIP MAPPING: FREQUENCY RATIOS ALONG DEFINED PATHS

We now have a very clear picture, as exemplified by the relational map, of just how the data entities are related. Mapping is a technique to represent those relations graphically.

The terms *relational link* and *path* were used interchangeably in the previous example on relational mapping. The use of these relational links as access paths to real data is a logical extension of the normalization and business rules principles.

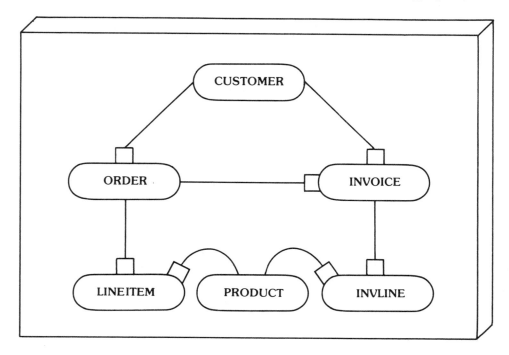

FIGURE 4.12 Relational Map Adding the INVLINE Junction

At this point we have Table 3.1, the table with the average frequency of occurrence of each relation as a ratio to the entity relations to which it is linked. The table resulted from an analysis of the business functions made in Chapter 3.

The task now becomes one of overlaying these average values and ratios on top of a copy of the relational map. First, record the approximate value of each entity somewhere within the circle. A typical customer entity might be coded as:

Next, utilizing the frequency of occurrence column, place a figure in the box at the end of the relational link to indicate the ratio of the entities involved in the relation with each other. On average there are five orders per customer in our example, coded as shown in Figure 4.14.

The simple rule to follow here is "Divide the volume of the one into the volume of the many." Repeat this exercise for the entire relational map, with the results as indicated in Figure 4.3.

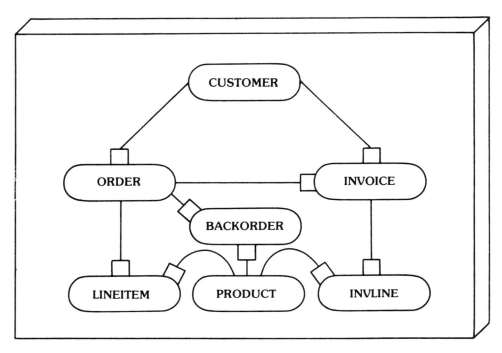

FIGURE 4.13 Final Relational Map After Adding the BACKORDER Entity

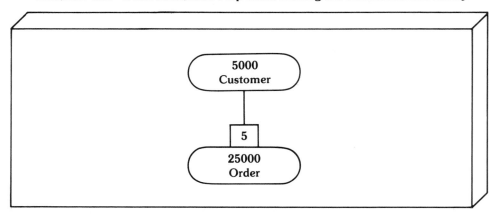

FIGURE 4.14 Ratio of Entities in a Relation

This technique is utilized by S. Atre, C. Finkelstein, and M.L. Rubin. The Finkelstein and Rubin mapping technique is based on simple entity ratios, while the Atre technique employs a more complex and thorough treatment of probability theory and mathematical expectation. Both techniques are simple tools that illustrate the methodology and have both a useful and a practical purpose.

Two ratios, INVOICE to INVLINE and PRODUCT to LINEITEM, were deduced from the volume of the entities in the relation. The relational map in Figure 4.15 shows the frequency of access along relational links, but only those links (paths) that are derived directly from the data. Figure 4.16 recapitulates the entire mapping process.

Every input or output operation against a data base uses a path through a set of relations. The relationship may be intrinsic to the data and expressed as a normalized relational link, or it may be artifically imposed by the designer for performance reasons. Nevertheless, following the paths and multiplying out the frequency ratios can give a designer a considerable amount of information.

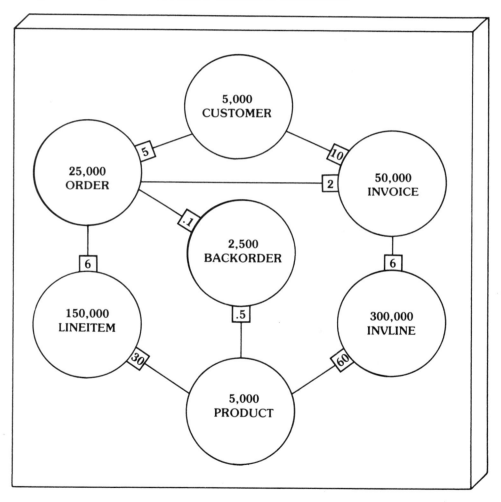

FIGURE 4.15   Relational Map with Frequency Ratios

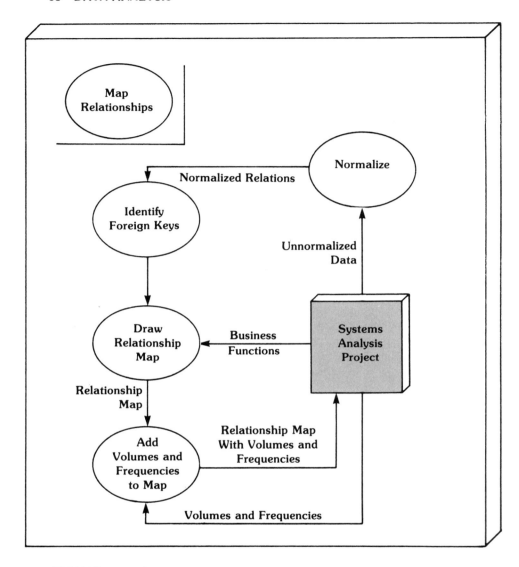

FIGURE 4.16 Stage 2—Map Relationships Data Flow Diagram

In order to develop a true feeling for the uses of the data for a particular system, as designer you must create some type of diagram for each function within the system in order to identify each system function along with its data requirements. Build paths from entity to entity, indicating the direction of the path in terms of the data requirements of the function. The paths you use for the most part should already exist as relational links. If necessary, you should construct new links in order to complete the function. This transaction mapping process is defined in detail in the next chapter.

5 Transaction Analysis

Attempt the end, and never stand to doubt; nothing's so hard but search will find it out.

Robert Herrick,"Seek and Find"

WHAT IS A TRANSACTION MAP?

Transaction analysis involves building diagrams of how the data is being used by individual transactions. Four questions are illustrated and answered by a transaction map.

1. Where does the transaction start (its entry point)?
2. What is the minimal number of entities needed to satisfy a transaction's data requirements?
3. What is the flow of the transaction from entity to entity?
4. What type of access is required of the entity selected (read, update, delete, etc.)?

The diagrams constructed are really bubble charts showing the logical order of data access for each transaction. As stated *earlier* in Chapter 1, this is qualitative analysis; no loading or number calculation is done here. Start the process by answering the four questions to the best of your ability.

To determine the entity point or starting entity, determine what data you know before you start the transaction. In particular, take note of what key values you know. When starting any transaction you must always enter at some known point and then utilize the data structure to get to your unknowns. Compose a shopping list of attributes needed to satisfy a transaction's data requirements. Some you will know already; some you will need to retrieve. Figuring out what to retrieve and when to retrieve it is the process of transaction mapping.

In order to determine the entities required, look at your list of unknown, but needed, data attributes. On what entities do these attributes reside? If a needed attribute resides on more than one entity, select the entity that has other values that are needed but only reside in one location. In this manner you will retrieve only the minimal entity set.

In order to determine the flow from entity to entity, try and visualize an ideal structure in which any record access is possible. Do not worry about having "the right keys" to get from one entity to the next. Get an entity only if it has data elements on it that you need to display or modify. This should further limit the number of entities accessed. Obviously, ignoring transportation requirements will not save you from doing something about the problem. Just put off this task for a while. You will have a better method of dealing with it later. Branch from entity to entity by satisfying your data attribute shopping list. Make believe that conditions are ideal. Make believe that all the data records you need are arranged to suit your purpose. You decide what are these ideal conditions.

Last, determine what you are doing to the attributes required. Are you just reading them? Are you updating them? What kind of processing option do you need on each entity being accessed. Indicate that need with a letter code such as this:

R = Read only
U = Update
I = Insert
D = Delete
L = Load

Sample transaction maps for the E-Z Chair Corporation will be built to illustrate the technique.

BUILDING TRANSACTION MAPS FOR E-Z CHAIR

Thus far data analysis has proceeded step by step, handling functions or relations one at a time, then combining the result of each analysis into a composite structure of some type. When two different composite structures existed, the relational map and the transaction usage map, they became a composite logical structure.

The techniques for resolving the access paths do not differ from this pattern. The process builds on the previous results and adds to them by again analyzing each system function and calculating a path for each. When all functions have been calculated, combine the results into a system composite map.

Now take the E-Z Chair order example and start building transaction maps for each function. First identify some possible functions of the order-invoicing system.

a. Create an order.
b. Create an invoice.
c. Update a backorder.
d. Inquire about all customers' orders/invoices/products.
e. Inquire about all customers' backorders.
f. On how many invoices does a particular product occur?
g. Any backorders for a product?
h. What customers have ordered this product?
i. How many orders for this product?

Each of the functions in this list of examples is labeled for easier identification later during the mapping process. (See Figures 5.1–5.9) Determine where you start by determining your known factors. Start with the entity that contains the "known," and proceed from there to the unknowns. Determine what entities you need by obtaining *only* those entities that contain the fields necessary to satisfy your transactions data requirements. The flow is determined by picking an optional process order that may or may not be represented in the relational map.

Create an order.   The order taker knows ORD#, DATE, all the product numbers, and all the quantities ordered. The transaction must create the order document. The unknown information is pricing and description information. For this the ORDER is a starting point. Additional data requirements are for inserting LINEITEM, reading CUSTOMER, updating PRODUCT and inserting BACKORDER information. A diagram of this structure is shown in figure 5.1

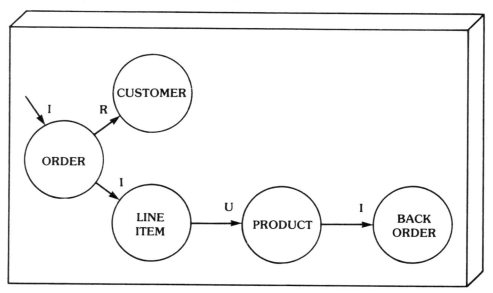

FIGURE 5.1   Usage Map for Transaction a

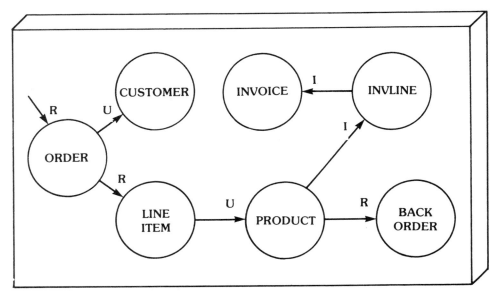

FIGURE 5.2   Usage Map for Transaction b

Create an invoice.   This task requires reading the order information and creating the invoice. Create additional entities—INVOICE and INVLINE.

Update a backorder.   The starting point here is PRODUCT. When there is enough to satisfy a backorder, cancel the outstanding order and delete the BACKORDER.

Customer full inquiry.   Start at customer, go to ORDER, follow through to BACK-ORDER and PRODUCT to pick up that data. Proceed for ORDER to INVOICE and INVOICE to INVLINE for that data.

Customer backorder inquiry.   Start at CUSTOMER and proceed to ORDER to see if there are any backorders attached. If so, proceed to BACKORDER.

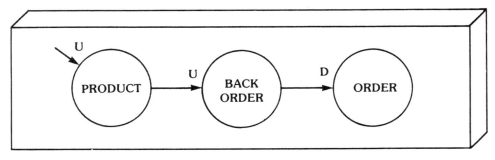

FIGURE 5.3   Usage Map for Transaction c

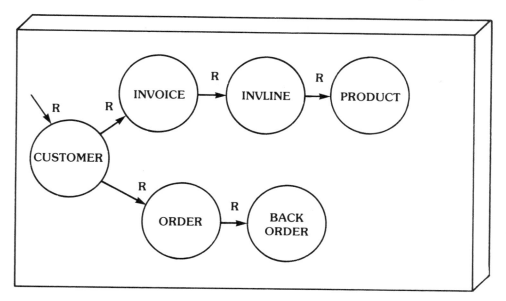

FIGURE 5.4   Usage Map for Transaction d

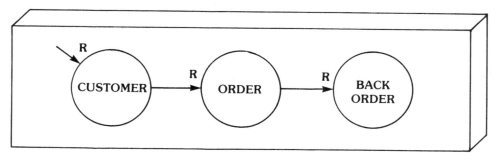

FIGURE 5.5   Usage Map for Transaction e

Number of invoices per product.   Start at PRODUCT and proceed to INVOICE totaling up each time there is one encountered.

Backorders on a product.   Start at PRODUCT and proceed to BACKORDER.

What customers have ordered this product.   Start at PRODUCT and proceed to ORDER to get customer number, and from there go to CUSTOMER.

How many customers for this product.   Start at PRODUCT and proceed to CUSTOMER.

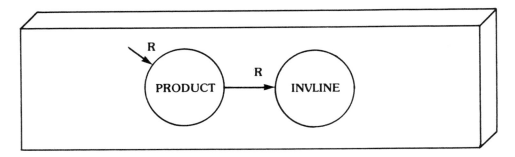

FIGURE 5.6   Usage Map for Transaction f

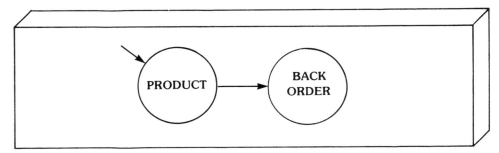

FIGURE 5.7   Usage Map for Transaction g

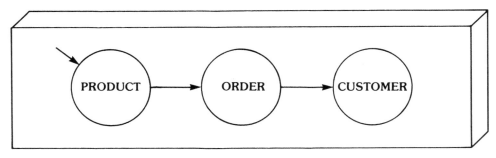

FIGURE 5.8   Usage Map for Transaction h

The process now is to symbolically represent each of these transaction diagrams on the entity map. A combined usage picture or transaction map would look like the structure in Figure 5.10. Notice the similarity of this diagram to that of the relational map.

Although the preceding example includes only some aspects of the entry order process, even this limited application of an entity usage map is of interest for data base design. That is because even this rudimentary mapping device has identified three key points:

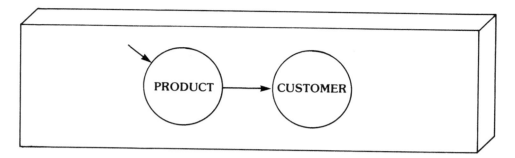

FIGURE 5.9   Usage Map for Transaction i

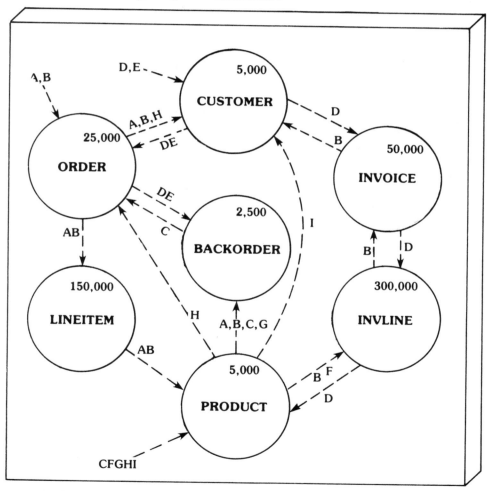

FIGURE 5.10   Sample Combined Transaction Map

1. The three distinct entry points into the system provide the designer with definite clues as to the ways in which the data might be indexed.
2. Every entity was utilized as described; therefore, there is some indication of the usefulness and validity of the entity.
3. Certain paths have a high degree of traffic flow from multiple functions (more than one transaction uses the same path) and therefore must be maintained.

COMPOSITE OVERLAY MAPPING

The structure can become even more useful if it is now superimposed over the relational map drawn earlier. However, the problem now becomes one of differentiating between relational paths and usage paths. In the composite map, Figure 5.11, dashes signify paths and solid lines signify relational links. Usage paths between the same two entities going in both directions are signified by double arrowheads. The transaction letter near the arrowhead indicates that transaction's usage path direction. The resulting structure looks like the one described in Figure 5.11.

The structure illustrated is called the composite map. What remains to be done to this structure is that any differences between the relational and transaction usage paths must be resolved. This methodology of overlaying a transaction derived usage map on top of a theoretically derived relational map, first employed by Finkelstein, is a major step forward in matching theory with a practical methodology. The resultant structure should now be reviewed.

When a usage path is encountered without a matching relational link, check the following:

1. Are all entities in third normal form?
   If not, normalize and re-do the relational map.
2. Is the path an M:M relation that was normalized to two M:M relations?
3. Consider alternate path choices in terms of performance as opposed to usability.

The sample structure has two unmatched transaction paths, one between PRODUCT and ORDER and another between PRODUCT and INVOICE. Remember that this M:M link was resolved in first normal form by creation of LINEITEM and INVLINE respectively. These two entities have the invoice number and order number keys necessary to accomplish the usage link required in the sample problem. Therefore revise the two paths to go through LINEITEM and INVLINE.

The use of this alternative path lengthens the total path and creates additional overhead to any function utilizing the path. However, constructing the M:M link also incurs overhead. Reconstruct links if it will eliminate overhead, if and only if the functional improvement outweighs the cost of that additional overhead. The next chapter describes such reconstructions in detail.

When an entity with a relational link lacks a transaction path, review the relationship to see if it was normalized properly. If it still remains valid, try to determine if the

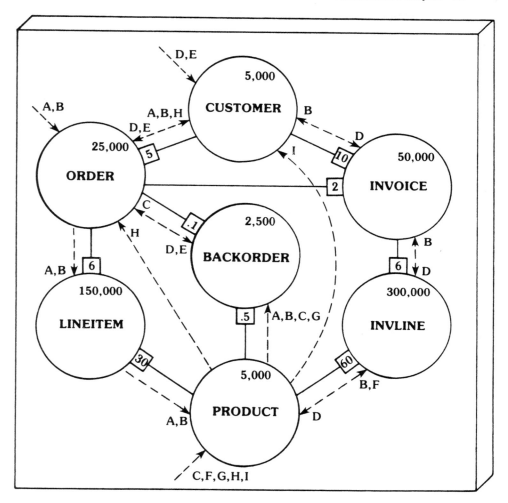

FIGURE 5.11 Composite Overlay Map

relationship should be maintained either for clarity or future flexibility. If the entity could have some future access path brought on by the future system requirements, maintain it. Does maintaining the entity separately give some clarity or consistency to the logical structure that would help the designers and users better understand or better utilize the data? If so, maintain the entity. If none of the above seem relevant, remove the entity. This should not happen too often.

Finally, through the process of composite mapping is derived a complete logical structure. See Figure 5.12. This structure is now ready for the final step of data analysis—estimation of the access loads and creating the finalized data model. Figure 5.13 illustrates the steps used to develop this composite map.

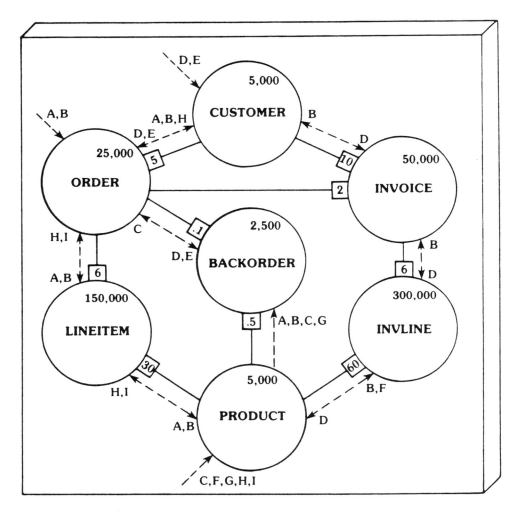

FIGURE 5.12 Complete Logical Structure

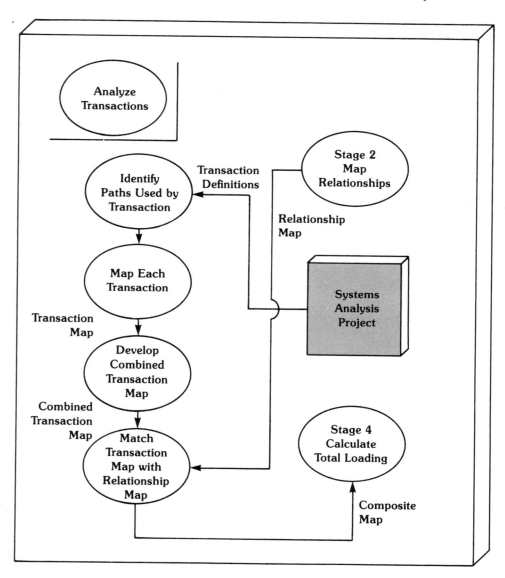

FIGURE 5.13   Stage 3—Transaction Analysis Data Flow Diagram

6 Constructing the Data Model

Whatever a man prays for he prays for a miracle. Every prayer reduces itself to this:
        "Great God, grant that twice two be not four."

                  Ivan Sergeyevich Turgenev, Prayer

QUANTITATIVE ANALYSIS OF THE FUNCTIONAL MODEL

The purpose of the chapter is to assess the cost of each transaction and eventually evaluate that cost to the whole system. The cost is basically determined by quantifying the input/output activity. Far and away the greatest component of response time is this I/O activity. The actual manipulation and conversion of data is a very small component of the total time spent processing a transaction. Therefore constructing the loaded data model will focus on determining the average number of input/output operations associated with each transaction.

Use the term *transaction* to describe the individual system functions. The order-invoice example in the previous chapter discussed such system functions or transactions. Let's look at them again using quantitative analysis.

The task is now one of stepping through each transaction and recording the access path (entity to entity), the type of access (read or update), the average number of times the path occurs (derived from ratios), and then determining the number of times the path is used for that transaction and alternatively for some peak-load time parameter. Each access path in a transaction will have a given value for these items. In a real situation the user determines this number. When all the access paths are complete for a transaction, the total number of logical references for that transaction is also recorded by multiplying the number of paths used by the number of uses for each path.

THE TRANSACTION PATH ANALYSIS FORM

The form for completing this information would look like Figure 6.1. The form is divided into three sections. Section 1, the *heading*, contains the TRANSACTION-ID, this in our example would be *a* to *i*; A DESCRIPTION field that briefly gives a text description of the transaction and, last, a peak volume number that determines the number of times this transaction is scheduled a specified time period.

Section 2, the *path descriptions*, is divided into four fields, UNIQUE-ID, FROM ENTITY, TO ENTITY, and ACCESS. Notice that a unique path-ID can be assigned each path. This will make the identification for load matrix compilation much easier later. A simple technique for assigning a unique path-ID would be to assign each entity in the system a unique number, such as 1 for CUSTOMER and 2 for ORDER. Then the path-ID from CUSTOMER to ORDER would be 1-2 and the reverse path from ORDER to CUSTOMER would be 2-1. Entry points or paths would be indicated by a zero thus entry on CUSTOMER path-ID would be 0-1, entry on ORDER would be 0-2. "From entity" and "to entity" contain the names of the entities being accessed along this path. On entry, the "from entity" field will be equal to zero or asterisk to indicate entry from outside the data map. The access field will contain a letter indicating the type of access to the "to entity" R = read, I = insert, U = update, and D = delete.

Section 3 contains six fields, called, respectively, AVG, MULT, DURING ONE TRAN, ACC WT, ADJ, I/O, and DURING STRESS PERIOD. These six fields contain numbers. The AVG field contains the average number of times this path occurs in the relational map. The number can be determined by looking at the relational map and putting the number beside the "to entity" along the path being used. For example, in the E-Z Chair map, the number beside the "to entity" in the CUSTOMER to ORDER path would be 5. In the ORDER to CUSTOMER path, the reverse direction, the number would be 1.

The MULT field is the multiplier, a number greater than zero and having a maximum value of 1. It signifies how many of the available "TO ENTITIES" this transaction will access. The value 1 would indicate that all available "TO ENTITIES" would be accessed. The value of MULT for any number less than all would be the fraction created by dividing the number of paths desired by the total number of paths available. For example, if the possible number of "to entities" is 60, but for this transaction you are only looking for a particular "to entity," the value of MULT would be 1/60.

The DURING ONE TRAN field contains the total number of TO ENTITIES being accessed during one transaction. This number is *always* determined by multiplying the number of FROM ENTITIES for this path times the AVG times the MULT.

ACC WT. is used to assign a weighting factor for each type of access. Different kinds of access require different I/O costs. Reads are the cheapest. Inserts cost more than reads, deletes more than inserts, and updates cost the most of all. ACC WT. will reflect these weighted costs by assigning numbers to each kind of access. In the examples listed in this book, reads will be assigned a cost of 1, inserts and deletes a cost of 2, and updates a cost of 3. These numbers vary from system to system and

Transaction Path Analysis Form

Transaction ID   **Description**   **Peak Load**

	Path Description				Number Times Path Occurs		Number Times Path Used			
Unique ID	From Entity	Num	To Entity	Access	Avg	Mult	During One Tran	Acc Wt	Adj. I/O	During Stress Period

FIGURE 6.1   Transaction Load Calculation Form

DBMS to DBMS. The numbers generally reflect the additional reads, writes, and logging required by inserts, deletes, and updating.

ADJ. I/O is obtained by multiplying the DURING ONE TRAN field by the ACC WT. This will tend to give a more realistic cost of the actual I/O being done along each path by the transaction.

The last field, DURING STRESS PERIOD, is obtained by multiplying the value in the ADJ. I/O field by the PEAK LOAD fields value. The process involves tracing the usage path for the transaction and filling in the form every time the path enters an entity. On entry the values for AVG, MULT, and DURING ONE TRAN will always be 1! As an example start with transaction Figure 6.2; first, enter the ORDER entity. Attributes in the ORDER relation will be modified; therefore, the access type is update. The path frequency is 1; MULT is 1 only one ORDER entity is required per order. Because the access is update put a 3 in ACC WT. This also means there is one logical access of the ORDER entity along this path for this transaction. If there is a maximum of one order transaction every minute, there will be 60 transactions per hour on a peak-load basis. The peak time slot is filled in by multiplying the number of logical references per transaction by 60.

The next path is from ORDER to CUSTOMER; the purpose is to read the customer entity to get things for the order, such as customer name and address. The access type is therefore read-only. Path frequency is 1, MULT is 1 all paths are used only one customer per order. ACC WT. is 1. Logical references are 1 and 60 as in the first path. The number of FROMS, ORDER is 1; AVG is 1, MULT is 1 therefore,

Transaction Path Analysis Form

Transaction ID   A   Description   Create An Order   Peak Load   60

| Path Description | | | | Number Times Path Occurs | | Number Times Path Used | | | |
Unique ID	From Entity	Num	To Entity	Access	Avg	Mult	During One Tran	Acc Wt	Adj. I/O	During Stress Period
0-2	•	1	ORDER	U	1	1	1	3	3	180
2-1	ORDER	1	CUSTOMER	R	1	1	1	1	1	60
2-3	ORDER	1	LINEITEM	I	6	1	6	2	12	720
3-4	LINEITEM	6	PRODUCT	U	1	1	6	3	18	1080
2-5	ORDER	1	BACKORDER	I	.1	1	.1	2	.2	12
									34.2	2052

FIGURE 6.2 Transaction: Create an Order

$1 \times 1 \times 1 = 1$, and 1×60 is 60. A box labeled NUM has been provided to record the number of froms.

LINEITEM is entered next for update, and this is the first path frequency change takes place. It has been determined in the analysis of the business functions and recorded in the relational map that in an average order, 6 LINEITEM entities are created. Because you must look at all LINEITEM entities, the MULT is 1. The path from ORDER to LINEITEM is crossed 6 times. This then translates to 6 logical references per transaction and 6×60 transactions per hour or 360 references per hour. ADJ. I/O will be 3 times 6 or 18 per transaction, making 1,080 per hour.

The path from LINEITEM to PRODUCT reads and updates the product information for each LINEITEM, the purpose being to read the product description and price and to update the product inventory amounts and set BACKORDER processing switches if necessary. The path frequency is only 1 because each LINEITEM accesses only one product. The logical references to a PRODUCT entity, however, is equal to the number of lineitems in an order, with an averge of 6. The peak time references to PRODUCT are 6×60 or 360. The formula FROMS $\times$ 1 AVG $\times$ 1 MULT equals 6. $6 \times$ ACC WT. of 3 is 18 and 18 times PEAK LOAD of 60 is 1,080.

The system must maintain backorder information if there is not enough product to satisfy the order. This will utilize the path from PRODUCT to BACKORDER. However, since typically only half the products have backorders, this path is only used a frequency of 0.5, which at 6 products per order would give a logical reference per transaction of 3 and a peak-load reference of 180. This PRODUCT to BACKORDER path, however, is not really based on the view from backorders but on the number of backorders for an order. The ratio of ORDER to BACKORDER is 1 to 0.1. Thus a new BACKORDER entity would be created only 10% of the time; therefore, the path frequency is really 0.1, the logical reference per transaction is 0.1, and the peak load reference is 0.1×60 or 6.

When calculating paths, carefully consider the ramifications of using alternate paths to an entity and the ratios along that path. The ORDER to BACKORDER path is based on orders. The PRODUCT to BACKORDER path ratio is based on backorders. You will see the use of this path when you describe the backorder status transaction.

Completing the same exercise for transaction b, notice that transaction b while creating an invoice, traces over much of the path utilized when creating the order. However, this time through, the paths dealing with order access are for information, not update, and are therefore of a read-only type. See Figure 6.3. You will notice that in all cases for this transaction the value of MULT was 1. This is because in every case we wished to use all paths.

Transaction b, as with the order transaction, is keyed to entry on the ORDER entity. Information on the customer, the order, lineitems, and outstanding backorders against the order are gathered through access paths exactly the same as the order creation transaction, transaction a.

One new path crossed is PRODUCT to INVLINE. This path is utilized once for every LINEITEM in an order, which in our example is 6. Thus, on the form the AVG is

Transaction Path Analysis Form

Transaction ID B　　　　**Description** Create An Invoice　　　　**Peak Load** 60

Path Description				Number Times Path Occurs		Number Times Path Used			
Unique ID	From Entity	Num	To Entity	Access	Avg	Mult	During One Tran	Acc Wt	Adj. I/O	During Stress Period
0-2	·	1	ORDER	R	1	1	1	1	1	60
2-1	ORDER	1	CUSTOMER	U	1	1	1	3	3	180
2-3	ORDER	1	LINEITEM	R	6	1	6	1	6	360
3-4	LINEITEM	6	PRODUCT	R	1	1	6	1	6	360
2-5	ORDER	1	BACKORDER	R	.1	1	.1	1	.1	6
4-7	PRODUCT	6	INVLINE	I	60	1/60	6	2	12	720
7-6	INVLINE	6	INVOICE	I	1	1/6	1	2	2	120
									30.1	1806

FIGURE 6.3　Transaction: Create an Invoice

60 but the MULT is 1/60, the logical references per transaction is 6, because we have 6 "FROMS" or LINEITEMS. And the total references during a peak period is $6 \times 60 \times 2$ or 720 logical references. The ACC WT. of 2 concerns the insert weighting.

After completing all the INVLINES, access the path from INVLINE to INVOICE to create the body of the invoice, which is very similar in content to the ORDER entity. Record the total invoice amount here, and update this amount on the customer's running balance; an access from ORDER to CUSTOMER, also if update type, is crossed. Both paths have a AVG of 1, in order to obtain only 1 logical access per transaction and 60 access per peak load the MULT must be 1/6.

The next transaction from which to determine the load is the backorder update, transaction c. See Figure 6.4. The entry point here is through PRODUCT because only when a new product is created can the backorders be relieved. This type of transaction usually occurs as part of a batch processing mode in an actual order processing system, but for this example the business rules determine on average that 3 backorder update transactions occur every hour. Therefore, the entry PRODUCT path loads, would have a path AVG of 1, A MULT of 1, a logical access of 1 per transaction, and a peak load logical access of 3.

The PRODUCT to BACKORDER path frequency is determined by the ratio of 1 to 0.5; thus the logical references per transaction are 0.5, and the peak references are 3×0.5 or 1.5. MULT is 1 here because we always want every BACKORDER available.

Transaction Path Analysis Form

Transaction ID C **Description** Update a Backorder **Peak Load** 3

Path Description				Number Times Path Occurs		Number Times Path Used			
Unique ID	From Entity	Num	To Entity	Access	Avg	Mult	During One Tran	Acc Wt	Adj. I/O	During Stress Period
0-4	•	1	PRODUCT	U	1	1	1	3	3	9
4-5	PRODUCT	1	BACKORDER	U	.5	1	.5	3	1.5	4.5
5-2	BACKORDER	.5	ORDER	U	1	1	.5	3	1.5	4.5
									6	18

FIGURE 6.4 Transaction: Backorder Update

For every BACKORDER entity there is a path to the ORDER entity. The remaining transactions are all queries, and read-only ACC WT. will always be 1.

Customer backorder inquiries are done at the rate of 6 per hour in the sample online system. This transaction is entered through the CUSTOMER entity. There are on average 5 orders per customer on the data base at any one time; therefore, the path frequency of the CUSTOMER to ORDER path is 5. Since 10% of all orders are backordered, the path frequency is 0.1 between ORDER:BACKORDER. Five orders per inquiry leaves a logical reference number of 0.5 (0.1 × 5 orders). There is always a path from BACKORDER to PRODUCT; thus the frequency is 1. The logical references are the same as the number of references for BACKORDER, (0.5). See Figure 6.5.

The customer order inquiry transaction, see Figure 6.6, has a peak-load volume of 10 per hour. This particular inquiry has rather a severe impact on the entities within the sample system because it touches every entity, and the MULT is always 1.

The entry to this particular transaction is through the customer entity. Looking at all orders and line items under them, plus all invoices, involves considerable activity. The CUSTOMER:ORDER path occurs 5 times on average for each customer. This is a logical access of 5 per transaction and 50 per peak-load interval. Each of the 5 orders has 6 lineitems, which indicates 30 logical accesses per transaction and 300 per peak load. The one-to-one ratio of LINEITEM to PRODUCT also indicates similar values along that path.

The ORDER to BACKORDER path has a frequency of 0.1. Logical accesses to the BACKORDER entity are then 0.1 times 5 orders per inquiry. This is 5 accesses over the peak-load period. There are twice as many invoices as orders for each customer as determined in the business rules. Thus the ORDER to INVOICE path

Transaction Path Analysis Form

Transaction ID E   **Description** Customer Backorder Query   **Peak Load** 6

Unique ID	Path Description				Number Times Path Occurs		Number Times Path Used			
	From Entity	Num	To Entity	Access	Avg	Mult	During One Tran	Acc Wt	Adj. I/O	During Stress Period
0-1	•	1	CUSTOMER	R	1	1	1	1	1	6
1-2	CUSTOMER	1	ORDER	R	5	1	5	1	5	30
2-5	ORDER	5	BACKORDER	R	.1	1	.5	1	.5	3
5-4	BACKORDER	.5	PRODUCT	R	1	1	.5	1	.5	3
									7	42

FIGURE 6.5   Transaction: Customer Backorder Inquiry

Transaction Path Analysis Form

Transaction ID D   **Description** Customer Order Query   **Peak Load** 10

Unique ID	Path Description				Number Times Path Occurs		Number Times Path Used			
	From Entity	Num	To Entity	Access	Avg	Mult	During One Tran	Acc Wt	Adj. I/O	During Stress Period
0-1	•	1	CUSTOMER	R	1	1	1	1	1	10
1-2	CUSTOMER	1	ORDER	R	5	1	5	1	5	50
2-3	ORDER	5	LINEITEM	R	6	1	30	1	30	300
3-4	LINEITEM	30	PRODUCT	R	1	1	30	1	30	300
2-5	ORDER	5	BACKORDER	R	.1	1	.5	1	.5	5
1-6	CUSTOMER	1	INVOICE	R	10	1	10	1	10	100
6-7	INVOICE	10	INVLINE	R	6	1	60	1	60	600
									136.5	1365

FIGURE 6.6   Transaction: Customer Order Inquiry

Transaction Path Analysis Form

Transaction ID F   **Description** Product Invoice Query   **Peak Load** 2

Path Description				Number Times Path Occurs		Number Times Path Used			
Unique ID	From Entity	Num	To Entity	Access	Avg	Mult	During One Tran	Acc Wt	Adj. I/O	During Stress Period
0-4	•	1	PRODUCT	R	1	1	1	1	1	2
4-7	PRODUCT	1	INVLINE	R	60	1	60	1	60	120
									61	122

FIGURE 6.7   Transaction: Product Invoice Inquiry

frequency is 2 per order. This tallies as 10 logical accesses to the INVOICE entity for each transaction, which is 100 accesses along their path during peak load time.

There are 6 invoice lines for every invoice, so the INVOICE to INVLINE path frequency is 6. The logical accesses per transaction, for each INVLINE under a specific customer, would be 6 $\times$ 10 invoices per customer or 60. The peak load across for this path would be 600.

The total for all the logical accesses for the entire transaction is 1,365. Note that this figure is from 7 to 20 times greater than any of the transactions generated thus far.

The PRODUCT-INVOICE inquiry transaction (see Figure 6.7) in the sample system is a low-volume inquiry of only 2 per hour. The purpose of the transaction is to determine the number of invoices for a particular product. The only key available to the inquiries is the product number. The inquiry must proceed up the PRODUCT:-INVLINE path and total the lines and record the invoice number.

The inquiry enters at the product and then interrogates each INVLINE entity to get the invoice number. (This key could be used to retrieve the INVOICE entity if it is required later.) The frequency along the PRODUCT;INVLINE path is 60. Total logical accesses are 60 per transaction for the INVLINE entity, 120 logical access per hour.

As an exercise, complete the usage path analysis load maps for the remaining transactions. Use the peak-load values of 5, 5, and 10 for the remaining 3 transactions in the sample system.

Always remember the following rules when using the transaction path analysis form.

1. On entry the values for NUM, AVG, MULT, and DURING ONE TRAN will always be one.

2. Determine the "number of froms," NUM, by finding the FROM ENTITY name in the TO ENTITY column and putting the DURING ONE TRAN number for that path in NUM.

3. The value of MULT will always be 1 if you desire to use all the paths.

4. When a specific "to entity" is desired or a known specific number of "to entities" is to be accessed, the value of MULT is that number over AVG.

5. Determine the value of DURING ONE TRAN by multiplying the NUM times the AVG, times the MULT.

6. Obtain ADJ. I/O by multiplying the ACC WT times the DURING ONE TRAN.

7. Totaling up all the ADJ. I/O fields gives the total number of logical entity accesses for the transaction.

Solutions to all sample problems are found in Appendix A. Appendix E will review the "how to's" of the path analysis form on a field-by-field basis.

USING MATHEMATICAL PROBABILITY TO PREDICT ENTITY FREQUENCY

The previous methodology is somewhat different from the mathematical probability theory approach to load calculation developed by S. Atre. Atre states the following:

> To access segment B from segment A one needs to know all the segments that have to be touched on the way. One can estmate the number of I/Os necessary for accessing segment B from segment A if the probabilities of I/Os are known for all intermediate segments.[4]

Basically, the probability theory approach boils down to this: the probability that an event will take place is represented by a number someplace between 0 and 1. Zero means the event never happens, and 1 means the event always happens. The classical probability definition is as follows:

> The probability of an event occurring (p) is equal to the ratio between the number of cases which are favorable to this event (a) and the total number of probable cases (c), provided that all cases are mutually symmetric.[5]

Expressed mathematically as

$$p = \frac{a}{c}$$

Likewise, the probability of an event not occurring (q) determined as $p + q = 1$, or

$$q = 1 - p, \quad \text{or} \quad q = 1 - \frac{a}{c}$$

The crux of the problem here is to determine a and c, and this is done in a manner precisely like that noted on the transaction path analysis form.

Once designers determine the probability for a particular entity segment type, they can also determine the mathematical expectation of a particular entity of a particular length occurring in the data base.

Since length is always a discrete positive whole integer having some value between 1 and n, it is called a "discrete valued random variable." Variates of the type will have a mathematical expectation equal to

$$E = (v1 \times p1) + (v2 \times p2) + (v3 \times p3) + \ldots (vn \times pn)$$

or

$$\sum_{i=1}^{n} vi \times pi,$$

where $v =$ the variable length and $p =$ the probability. Moreover this implies

$$p1 + p2 + p3 + pn = 1.$$

If we substitute the ratio a/c for p, the equation reduces to

$$\frac{\sum_{i=1}^{n} vi \times ai}{c}$$

Atre uses this formulation to calculate the average entity length for the distribution of the length of an entity.

THE LOADED MATRIX

The easiest way to assimilate all the load data built in the load maps is to construct a table of the data. This table is called the load matrix. The matrix will show the entity-to-entity count for each transaction, the combined peak usage figure of every path, the ratio of each entity involved in a path relationship and finally, the total of the average number of entities accessed along each path per transaction and per peak-load interval. The technique is a refinement of the data element cross-reference tables that have been used by data base designers for years.

The transaction path analysis forms completed in the previous chapter are now reviewed in order to tabularize the usage and loading for the entire system on the matrix. The matrix is merely a convenient way of expressing the contents of the transaction path analysis form on one line in the matrix sheet. See Figure 6.8 for sample load matrix.

This form is used to consolidate the several pieces of paper resulting from the transaction path analysis. The form consolidates the key figures from each form onto a single line of the load matrix. The process is merely transcribing the path analysis number onto another sheet of paper. This results in two major benefits.

First, the relative cost in logical accesses for each transaction can now be seen at a glance, and it is very easy for the designer to determine which transactions are going to be fast and which are going to be slow. You might call it separating the pigs from the gazelles. The transactions with the highest number of logical accesses obviously have more work to do than transactions with fewer accesses; therefore they will take longer to finish their task.

Second, and more important, the load matrix gives the designer the opportunity to look at the activity across each path in the system individually. Each individual path has a specific column on the form. No path should be repeated! If a path is utilized on more than one transaction, the stress period numbers corresponding to that path are entered in different boxes under the vertical path column at a position corresponding to the appropriate transaction. When all the transactions and paths have thus been mapped, the designer goes down each path column and totals the figures for that path.

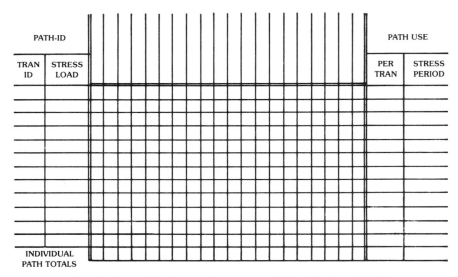

COMPOSITE TRANSACTION PATH LOAD MATRIX FORM

FIGURE 6.8 Sample Load Matrix Form

This provides the designer with vital information regarding the relative usage and therefore the relative importance of this path.

The total number of accesses for each transaction is the sum of all the counts for each path used in the transaction. The peak totals are the sums of all the paths times the peak usage.

Through this simple technique, you the designer have the values in a form simple enough to easily construct a full loaded data model, and certain paths are identified as high usage, along with certain transactions.

	Transaction	Peak Usage
a	Create an order	60
b	Create an invoice	60
c	Update a backorder	3
d	Customer order inquiry	10
e	Customer backorder inquiry	6
f	Product invoice inquiry	2
g	Product backorder inquiry	5
h	Product customer inquiry	5
i	Product order inquiry	10

The solution can be found in the load matrix Figure 6.9; you can draw the loaded data model pictured in Figure 6.10. The paths, direction, and volumes are now combined in a single structure that can be easily examined in the final stage of data analysis. The data model is constructed by drawing the relational map and replacing the path occurrence numbers with the path total figures.

It was stated earlier that the importance of dealing with stress periods would be explained. The reason stress periods are important is that they are essential to understanding and interpreting response time. Stress periods in today's environments must typically be expressed in very short intervals of time. One must know the amount of work to be done and the amount of time there is available to do it. Sometimes simple mathematical division is not enough.

As an example take a small on-line order system: the system is on-line 10 hours a day and handles 6,000 transactions per day. Simple division tells us that this is 600 transactions per hour or 10 per minute. If you proceed to design your system on this assumption YOU ARE IN BIG TROUBLE!!

Why? Because actual system use is as shown in Figure 6.11. The system runs from 8 A.M. to 6 P.M., but people put the majority (80%) of work through the system between 9:30 A.M. and 12:00 noon. At lunch time from 12:00 to 1:00 there is virtually no activity! There is a small peak after lunch (on Fridays even that disappears) and most everyone goes home at 5:00. So the period from 5:00 to 6:00 P.M. has virtually no activity either.

During the stress period just prior to lunch the actual transaction rate approaches 50 per minute, 5 times the predicted average. Hence determining the

Tran ID	Stress Load	0-2	2-1	2-3	3-4	2-5	4-7	7-6	0-4	4-5	5-2	0-1	1-2	1-6	6-7	4-3	3-2	5-4	Per Tran	Stress Period
A	60	180	60	720	1080	12													34.2	2052
B	60	60	180	360	360	6	720	120											30.1	1806
C	3								9	4.5	4.5								6	18
D	10			300	300	5						10	50	100	600				136.5	1365
E	6					3						6	30					3	7	42
F	2						120		2										61	122
G	5		150						5	2.5									1.5	7.5
H	5								5							150	150		91	455
I	10								10							300	300	3	61	610
Individual Path Totals		240	390	1380	1740	26	840	120	31	7	4.5	16	80	100	600	450	450	3		

Path-ID

Path Use

Composite Transaction Path Load Matrix Form

FIGURE 6.9 E-Z Chair Load Matrix

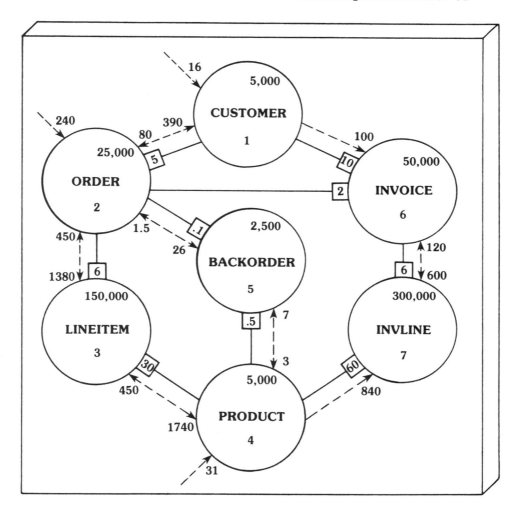

FIGURE 6.10 E-Z Chair Loaded Data Model

stress period is extremely important in order to determine the real load on the data model.

IMPLICATIONS AND FACTORS IN PHYSICAL DESIGN

The task at this point is to examine the most frequently used paths and prejudice the physical design implementation in their favor. Examples of this are the ORDER;LINE-ITEM and LINEITEM;PRODUCT paths, which are symbolic of the M:M relationship that exists between order and product.

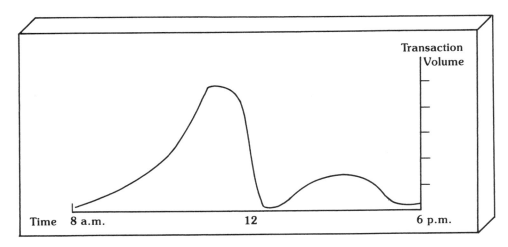

FIGURE 6.11 Finding the Stress Period

Alternatively, in transactions with very high numbers of logical accesses, such as transaction h, the product-customer inquiry may fair better if a product-customer entity were created to directly bridge the two. A business function may be discovered that finds a ratio of 20 products on order by a customer at any one time. This would indicate 100,000 product-customer entities and a corresponding ratio of 20 to 1 customer-product to product. Mapping transaction in both ways results in the comparison found in Figure 6.12.

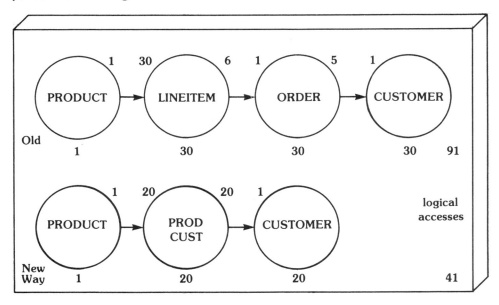

FIGURE 6.12 Alternative Path Creation

If the ratio of product-customer entities can be shown to be anything less than 45 to 1, the new path will be more economical. Does the new entity provide for greater flexibility in the structure? Are there any attributes of the entity other than the key? Does the creation of the entity lend any new information about the logical structure of the data? Does the alternate path provided through the creation of the new entity offer enough savings to justify its existence? If the answer to one or more of the questions is yes, then the entity may be valid, and it certainly warrants more than cursory investigation.

What is important to remember at this stage of design is that the logical structure is not cast in steel. It is still quite possible (even necessary) to alter the structure at this stage.

Besides the previous example dealing with path usage lengths and their complexity, another consideration has to do with data stability. Data can be static or dynamic. Certain data such as dates (birthday, employment, termination) and names (customer, product description) are usually quite static, and once written are rarely, if ever, altered unless they were originally entered improperly. Other data is quite dynamic and changes often. Amounts, cash totals, and salary taxes all change relative to time.

The temporal relationship of the data may be significant enough to justify further restructuring of the data. During the discussion of normalization in Chapter 2 this type of restructuring was referred to as *vertical partitioning*. An example of vertical partitioning follows:

Customer
Customer number, name, address, start date, termination date, current balance, credit status discount rate

The customer entity might better serve if it were broken into two entities based on the volatility of the attributes:

Customer-static
Customer number, name, address, start date, termination date
Customer-dynamic
Customer number, balance, credit status, discount rate

Entity of segment (borrowed from the IBM Information Management System) size may require the combining or further breakdown of the data. This is a purely physical constraint based on the choice of the DBMS or the hardware upon which the data base is to function. It also relates to possible data base recovery problems either because of data base segment size or because of the sheer total number. Some type of horizontal partitioning or record grouping may offer integrity advantages, or enhancements to the speed or simplicity of recovery. In fact, a gamut of integrity or security functions might necessitate the separation of some otherwise similar attributes into separate entities.

The primary concern in any data base design is to minimize the effect of change. Therefore derive the logical structure from the data itself, using third-normal-form

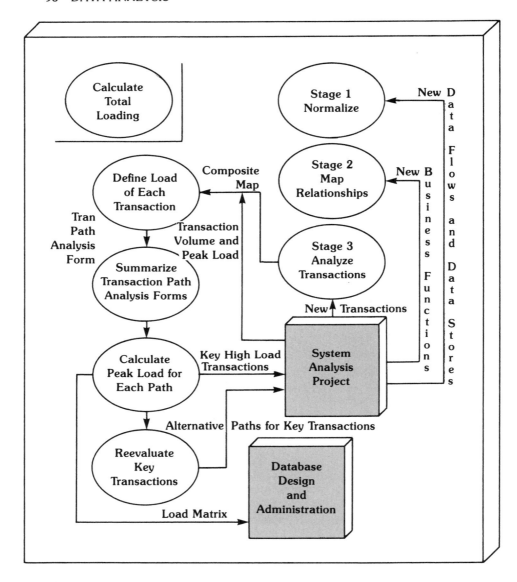

FIGURE 6.13 Stage 4—Calculate Total Load—Data Flow Diagram

relations. Do not restrict the structure of a new system to the structure of the system it is replacing. Above all follow the SIBKISS principle.

SEE it big—keep it simple and straightforward!

A simple design is a clear design, and a clear design is understandable and maintainable by others.

Another word to keep in mind when designing data bases is "ITERATION." The entire design process is one of do and review. New discoveries about data and its use must constantly be recycled. As you can see in Figure 6.13, the stages of data analysis provide for and require the designer to do just that. The final point in data analysis and design is to document your analysis well. Keep the relational and usage maps up to date. Be sure to record the business functions and the analysis of business functions. Your design may not be perfect using this methodology, but is most assuredly will be better than if you had not been very analytical and very methodical.

For readers who wish further practice in data analysis, please turn to Appendix F in which two additional sample case problems will be found.

NOTES

1. S. Atre, *Data Base Structured Techniques for Design Performance and Management* (New York: John Wiley, 1980), pp. 288–301, Appendix C.
2. Clive Finkelstein, *Data Analysis and Design Information Systems*, (Gordon. N.S.W., Inforcom, Australia: 1980).
3. Martin L. Rubin, *Documentation Standards and Processing for Combie Systems*, (New York: Van Nostrand Reinhold, 1979), pp. 161–181.
4. S. Atre, *Data Base Structured Techniques*, p. 295.
5. Harold Cromer, *The Elements of Probability Theory and Some of Its Applications* (New York: John Wiley, 1958), p. 13.

Part Two
DATA BASE DESIGN

7 Data Base Management Systems: Their Architecture and Evolution

Throughout is a single work of art, and as such subject to the primary laws of every work of art namely, that it shall be framed upon a single, noble motive, to which the design of all its parts in some more or less subtle way, shall be confluent and helpful.

Robert Vaux, 1858

PRIMARY DBMS ARCHITECTURES

A data base management system (DMBS) is "the data processing system providing the means to access, organize and control all information stored in the data base." From this rather basic definition, borrowed from the April 1971 report of the CODASYL Data Base Task Group,[1] a string of new terms, and in fact a whole language, has evolved concerning DBMS methodology and technology.

An understanding of the basic DBMS architectures currently available centers upon an understanding of physical access methods and logical data structures. It is these two areas from which spring the language, methods, practices, and techniques of data base.

Data base access methodology concerns the input and output operations involved in handling data within the data base. Basically there are only two ways of accessing data from a mass storage device such as a tape or a disk. Either the physical address of the data is known, and that it can be retrieved directly; or if the address is not known, the relevant part of the data base is scanned until the data is found.

In sequential processing, the next record required is the next record on the files; its location is determined by its position relative to the current record being processed, and its physical address on the file is of no consequence. All other basic access methods, however, are concerned with providing the physical address of the record. There are several possibilities in the implementation of the address approach to data access:

Chains or *Pointers*

The address of the next record to be processed is contained in the current record. Locating the first record in the chain is problematical.

Random File Structure

An address-generating algorithm or randomizer can be used that operates on the key of the required record. This is called a random file structure because the physical sequence of the records need not bear any resemblance to the logical sequence of the data structure. The major problem is that more than one key can generate the same address (synonyms). Random file access techniques are, in general, the most rapid method of gaining access to data.

Index of Record Keys

The address of the required record is obtained from an index of record keys. The problem here is to locate the index entry. This is usually accomplished through making serial or binary searches and addressing algorithms or a higher level index. The indexes themselves are just simple files, and, as such, import certain storage and access overheads to the system.

Because access methods by themselves do not provide the necessary complex file structures, there is a need for *logical data structures*. These structures are defined by the DBMS software as something called a schema, which can in turn, be interpreted in terms of basic structures. Logical data structures fall into one of the following three classes:

Simple

All the units of data are *independent* and *logically equal* in significance. The units can either be ordered or unordered.

Hierarchic

Units of data are *dependent* and can logically be arranged in a hierarchy of levels in which units have a single owner and/or own one or more other units. A hierarchy is the perfect structure to handle the one to many relationship. Hierarchic files are always logically ordered.

Network

Units of data are dependent, but in a *more complex structure* than in a hierarchy, networks allow units to have more than one owner, as well as own one or more other units. This type of structure accommodates the many-to-many relationship as well as the one to many.

Each of the above structures is supported by a number of file organizations. The file organization, though a logical structure, corresponds directly to the access method being used.

The first and most basic file organizations are the types that require processing in sequential order. If the file is unordered the organization is called *serial*. The only way to update a serial file is by recopying it. Files that are ordered and sequentially processed are called *sequential*. Sequential files can be represented hierarchically because relationships are indicated by relative record position and record keys.

Therefore, complete keys are redundant. If all the keys are unique the structure is termed *generalized* (Figure 7.1).

Indexed files are the next organizational structure to be considered. Indexed files can be randomly ordered or sequentially ordered. Nonordered indexed files are best

Serial Files

Records

Domains	E37B8	A16A9	A16X3	A21P4	E37B8	T14A7	E37X2	E37A9	D21P4		

Sequential Files

Records

Domains	A	A	A	D	E	E	E	E	T	Major Key
	16	16	21	21	37	37	37	37	14	
	X3	A9	P4	P4	A9	B8	B8	X2	A7	Minor Key
										Data

Generalized Files

Variable Length Records

Domains	A			D	E			T	Major Key
	16		21	21	37			14	
	X3	A9	P4	P4	A9	B8		X2	A7	Minor Key
										Data

FIGURE 7.1   **Simple Data Structures**

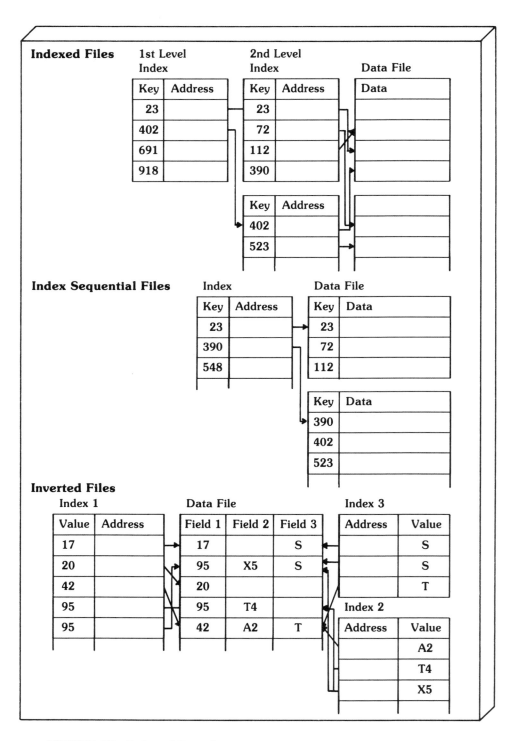

FIGURE 7.2   Indexed Data Structures

104

suited to direct processing. They consist of blocks of data and one or more levels of indexing that list the keys of all the data records along with their physical addresses.

Hierarchies can be expressed in an indexed structure by the sequence of indexed entries. The index must contain a full key for each record, but the full key need not be repeated within the data record itself.

Indexed sequential files may be processed either directly or sequentially. Here the files consist of blocks of data sequenced by record key plus one or more levels of index. These levels of index usually point to the required block in which the candidate record can be found by either sequential or binary search. In a hierarchical representation, indexed sequential records must all contain a complete key.

Files based on a randomizing address algorithm are called *random files*. This type of access was discussed earlier. Most DBMSs process these files directly or serially. Do not use generalized files, because all files should carry a complete key and because synonyms would cause confusion. This type of organization is rarely used in hierarchies, except to point to the head of a chain or string, because to move up or down in the hierarchy requires the key of either the previous or next record.

The last type of indexed organization is the *inverted file*, which is an extension of the indexed concept whereby no restriction is placed on what field or how many fields are indexed. You can quickly retrieve data using any combination of attributes instead of just using a key field. This type of structure is extremely well-suited for applications requiring complex or multifaceted inquiries. As can be imagined, the overhead for maintaining multiple sets of indexes can be considerable. In many cases the storage occupied by the indexes is greater than that occupied by the file itself. If the data being organized in this manner is highly dynamic, then updating can be difficult and expensive, because one or more indexes would also have to change. To cut down on this expense, reduce the number of candidate key fields to a select group. This is referred to as partial inversion (see Figure 7.2).

The alternatives to the index types of organization are the pointer types of organizations. Pointer structures are the list, ring, tree, next and network file organizations.

The most elementary of the pointer structures is the *list file*. These are ordered files in which all records are related by pointers. Process these files in logical sequence rather than physical sequence. There may also be more than one set of pointers so that a file may be processed in more than one logical sequence. However, to add new records, the system must chase down the pointer chains and properly connect the chains after the appropriate location is found for the new record. List files are frequently indexed to provide partial inversion. The ADADAS DBMS has such an inverted list type of structure.

Ring or *chain files* are just extensions of the list structure. The only difference is that the last record in the list now has a pointer back to the top of the list, which has the effect of producing a continuous processing loop. If indexes are provided for records within the loop, and forward and backward pointers are provided for each record, the entire set of records can be processed in either direction (see Figure 7.3).

Tree files (or upside down trees) provide a means of representing hierarchies through the use of pointers. Each record in the hierarchy is linked to and dependent

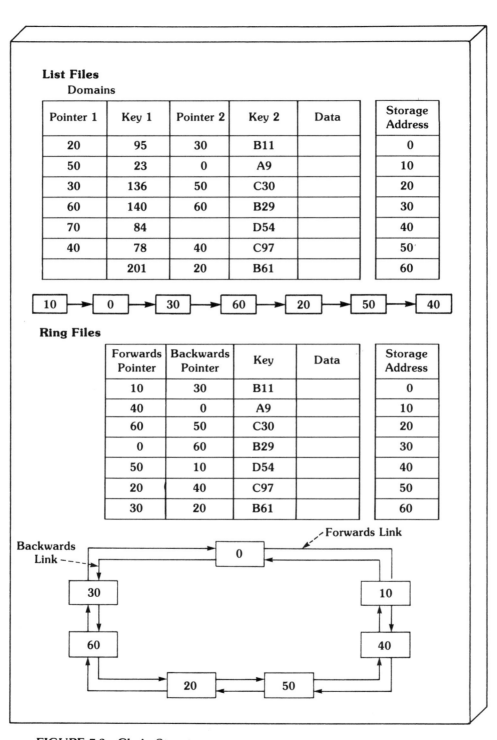

FIGURE 7.3   Chain Structures

on the record immediately above it (the owner) and to the records below in which are dependent on it (the members).

The top record in a tree structure (always an owner) is sometimes called the root. Once the root is located, it is possible to process up or down the hierarchical tree. Add new records by simply storing the record where space permits (usually in the same or adjacent block) and creating a pointer to it, from its owner, and from it to its members (see Figure 7.4).

Net files use a combination of tree and ring structures. Each level in a hierarchy is represented by one or more rings, or sets, in which a single higher record in the owner and the lower records is a member. These members can in turn be owners of sets even lower in the hierarchy. This structure is different from a tree in that the related records at each level—the members—are linked to each other. Obviously, with all this pointing and chaining, the pointer overhead can become quite significant.

Network files provide even further extension of the use of pointers to represent entity interrelationships. In a network, a record may have several owners in addition to owning several numbers. The only restriction is that the data structure must be internally consistent. Owners can have members, and they in turn can own other members; however, the other members cannot own the original owner. Simply put, this means that A owns B, B owns, C, but C cannot own A.

Data base management systems use these techniques solely or in combination in order to accomplish their purposes. These structures and access methods evolved over time into the myriad DBMS products on the market today.

EVOLUTION OF DATA BASE

The primary concepts for data base were laid in the early days of programming, when file linkage routines were moved out of the application programs and put into common access libraries, and common file descriptions were removed from programs and placed into copy libraries.

IBM created an extension to one of these file linkage routines called the *bill of materials processor* (BOMP). This was an early attempt at a chain structure organization. The application through a call to BOMP could follow a predefined set of pointers through related data files. Programmers did not have to maintain the forward and backward pointers provided by BOMP; however, programmers needed to have an intimate knowledge of the structure of the data to be able to navigate within the structure. Thus the program had to specify to BOMP just which chains had to be followed and just which data was needed.

This structure was more independent of the data than conventional file processing systems. But since the logic required to access the data was so directly tied to the application program, the program was inexorably tied to the data structure. Thus if the data structure changed, the programs also had to change with it.

The data dependence resulting from this situation led to an enhancement of BOMP into *database organization and maintenance processor* (BOMP). This newer product provided a higher level of access with some measure of data independence so that programmers could restructure the data without rewriting the application program.

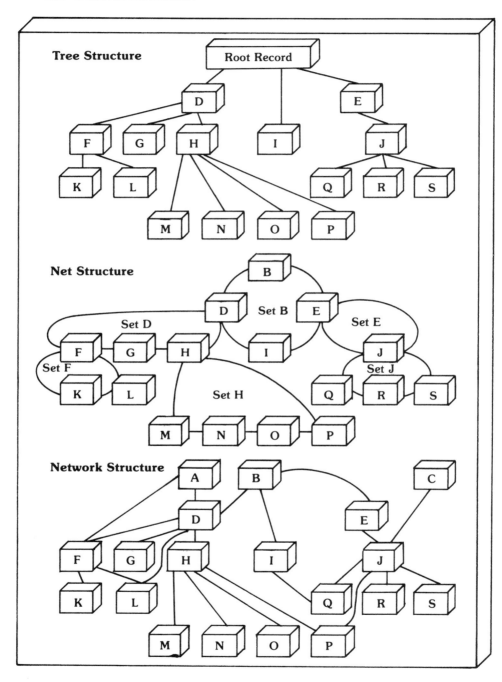

FIGURE 7.4 Complex Structures

TOTAL

Other people were also attempting to improve BOMP. In 1967 three former IBM engineers created TOTAL. TOTAL is a chain file processor with significant improvements over BOMP. The product has proved quite popular and is available in several software versions that enable it to operate on a wider range of computers than any other DBMS available today. TOTAL is network structure based on separate data sets and files for each record type.

Two types of files are defined for the system: MASTER files and VARIABLE-ENTRY files. (See Figure 7.5) Master files are accessed according to a key value for each record. TOTAL uses a randomizing algorithm to compute a physical address for each record. The master files are therefore referred to as "single-entry" files.

The variable-entry files, on the other hand, are related to the master files by means of forward and backward pointers. The chain starts at the master record and points to all the variable-entry records related to it. The master file record is the owner. The variable-entry files consist of fixed-length records of one record type or multiple record formats. The pointers between the master record, and the variable-entry records constitute the linkage path.

The big drawback to TOTAL is that there is no way to construct a linkage directly from one master file to another master file or directly from one variable-entry file to another variable-entry file. However, this relationship can be developed through the construction of artificial master or variable-entry files to act as conduits.

As with BOMP, TOTAL is accessed via a call. It can be coded COBOL, FOTRAN, BAL, or other programming languages. Data independence with TOTAL is PL/1 largely achieved through field independence because the application program has the ability to request only those fields it requires for processing. Therefore the record could change without the program requiring recoding and recompilation.

TOTAL requires that the application program know the physical structure of the data base. The programmer must navigate around the data base by supplying the appropriate files to be accessed and the linkage paths to be followed. Any major restructuring of data that also involves changing the linkage paths may require program modification.

INFORMATION MANAGEMENT SYSTEM

IBM, disappointed with the limitations of DBOMP, looked for new pastures. They became interested in a problem at Rockwell International Corporation, which eventually developed into a joint project. This project evolved into the Information Management System (IMS). The Rockwell problem was one of handling a one-to-many relations between header and trailer records by expressing them in a hierarchy of owner to members. This owner to member terminology was expressed as "Parent to Child." The analogy was further expanded to incorporate "*twins*," children of the same type, and on the same level, that have a common parent. These new terms and concepts facilitated the representation of very complex data relationships to minimize system input-output activity and therefore improve performance.

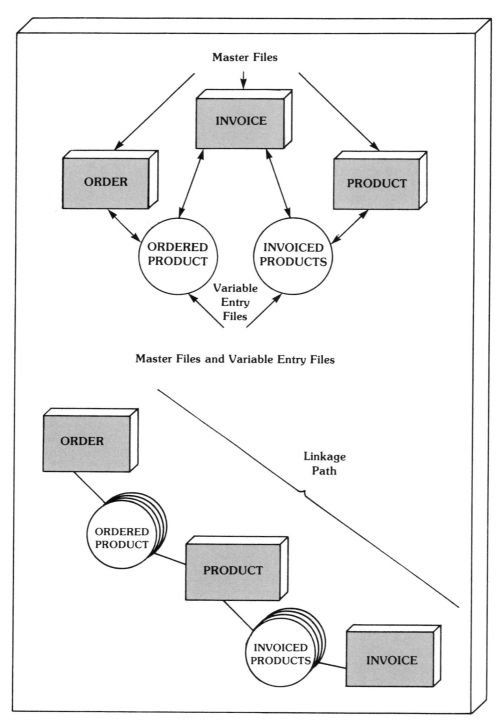

FIGURE 7.5 Example of TOTAL Structure and Linkage Path

By 1971 IBM had announced its intention to continually enhance IMS and interface it with two other strategic products CICS, Customer Information Control System, and GIS, Generalized Information System. In May 1979 IBM reaffirmed its commitment to IMS and IMS users despite the rumored substitution of the product for one involving a relational architecture.

The language of IMS is named DL/1, Data Language one. As with most DBMS products, a call is issued from an application program to retreive the data. The application program can be coded in BAL, COBOL, or PL/one.

The key to IMS, however, is the degree of data independence available to the programmer. The physical constraints and constructs of the data base, the schema, are defined in a control block called the DBD, Data Base Description. The application or logical view of the data base, the subschema, is defined in a different control block called the PSB, Program Specification Block. The PSB can be defined to mirror the logical structure, which can be quite different from the physical structure.

Data independence with this type of arrangement is quite good, for even if the physical data base changes, the program view as seen by the PSB remains the same. Through implementation of the subschema, the programmer can turn in his sextant and compass and leave the navigation up to IMS.

Figure 7.6 illustrates a sample IMS hierarchy. Entities are implemented into units called segments, and they in turn, consist of logically related fields, the entities' attributes. An IMS schema has a limitation of no more than 255 different segment types and a hierarchy of no more than 15 levels.

Relationships are maintained between parent and child in the physical structure via physical parent (PP) and physical child (PC) pointers. Relationships of twin to twin in the physical structure use physical twin (PT) pointers. Logical relationships such as the illustrated PRODUCT to ORDER relationships utilize logical child and logical parent pointers (LP, LC).

CODASYL

The Conference On Data Systems Languages (CODASYL) developed in 1959 as an outgrowth of the development of the General Electric Company's data base management system called Integrated Data Store, or IDS. Initially some 40 concerned organizations representing government, industry, and computer manufacturers initiated CODASYL. The initial task of the conference was to establish specifications for COBOL.

In the mid 1960s a task force on list processing became known as the Data Base Task Group of CODASYL (DBTG). The purpose of this group was to develop specifications for a new data base standard. The first formal publication of this task group was the October 1969 DBTG report.

The report detailed the structure and syntax for a *Data Description Language* (DDL) and a *Data Manipulation Language* (DML). The DDL was to define the data base, and the DML was a host language incorporated facility that manipulated the data in the data base defined by the DDL. In April 1971 a new report of the committee was issued that incorporated over 120 changes into the 1969 report.

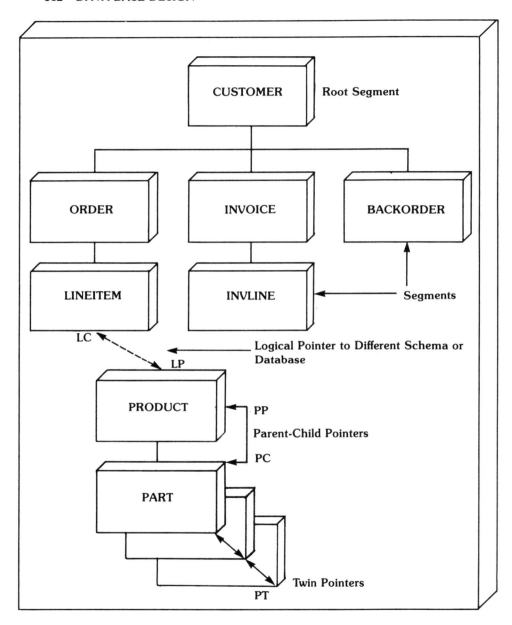

FIGURE 7.6   Typical Information Management System Hierarchy

The biggest and most important change was the development of the subschema. The role of the subschema is to provide a logical subset of the total data base (schema) which is program oriented and understandable to the host language. A syntax for the COBOL version of the subschema was recommended in the report.

Since that time splinter committees have been formed, such as the Data Base Language Task Group (DBLTG), which published further enhancements in the COBOL *Journal of Development* (JOD) in March 1973 and January 1978. With all the changes in the last few years the DBTG specifications have yet to be ratified by CODASYL as the data base standard.

While the standard was evolving, B.F. Goodrich Rubber Company developed a DBMS based very much on the CODASYL standard called IDMS. It was purchased by Cullinane Corporation and was enhanced and marketed as IDMS, ostensibly to run on IBM/370. IDMS marketing and development rights subsequently were sold to Digital Equipment Corporation (DEC) and International Computers, Limited (ICL), which in turn produced IDMS for PDP 16, DBMS 11, and ICL 2900 series computers.

Univac also purchased the B.F. Goodrich product and developed DMS90. Univac on its own developed DMS 1100 for its 1100 series computer. DMS 1100 was loosely based on the April 1971 DBTG report.

Other companies developed their own systems. DEC independently developed DBMS10 to run on its DEC10 and DEC20 computers. DBMS10 is also based on the DBTG recommendations. In addition, Control Data developed DMS170, generally implementing only the CODASYL DDL specifications.

The CODASYL DBTG has been the basis for several new DMBS products; there is a CODASYL type DMBS for practically any computer one wishes to purchase. See Figure 7.7 for an illustration of a CODASYL network implementation.

INVERTED LISTS

Inverted structures, as outlined earlier, were also developing during this period. In Germany, Software-AG of Germany developed ADABAS utilizing inverted multi-index lists. ADABAS (Adaptable Data Base) has all the virtues of the inverted list structure for handling multifaceted inquiries.

In the United States MRI Corporation developed a DMBS called System 2000, which was a compromise between IMS and ADABAS, an inverted list hierarchy. The idea here is to give the inquiry the flexibility of inverted list structure and also to provide the organization and performace enhancement for updatability found in hierarchical systems.

The architecture of inverted list DBMS products is quite different from that of the hierarchical and network structure defined earlier. Networks and hierarchies are structured around the use of pointers to establish the relationships between data entities or segments; inverted list structures are characterized by establishing relationships outside the data base. No internal pointers are embedded within the data base records. Typically the actual inverted list data base looks like the generalized file structure discussed earlier. For all intents and purposes it is a conventional file.

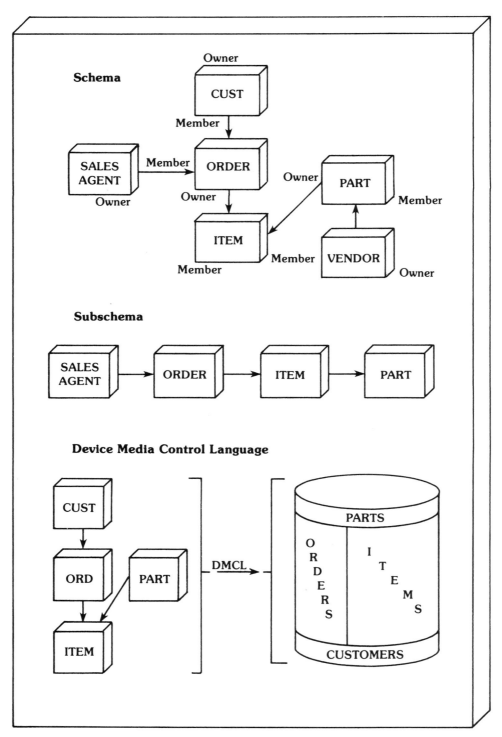

FIGURE 7.7   Sample CODASYL Network and Subschema

114

The difference is that certain fields within the files are designated as index keys. These fields are then used to access data base records, depending on their content in relation to the retrieval key. When the data base is loaded, the content of every designated key field is extracted from each data record and identified with the data base record in which it resides.

This association list is then sorted so that all occurrences of a particular key are brought together in some specified order, ascending, descending, etc. Figure 7.8 illustrates this inverted list architecture. In the example, if product name were an indexed field, all the "sofas" would be grouped together and all "rocking chairs" would be grouped together. A request to retrieve all product records with the value "rocking chair" would be resolved by accessing the sorted index and finding the location of every product record with the name "rocking chair."

Addition and deletion of records require index maintenance. This maintenance is done by the DBMS, but this activity can use up a considerable amount of overhead if the relists are many and the data is highly volatile.

Data independence is similar to TOTAL; it is dependent upon field-level independence. New fields can be added to an inverted list data base without requiring the reprogramming of existing applications. Data restructuring also has less impact because the data relationships are established outside the data base record and in the index lists.

Most inverted list structures provide utilities automatically establishing relationships between common keys that appear in different files such as part number or the customer-order file and part number on the vendor-part file. This is called *coupling*.

RELATIONAL DBMS

In Part I, the work of E. F. Codd on normalization and determining entity-relations was mentioned. In addition to developing a theory on data grouping, Codd proposed pure relational data bases as the only way to provide true data independence.[3] Though most DBMS products today provide a measure of physical data independence, logical data base independence is still rather limited. As has been previously shown, some DBMS products still require that the program have some knowledge of the physical structure of the data base it is accessing. True logical independence is achieved only when the application programs view the data base solely in terms of how that application works with the data and not how that data is physically arranged on the data base.

The relational model is a mathematical approach built around two basic concepts. The logical storage structure of the relationship is in third normal form (which in previous discussion is the type of relation with the optional properties for use in a data base), and the DML (data manipulation language) is based on the applied predicate calculus and is designed to operate on relationships. Together these two concepts provide an original approach with great potential.

With the relational calculus language the user does not operate directly on the data base. All operations are done to relations; each is constructed in a work area that is a logically separate space. This work area could be in a terminal buffer, in core, on disk or even in temporary links in the physical data base.

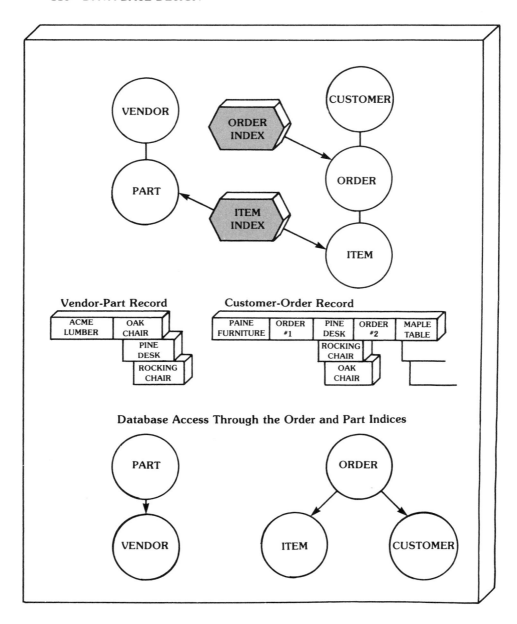

FIGURE 7.8   Typical Inverted List Architecture

Of the products discussed previously, the inverted lists bear the most similarity to the relation DMBS structures. Figure 7.9 illustrates a relational type data base file. The relational entities are really "two-dimensional tables," unique keys (one or several concatenated fields) and their normalized attributes. The relationships are established (coupled) on the basis of common keys within each entity.

There are several relational model data systems in use today such as MAGNUM, ORACLE, MIMER, INGRES, SQL/DS, RDBMS, QBE, and System/38. This text will use the QBE and System/38 as examples. The System/38 implementation is unique in that much of the software is implemented directly into the hardware's microcode. The DML utilized is an offshoot of the powerful and concise nonprocedural predicate calculus language, commonly referred to as Data sublanguage *alpha*.

System/38 is not a true or pure relational DMBS, but it has many of the attributes of relational, hierarchical, network, and inverted list architectures. As shown in Figure 7.9, there are two file structures in System/38, physical files and logical files.

The physical file represents the data as it is physically stored. It has one access path and one format. Therefore, all records in the file have the same attributes, fields, and size. These fields are ordered as defined in the access path to the file.

The logical file, on the other hand, represents the way the user would utilize the physical file or files for a particular application. The logical file may have one or more physical files within it and a different access path and one or more formats. It is the logical file that provides an alternate path and format to one or more of the physical files. It provides a user-view, or a subset or superset of the physical file(s). It is along the logical path that the physical data is reorganized, reordered, or otherwise formatted to conform to the user's view of the data base.

In this manner, different programs, using different logical files, can manipulate the same physical data in diverse ways. System/38 provides the control mechanisms for simultaneously updating and communicating information on changes in the system. New physical or logical files may be built at any time without requiring changes in the programs or the logical or physical file structures.

It is the System/38 physical file that is most like the relational two-dimensional table file. The key to a relational structure and its intrinsic relationship to another entity is the maintenance of key value fields in each entity that are common to both.

The logical file in System/38 is borrowed from IMS and the PSB concept. System/38 logical files represent the user view of data in a logical hierarchy. Since multiple logical views can be maintained in this manner, multiple views within a single application provide a function comparable with that provided in network architectures.

QBE, or Query-By-Example, is a high-level data base management language that provides a convenient "fill in the blanks" format in order to query, update, define, and control a relational data base. This software is not tied to a particular piece of hardware as is System/38.

The format of the language allows a nonprogrammer to make relatively sophisticated queries without requiring the user to know first-order predicate calculus.

For those wishing a deeper discussion in lay terms of predicate calculus and Codd's relational data language ALPHA, see the excellent work by A.T.F. Hutt, *A Relational Data Base Management System*. Hutt in his discussion of predicates

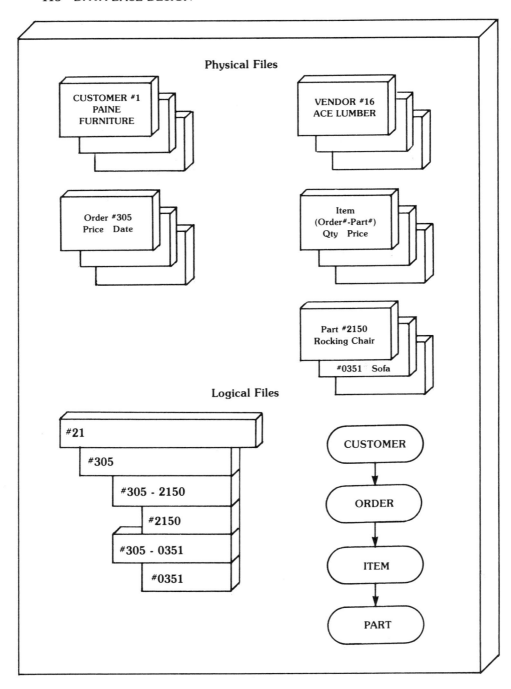

FIGURE 7.9 Relational DBMS Structure

explains that each entity set within an information environment may be governed by a predicate that states the conditions that an entity must satisfy in order to belong to an entity set or logical record group. Languages such as ALPHA and ICL's CSL utilize a series of propositions in either the propositional calculus or first-order predicate calculus for their format. As Hutt states "Propositional calculus (often mistakenly described as Boolean algebra) is a method of calculating with sentences or declarations, each of which produces a value 'true' or false'."[4]

The language itself has statements that establish the entity-to-entity connections such as SET, READ, UPDATE, CREATE, DESTROY, WRITE, and COPY. Further discussion of this topic will be conducted in Chapter 12.

NOTES

1. CODASYL, *Data Base Task Group, April 71 Report* (New York: Association for Computing Machinery, 1977), p. 7.
2. Ian Palmer, *Data Base Systems: A Practical Reference* (Wellesley, Mass.: QED Information Sciences, Inc., 1977), p. 33.
3. E.F. Codd, "Further Normalization of the Data Base Relational Model" R.J. 909 (San Jose, Calif.: IBM Research Laboratory, August 1971).
4. A.T.F. Hutt, *A Relational Data Base Management System* (Chichester, England: John Wiley & Sons, 1979), p. 108.

8 Data Base Design Methodology

Dictionaries are like watches; the worse is better than none and the best cannot be expected to go quite true.

Johnson, *Anecdotes of Samuel Johnson*, 1786

The previous chapters have discussed data base, the management of data, data analysis, normalization, and typical DBMS architectures. The purpose and goal of the rest of this book is to utilize what has been discussed earlier as the basis for a final data base design that can be implemented under a specified DBMS.

Good data base design does not just depend on a knowledge of a particular DBMS or its architecture and design constraints. They are an essential part of design, but just as important is an awareness of the specific data needs of the application being designed and a general understanding of an organization's general data requirements.

The question one must now ask is what happens to the model or products that have been developed in functional and data analysis. How does the data base administrator (DBA) use them to create the physical structure or structures that are the data base. If we could look over the DBA's shoulder what would we see happen? What is the DBA's role? What is a dictionary really? And most important of all, how do these things all relate to the actual design methodology?

Data analysis is a way of understanding the specific needs of an application. A different analysis tool is needed to understand the overall data needs of the organization. Data analysis works with reports, forms, and paperwork, the end results of an application, to provide a means of generating normalized data. This type of analysis gives only a narrow application view of the data. In order to gain a appreciation for the overall needs of a business make a top-down analysis of the functions within that organization—a *functional analysis*.

Functional analysis examines the basic purpose and mission of an organization asking what are its products, its markets, and channels, and what are the information needs of upper and middle management—its corporate objectives. These are the things that determine the policy and direction of an organization and therefore the direction and purpose of its information management systems.

The output of this analysis is a series of data lists that can be normalized into third-normal form relations. These new entities and attributes can be combined if they differ from those entities obtained from data analysis. What falls out from this type of analysis is the possible future direction and the new fields that an application design should take into account in order to touch all bases. Analyzing an application from both directions proves the pudding of the third-normal-form entities.

Because the ultimate responsibility of the data base implementor is to the enterprise and not the application, the implementor (in this case the DBA), must have a global view of the organization. There must be some arm of the organization that can provide an *analysis integration* service. Analysis integration is the blending of the various application views of the totality of an enterprises's data into some kind of cohesive approach to a single physical base or basis of data.

This is not an easy task. Within the constraints of the system, the DBMS, the access methods, and the hardware, what are the forces that come into play? Which forces work against the smooth translation of all the divergent logical views of the data into a performance-optimized physical structure? An applied methodology is needed for the design process as well.

This methodology will benefit from the consistent format developed as output from both functional and data analysis. By having a consistent format, the process of analysis integration becomes one of overlaying application composite maps on top of one another to construct system composite maps. The entity lists developed in each application analysis are also combined into system entity lists. What basically happens is that a vast pool of information about data within the enterprise is being generated. The natural collection point for such data is some kind of dictionary. (We shall explore the particulars of dictionaries later in the chapter.)

Data base design then must operate in a series of phases (see Figure 8.1). The first phase is entered after programmers obtain the input to design through data and functional analysis. The four phases of data base design are

1. Schema design
2. Subschema design
3. Integrity and security design
4. Operation and Performance design

Schema design is concerned with laying out the physical data base structures or schema. The third-normal-form entity list and the relational data model maps obtained from data analysis and functional analysis are used as input.

The various relations described in the relational map obtained from data analysis are identified as being one to one or one to many. Remember that the one to many

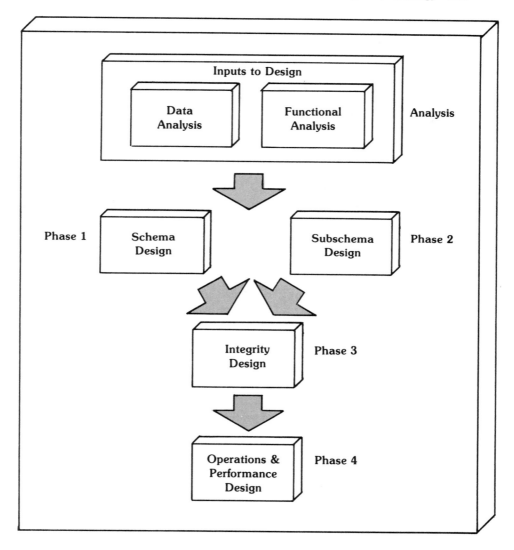

FIGURE 8.1 Stages of Data Base Design

illustrates a natural data hierarchy when repeating groups are involved. The relational map also indicates the frequency of occurrence of the specified entities.

With this information, designers can create a physical structure of entities (records or segments) and their intrinsic relators. When they combine this with information obtained from the usage map, such as what are the most likely paths for an application to take, which are query paths, which are update, plus what are the entry points and what are the primary and secondary keys, designers are better able to group data more efficiently and thereby shorten those paths.

By analyzing the loaded composite map, designers can identify heavy usage paths. When they have this information, designers are better able to group data more efficiently and thereby shorten those paths.

The four key points in order of importance, in schema design are

1. Entry point
2. Logical structure
3. Path activity volume
4. Directionality

The entire organization of a file or data base is primarily centered around the *entry point*, the way you enter the structure. Knowing the entry point determines root segments in IMS, location mode CALC's in CODASYL systems, and indexes or associators in the inverted list architectures. Even in flat files the primary sequence is determined by how you are to access the file. The composite map from data analysis answers this question for you.

The second most important aspect of schema design is to determine the underlying *logical structure*. What are the relationships between the records, the one to ones, and one to manies. The relationship map from data analysis provides the answers for this also. The one-to-many structures indicate the sets in the data base. This determines the "owners and member," the "parents and children," or the "ancestors and siblings," as the case may be.

The load matrix is instrumental in determining the third aspect of data base schema design, *path activity*. When faced with a situation in which record X uses many record Y's and record Z also uses many record Y's the designer has a problem. Where do I put record Y? Neither knowing the entry point nor the logical structure gives an answer to this problem. If the designer could determine which record, X or Z, used Y more, then Y could be placed accordingly. This is where path activity volume from the load matrix comes into play. Look at the X–Y path and the Z–Y path. Which has the highest activity? Place Y nearer the record that accesses it more often. In the case where the activity is more or less equal, look at the system use, on line in favor of batch, dailies over weeklies, and so on.

Last, look at *directionality* along the paths to help determine pointer options. Is a path used in both directions? Does this necessitate an owner or parent pointer, as well as next and prior pointers? Use the composite logical structure to aid you in this decision.

All of this produces a preliminary schema model for the application.

Phase 2, *subschema design* can now begin. The subschema is the user's view of the data base. This analysis utilizes the same inputs as schema design, in particular the usage map from data analysis. These "user-views" present a logical data base that is a subset of the physical data base structure (schema). At this time access controls for both security and audit should be included in the subschemas. Which views are read-only? Which are update? How much data can be seen from any particular view? What segments? What fields?

Common logical views—those with the same access controls and security—are grouped together. A separate preliminary subschema is then created for each user-view.

Integrity and security design is the next phase. It is at this point that the designers bring the schema and subschema models together. The designer analyzes the security and audit requirements of the data base. Recovery/restart analysis is also part of this design phase. Based on this analysis some of the security audit and recovery/restart designs are implemented. The designer evaluates the schema and subschema design models and makes modifications where necessary.

The last phase in data base design is the *operations performance design*. The designers examine operational aspects relating to the data and how it is held in the data base and how it is to be processed. Then they consider questions relating to archiving, data accessibility, data storage, and data base performance. When system requirements change or the total number of transactions increases, data must remain flexible enough for designers to be able to reorganize and restructure the data base.

Other operational considerations are the timing and integration of this new system into the current production systems. How will the new system affect the production environment? What intersystem interfaces are needed?

At this point the schema and subschema models undergo a final scrutiny so that designers can evaluate and assess the impact of various batch and on line activities upon performance. The integrity design requires audit trails and integrity controls; this entails system logging and a considerable performance overhead. Designers must consider any criteria that may compromise data independence in favor of shorter paths and faster access during this final phase.

During this phase the designer also defines physical data base record sizes. They implement the types and numbers of pointers and indexes at this point. They also determine buffer and page sizes. In addition, they reevaluate the total I/O activity for the entire data base and again modify the appropriate schema and subschema models.

In summary, the various stages are necessary, not only to make sure the design satisfies the applications requirements, but also to make sure that the design performs satisfactorily.

Let us examine this design process in detail. The nature of the DBMS imposes certain constraints upon the physical structure of the data base. The earlier analysis resulted in a logical data structure that was DBMS independent; now is the time for designers to apply DBMS dependencies in order to optimize the potential performance of a system and modify the structure to fit the DBMS architecture constraints. The process involves examining the relational and composite maps, figuring the architectural constraints, and grouping together entities that have heavily used reference paths between them. The record grouping can have positive performance benefits for those access paths that are heavily referenced and perhaps negative performance characteristics for the lesser used paths.

RECORD GROUPING AND DBMS ALTERNATIVES

The loaded composite map illustrated in Figure 8.2 was derived in Chapter 4 and will serve as our example. Figure 8.2 illustrates a sample record grouping that should be incorporated into this schema design. This preliminary grouping was derived by keeping those entities together that demonstrated high-usage paths between them in the data analysis portion of design.

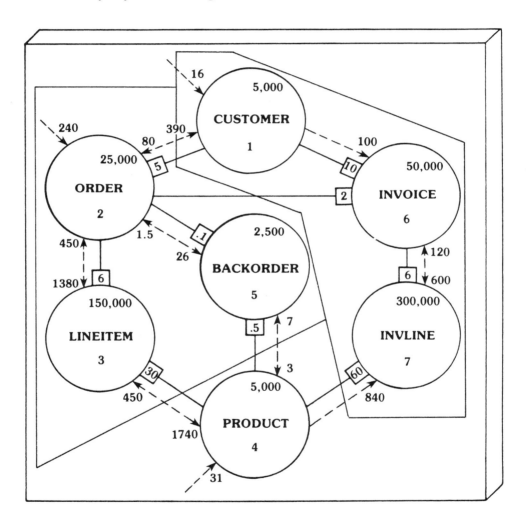

FIGURE 8.2   Sample E-Z Chair Loaded Composite Map with Preliminary Record Grouping

REVIEW OF SCHEMA DESIGN

Data in optimal third normal form along with the corresponding relational and composite maps provide all the data necessary to develop a schema for any of the DBMS architecture types. The individual peculiarities of the DBMS products can impose some constraints on the schema. The closer the architecture is to a relational structure, the easier the logical data structure can be mapped to a data base schema.

What data analysis has provided for the designer are stable data forms, lists of all the keys, knowledge of all possible primary and candidate keys, and the directions and loads along the usage paths between the data entities. Schema design is a stepwise process based on the material developed in data gathering processes of data analysis and functional analysis.

1. The record and/or segment layouts can be directly determined from the physical entity formats created by normalization.
2. The physical data relationships illustrated in the relational map establish the relationships required by each DBMS, owner to member, parent to child, master to variable, or record to periodic group.
3. The usage map diagrams the primary and secondary keys along with the access paths to be used for the application.
4. The loaded composite map indicates the most heavily referenced paths and otherwise aids in determining the best record grouping for performance reasons. It can also indicate the trade-offs for such grouping.
5. The architectural constraints of the DBMS then come into play to optimize the record grouping.

Out of the entire process emerges a model for the preliminary schema. The most difficult part of the design stage up to this point will be dealing with the DBMS architectural constraints. Up to this point, the entire design process could have been conducted by a non–data base professional. Now when the DBA types are called in, the data available to them is in the ideal format for them to carry the design process to a successful conclusion.

The next stage will deal with the cooperation between the systems analyst and DBA and the steps that are followed to conclude the data base design process successfully. Now that a physical plan for the data base has been derived, the various logical schema or subschema can be created. The resulting logical views are each reviewed for similarities and synthesized into several common views, a "logical synthesis" of application objectives.

LOGICAL SYNTHESIS

Subschema design takes the user-view of the data base (developed from the transaction analysis employed in making up the usage map) and creates a separate schema for each transaction. These separate views are then compared for similarity (order of access, entities accessed) and merged with each other when they conform. This process, which is called *logical synthesis*, can reduce the dozens of separate logical views to three or four views.

The process of logical synthesis not only takes into account similar logical views of the data base, but also flavors the selection with information on the type of access activity taking place along this logical view. Whether or not a logical structure reads or updates can determine (depending on the DBMS) whether or not two views which are similar in all respects except access have to be maintained as separate views because of security and audit constraints.

The usage map indicates the access paths and direction of access for each transaction within the application. Each transaction defines a user view.

The purpose of logical synthesis is to create the subschema design. Logical synthesis combines the user views, grouping together those transactions with a consistent view of a subset of all the data base entities along a particular access path, which has similar audit constraints or security authorization.

Access and security controls for the data base must be determined by the DBA depending upon user requests, audit controls, organization standards, and the needs of the DBMS.

The task now remains to find out all the user-views for the application being designed. This has already been done in Chapter 3 for the sample organization the E-Z Chair Corporation. Figure 8.3 presents all nine transactions and their associated user-views of the data. Also illustrated is the type of access (R for read, U for update), for each entity.

The process now involves consolidating the views where possible. Each of the consolidated views is broken into separate user-views again based on security and access evaluation. In this manner the minimum number of views, or subschemas, necessary for carrying out all the functions of the application, consistent with the security and access problems, can be defined to the DBMS.

Figure 8.4 illustrates the consolidated user-views, which will serve as a basis for completion of a subschema design. Transactions a and b most likely would be done by the same program and person; therefore, the security access is not going to be a problem. If the authority is there to create an order, most likely the authority is also there to create an invoice.

Transactions c and g could be combined; however, here the person or program making the update might not be the same one making a query. Therefore, the views are kept separate.

Transactions d and e and transactions h and i are combined even though person using transactions d or i does not need access to other segments. However, the program using this view would not be adversely affected by additional segments. And most likely the person doing the query would be the same. If for some reason this is not the case, keep them separate.

Thus with IDMS and other CODASYL type DBMSs several options are available to the designer for implementing specific subschema access security. All the information needed to define the various program subschemas is available now to the designer. The descriptions exist external to the program and are dynamically addressed by the program utilizing them.

SUMMARY OF SUBSCHEMA DESIGN

The usage map developed from data analysis determines all the separate user-views from the application being designed. From the usage map the designer is able to create subsets of the physical records and segments needed to satisfy the various application requests for data (transactions).

From these subsets of data and the various user-views, the designer then proceeds through a process of logical synthesis. Logical synthesis is the combining of similar user views into one view or subschema, taking into account the security and audit controls that might necessitate keeping two otherwise similar views separate.

The security and audit evaluation requires that the designer compare the various user-paths with each user-view and the types of access activity being done (read-only, update, add, and delete). When designers have completed this evaluation, they can then design various controls for each subschema.

The specific implementation of subschemas and their security controls varies greatly from DBMS to DBMS. However, most DBMSs do have some way of implementing a subschema and providing security for it.

Systems that remove the security and subschema design from the program and implement it through outside logical file utilities offer the greatest flexibility and data independence for the programmer along with simplicity and ease of control for the DBA.

Ideally expressed, subschema support in a DBMS should allow for a high degree of data independence with a minimal amount of programmer interaction. The DBMS should do the "navigation" through the data base, not the program. The DBMS of choice is one that can provide a logical structure, suitable for the application and yet independent of the physical structure of the data base. In addition, this DBMS is one that does not require serious system overhead. Additionally, the maintenance of the logical structure should be a separate, distinct, and controllable process by the data administrator or DBA staff.

OVERVIEW OF INTEGRITY SECURITY AND AUDIT DESIGN

The third phase of data base design involves considering the schema and subschemas designed thus far in terms of integrity, security, and audit controls. Mair, Wood, and Davis state the following.

The new causes of exposure that arise under data base management systems include:
- Unlimited access
- Destruction of files
- Software failure
- Slow response

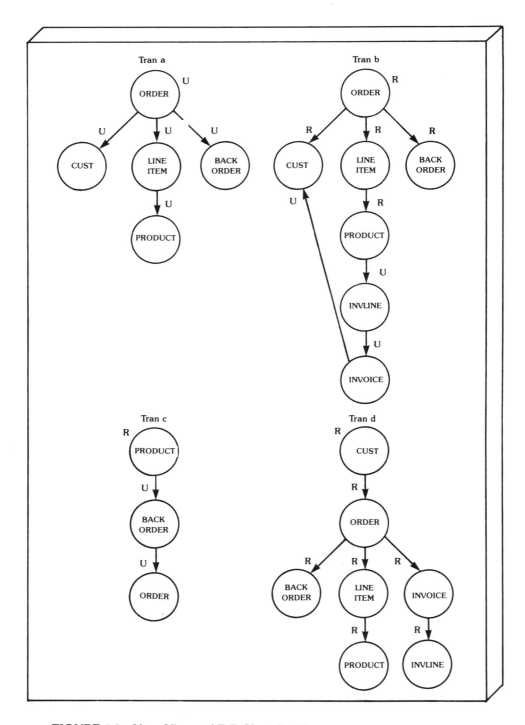

FIGURE 8.3 User-Views of E-Z Chair Problem

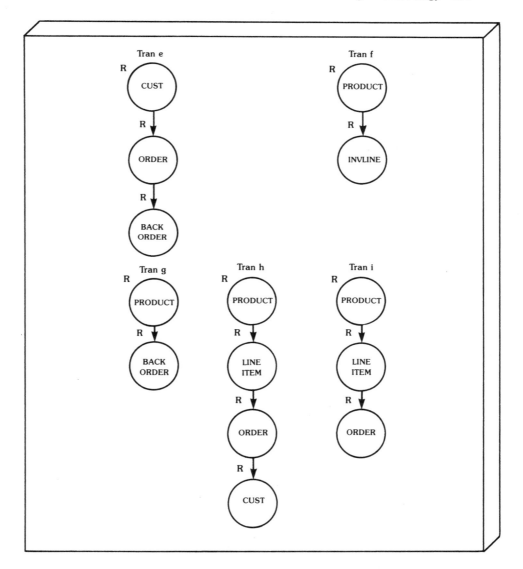

FIGURE 8.3   User-Views of E-Z Chair Problem (continued)

The increased concerns regarding unlimited access to file contents arise due to increased concentration of information assets. Without data base systems, an application program can only access information in specific files provided to it. The data base system effectively eliminates all "library controls" over files and allows unrestrained access to any file at any time.[1]

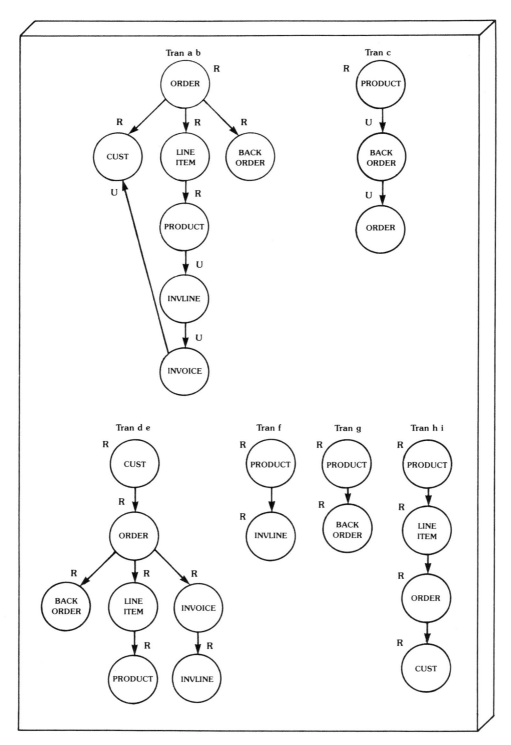

FIGURE 8.4 Consolidated User-Views

132

The controls generated here go beyond the security considerations imposed during subschema design. Security is not only enforced through defining privacy locks and passwords as seen in the Chapter 7, but also through restricting access to the hardware. What type of controls do the different DBMS products provide in this area? Some types to consider are logon/password security, location and line security tables (which isolate certain transactions to certain physical locations), and system command security, which restricts the menu of command selections available to any particular terminal.

The Institute of Internal Auditors (IIA) points out:

> The massive volumes of records actually associated with data base systems also complicate the development of adequate backup files for recovery purposes. A device failure or an application program may cause the destruction of machine-readable information just as readily as it could without the data base. Because the medium on which the data base is maintained does not readily permit a grandfather-father-son backup procedure, the volume of storage makes special backup operations much more costly. The situation could be likened to the effort required to copy every file in the entire library of a major information processing facility.[2]

Audit controls may introduce certain validity and consistency checking routines and/or requirements for tracing inquiry transactions, as well as transactions that update data. Some DBMS products embed this type of control in the schema such as the CODASYL type "CHECK" clause coded in the schema DDL or special user exit routines which are automatically invoked by the DBMS as found in IMS or TOTAL.

Auditors have concerns that should be taken into account by designers as they design the data base. Auditors are looking for documented controls such as password lists, authorization tables, and file maintenance procedures. Auditors are watching for adherence to company policies, standard business practices, and the methods and procedures of the application being audited. Auditors look for a disciplined and controlled environment. Above all, they look for a certain reasonableness in the system: Does the data base perform its work in a logical, acceptable, and reasonable manner?

The options open to the auditor are as follows:

1. Does the system control and DBMS software function properly?
2. Is the system being used properly?
3. Do any system controls exist, and are they in effect?

The auditor evaluates these options by auditing the system controls for security, integrity, and recovery. The role of the designer in all this is to try to provide the following controls in the system being designed.

For security, determine

What are violation criteria?
Which resources are protected and which unprotected?
What resources are or should be password protected?
What resources are or should be lock protected?
What are the security maintenance procedures, and how does the system replace them?

For integrity, determine

When to use program isolation
How frequent is data base backup up copy?
What are the implications of logical data repair and temporary data fixes?
How much data is being shared?
What controls exist remote access to data bases?
What is the storage, retention, and disposition of logs?

For recovery, determine

What are the criteria for judging failure?
Who is responsbile for recovery?
What are the recovery procedures for both on line and batch?
What are the procedures for both normal and emergency system restart?

Audit controls can have far-reaching implications in the selection and implementation of a DBMS. It is not the purpose of this chapter to detail theses procedures, but only to make you aware of the concerns the designer should address during this phase. Figure 8.5 is a summation of the control reliance and impacts and causes of exposure in advanced systems.

Integrity controls are geared to the particular problems of recovery/restart and data base logging. If the data base is damaged physically, users must be able to restore or reconstruct it. Designers must include recovery controls in the system so as to minimize the effects of the recovery procedures on the system's day-to-day operation. Thus the normal cyclic processing of a system requires that users periodically make copies of the data base image and keep and organize data base log tapes. The log is a mechanism provided by most DBMS products, which records a before and after image of the data on that portion of the data base being modified by a transaction. The DBMS products usually come with utilities that have the capability of utilizing the system log and/or image copy to restore the data base to an undamaged state. As pointed out by the IIA:

> By utilizing data base management systems, the organization becomes dependent upon another layer of software in addition to the operating system. This software is extremely complex and may fail due to inherent discrepancies or new types of violations devised by users and programmers.[3]

Advanced Systems Control Evaluation Table

Controls	Reference	Remote Batch — Loss of Data	Remote Batch — Distortion of Data	Remote Job Entry — Loss of Data	RJE — Distortion of Data	RJE — Unlimited Access	RJE — Computer Abuse	Switching — Loss of Data	Switching — Distortion of Data	Switching — Delay of Data	Switching — Misrouting of Data	Inquiry — Invasion of Privacy	Inquiry — Information Not Current	Inquiry — Distortion of Data	Update — Unlimited Access	Update — Hardware/Software Failure	Update — Unsupportable Results	Update — Human Data Entry Errors	Prog — Unlimited Access	Prog — Hardware/Software Failure	Prog — Unsupportable Results	Prog — Human Data Entry Errors	Prog — Computer Abuse	Prog — Destruction of Programs	Data Bases — Unlimited Access	Data Bases — Destruction of Files	Data Bases — Software Failure	Data Bases — Slow Response
Prevention Controls																												
Electronic security							2					2			2				2				2	2	2	2	2	2
Passwords			2		2	2	2		2			2			2				2				2	2	2		2	
Cyphers			2		2	2	2		2			2			2				2				2	2	2			
ID Cards					1	1	1					1	2		1				1				1	1		2		
Device identification				2	2	2	2		2		2	3		2	3				3				2	2	3	2	2	
Physical scanners				2	2	2	2		2		1	2		2	2	1			2	2			2	2	2	2	2	
Physical terminal security				2	2	2	2		2		2	2			2	2			2	2			2	2	2	2	2	
Authorizations																												
Detection Controls																												
Line protocol	2	2	2	2			2	2			2			2	2	1		3	2	1		3	2	2	2		1	
Up-front edits		2	2	2			2	2			2			2	2	2	2	3	2	2	2	3	2	2	2	2		
Access logo											2			2									2	2	2	2		
Authorized user title			3	3	2		2	2			2	2			2		2	2	2		2	2	2	2		2		
Read-back	3	3	3	3			2	2					2		2			2		2								
Redundancy checks (vertical or longitudinal)													2		2			2		2								
Line control hardware	2	2	2	2	2		2	2		2				2				2				2	2	2				
Corrective Controls																												
Rotation of access controls											2			2		3		2		3		2	2		2		2	
Transaction log					2	2	2	2		2	2			2	1	1		2	1	1		2	2	2	3	2	
On-line Instruction					2	2									2	2			2	2							
Recovery journal	1	1													2				2								
Graceful degradation							2	2		2			1		2	2	1		2	2	1		2	1	3	3		1
Impact of Causes																												
3 - Very likely to occur	3	3	3	3	1	3	3	3		2	2	2	1	2	3		2	3	2	1	3	2	2	1	3	2	1	1
2 - Likely to occur	1	1	1	1	1	1	1	1	1	1	1	2	1	1	1	2	1	2	1	1	1	1	2	2	2	2	2	2
1 - May occur	2	2	2	2	1	1	2	2	1	1	1	1	1	2	1	1	1	1	1	1	1	1	1	1	3	3	2	
Blank - Generally little effect	1	1	1	1	1	1	1	1			1	1	1	1		1	1	1		1	1	1	1	1	1	1	1	1

Warning: Reliance and impact relationships must be tailored to individual circumstances.
© Touche Ross & Co. Permission expressly granted for reproduction.

FIGURE 8.5 Control Evaluation Table

135

Restart works hand-in-glove with the utilities provided by the DBMS and the log to satisfy the requirements of normal and emergency restart of an application or on-line system. Restart generally requires recognition of the processing that was only partially completed at the time of program or system failure.

The data base design for restart may require establishing a *checkpoint* logic, which will provide for intermediate restart points. These checkpoints are written to the log when a commitment is made by the program that everything processed before the checkpoint was written and is okay. In the event of program failure after the checkpoint, the program would only have to be restored or *backed out* to the oldest checkpoint, thus saving much time and program effort.

The data base designer must determine what a safe fallback point is and how extensive logging should be. Data analysis provides the designer with two tools that will aid in the integrity design process, the user-views and the composite load map.

A great deal of work is being done by the system because the DBMS log generally takes a before and after image of the data. This substantial activity against the data base must be accounted for in the load matrix, because it represents a large increase in the number of logical references to each entity. Designers must know how the individual DBMS products accomplish this logging activity in order to efficiently design or modify the model schema and subschemas produced thus far to accommodate this increased activity.

Integrity design, therefore, has two areas of concern: recovery from physical data base failure, which involves the recovery/restart consideration using checkpoints, image copies, and backouts; and recovery from logical data base failure, which involves the security and audit considerations for invalid use and/or access of data.

INTEGRITY DESIGN SUMMARY

In general, integrity design requires a separate analysis of the security and audit requirements of the system being designed. From this analysis the designer proceeds to determine the special audit requirements so as to define the various system audit controls. Designers also determine recovery requirements so that they can define data base recovery options. Then designers analyze restart requirements for both batch and on-line portions of the system so that they can produce a definition of batch/on-line restart. Finally, designers review the security aspects of the application so that they can define ways to enforce the security requirments of the system. When designers have completed the procedures, they may wish to alter the design of the schema and subschema models created from phase 1 and 2 of the design process. If necessary, designers then update the models.

Integrity design is basically an awareness exercise for the user to go through in order to make sure all security, audit, recovery, and restart goals can and will be met by the application. Users must eliminate roadblocks imposed by the schema and subschema that could adversely affect data base integrity.

FACTORS AFFECTING SYSTEM OPERATIONS AND PERFORMANCE

Traditional data base designers most often end their paper-and-pencil planning stage at phase 2 or 3. They usually work out the day-to-day operational considerations as well as the performance optimization and tuning problems on a real data base. By carrying out data base design through phase 4, designers can save the data processing department much unnecessary effort and cost.

Operations and performance design has as firm a basis in the design process as the schema design. The processes involved in operational and performance design cover two main areas as follows:

Operational Environment Considerations
Recognizing cyclic business functions impact
Accessibility and storage of data
Concurrent processing functions
Performance monitoring and tuning

Performance Considerations
Data base grouping and record sizing
Choosing an access method
Choosing secondary key selection
Implications of the various DBMS architectures

At this stage in the data base design process, 90% of the schema and subschema models are in their final form. The final steps of design should not be overlooked in the rush to start the implementation process. The pressure on the designer to put away his models, tables, and maps can be quite formidable. Unfortunately, for a great many data processing organizations progress is still measured in lines of code, reels of tape, and feet of stacked output!

In this final stage of data base design, the major objective will be to modify the schema and subschema models to optimize the data access for the application system functions. Designers scrutinize the characteristics of the data to determine whether they match the capabilities of the chosen DBMS. Each type of DBMS architecture has certain strengths and weaknesses. DBMSs handle some data characteristics very efficiently and handle other characteristics very poorly. It is at this stage of design we hope to minimize or eliminate the latter characteristics.

As. T. Jack McElreath states in *IMS Design and Implementation Techniques*:

> It may seem to go against some of the high ideals of data management when we begin to change our structural design purely for efficiency. Perhaps it is, and we must guard against building data bases which work well today, but which are inflexible to accommodate system enhancements or changes to the data or its characteristics. But, the best looking data base in the world won't help anyone if the functions cannot be accomplished in an acceptable period of time.[4]

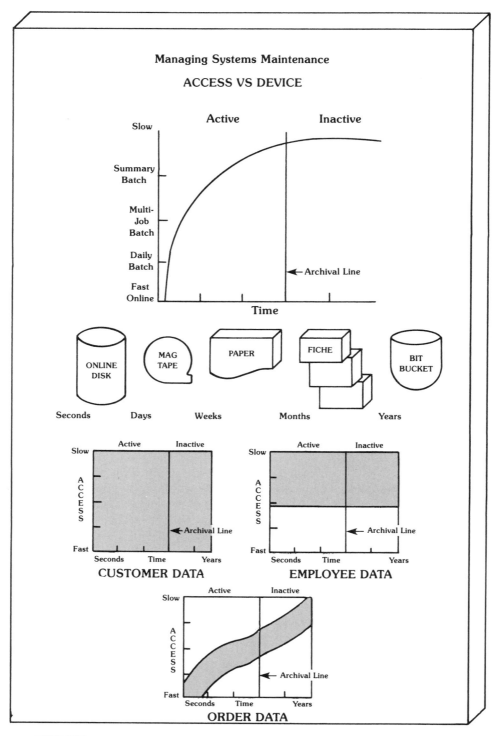

FIGURE 8.6   Managing Systems Maintenance: Data Accessibility versus Storage

A number of factors affect data base design in the operational area. One of these factors is recognizing the cyclic business functions of the organization and how these functions affect the corporate data resource.

Periodically during the business cycle, extra demands are made on the data processing departments over and above the daily running of applications. Along with standard processing there are monthly reports, quarterly cycles, and most demanding of all, year end processing. How does this affect the data base?

What the real question should be is "How does this affect the accessibility and storage of data?" What needs to be determined is what is the organization's policy for archiving data. What types of data does the organization need every day? What entities does it need weekly, monthly, or yearly? Perhaps of even greater importance, what data does it need once or twice and then never again?

The designer must establish a policy for the controlled removal of data from the active data base to archive files or throw the data away into the bit bucket. To establish this policy, the designer determines just what the access requirements are for the various pieces of data. The designer must determine the useful life cycle of the data. Data that is active and is needed fast or needed often should be kept separate from data that is inactive and needed slowly or rarely.

The designer must recognize the business life cycle requirements, the monthly, quarterly, year-end applications, and plot their functions against accessibility requirements over the business time cycle (see Figure 8.6). The figure graphically represents the trade-offs that can be made regarding data accessibility and how and when it is to be stored.

What the figure illustrates is the correlation between time and device and accessibility versus type of processing. The time device correlation illustrates that when the time period is short, the data needs to be on a device that would allow the most rapid access. Thus any access requiring less than one day turnaround should be stored on disk. Data required only weekly or monthly can still be on disk, but the disk files could be large and the data could be derived (virtual) and not stored directly. The amount of data requested could be voluminous, and physical data retrievals could be high. Monthly or quarterly passing of entire files should be done on tape. In most cases information requests on data a year or more old are so rare they can be handled with paper records or fiche.

The data accessibility-processing correlation reveals the relative need for speed dictating the processing function. The need for rapid access with response time measured in seconds or the need for the same information frequently dictates on-line type processing. When speed and frequency are not important, a slower type of processing can be used.

Looking at the plots of the various data types, you can more easily recognize when the data should be removed from the active data to the inactive data. The data types chosen for this particular example are general and in no way depict the use of such data in all organizations. The purpose is to demonstrate that the time spent plotting such usage is valuable to the design effort. Furthermore it does not mean the corollaries are absolute. Time and device criteria are not absolute, particularly at the points farthest from the axis. Not all data over 3 months old is stored only on fiche.

Bearing that in mind, you can make the following conclusions from the curves plotted for the various data types.

Employee Data
Rarely if ever a day-to-day access requirement, no on-line access required. Flurry of activity weekly, quarterly—most likely for payroll purposes. High degree of year-end activity probably related to taxing; then the information starts again for another year. Possible archiving of detail data and keeping the yearly summary data only.

Customer Data
High degree of activity when file is added initially and for day-to-day inquiries. The cyclic requirement for quarterly and yearly customer data decreases with time. No archiving of active data; monthly archiving of summary data.

Order Data
Plots a roller coaster type curve. The order builds slowly over time until it is shipped. Degree of inquiry on status jumps dramatically at this point. Each business cycle shows an increase because of monthly and quarterly status reporting. Possible archiving of closed order data from disk to tape on quarterly basis.

Data base designers should plan for concurrent processing when they develop the loaded composite map. The designer must match operations that operate in an on-line environment against the data base with those that process concurrently in a batch mode upon the same data. If this simultaneous processing requirement is not restricted by the DBMS, a reanalysis and regrouping of the data may be necessary.

Performance design has a component that is part of the operational design. Designers must set performance and tuning guidelines and must also develop procedures for maintaining the data base. As Finkelstein points out, "It is not sufficient to only design the data base to provide at least the required level of performance. It is essential that we design the data base also so that its performance can be monitored and tuned."[5]

The performance tuning story begins with two questions: Will response time be acceptable? What is acceptable? The designer must determine from the user what the relative functional or transaction priorities are. The designer follows through each system component and assigns a priority level to define "acceptable" for each system operation.

Is immediate response necessary? Is current response time sufficient? Perhaps a reasonable goal is 3 seconds for 50% of all transactions and no more than 9 seconds for 90% of all transactions. Maybe designers could perform calculations for each transaction. Figure 8.7 illustrates what the components of on-line response time are and how designers might measure response time.

This topic leads naturally into the final design topic: performance. Designers find ways to measure performance. They set up guidelines for what good performance is, and they monitor the system to see that the guidelines are adhered to. But what do

How Is It Measured?
The Same for All Transactions

Components of Response Time

Key in Data	Wait for Poll	Input Line Time	Input *Server Wait Time	Process	Output Server Wait Time	Output Line Time	Think Time
A	B	C	D	E	F	G	H

A and H	- almost impossible to measure (do we want to?)
B	- can be the largest component in some systems
C	- estimate (#chars × 8) BAUD RATE + DELAYS
D thru G	- log or journal statistics (i.e., type 31 and 36 records in IMS)
B thru G	- can be measured by some hardware monitors

*Server = message queue in IMS

FIGURE 8.7   Components of Response Time

they do to the schema and subschema designs in order to get acceptable performance?

One of the primary ways of getting good performance is with good record sizing and data set grouping. One of the goals to strive for in data base is developing a data base record size of uniform in length throughout the data base. Ideally records should be large enough to hold all the data necessary for handling the greatest number of requests in the same physical block. The designer must also take into account records that are unwieldy in size, especially if they are frequently accessed. For example, 98% of the records in a particular design fit into one 2,000-byte block each, and the other 2% require 25 such blocks. However, if that 2% account for 75% of the activity of the data base, then the processing time for this data would be excessive. The design must take this into account.

There is also an external system component of record grouping. How should the disk devices (DASD) be configured for optimal performance of the system? DASD performs well when the fewest number of disk drives is employed to provide the lowest wait time (called IWAIT by IBM). An IWAIT time of around 40 milliseconds is acceptable. One of the main factors in IWAIT time is how often is the pack upon which the data base resides busy when the DBMS wants to use the data base. A reasonable goal to strive for might be 35% maximum device busy.

Thus, in a good system that meets these criteria, there will be an average of nine physical I/Os per second.

$$(1 \text{ second}/40 \text{ millisecond}) \times .35 = 9 \text{ I/O per second}$$

Having multiple high-use data for different application transactions on the same disk device could adversely affect this performance. Another concern is keeping the seek time of the disk device under 50 cylinders by keeping the record grouped properly. As you can see, physical data base structure and storage, when viewed in terms of the type of processing planned, affect performance. The ability of the designer to group data and of the DBMS to accommodate that grouping plays a significant role in performance.

At this point the designer must also choose an access method. This choice will affect performance. Some DBMS products offer a wider selection of access methods than others. The choice of access method depends upon the dynamics of the data and the indexing and search techniques which users must employ to enter a data base and find specific records.

The dynamics of the data has to do with the volatility of the data values. Static data values are ideal values to use for keys and descriptors when applicable. Data that is very dynamic and always changing position, size, and value requires increased I/O overhead and may require a direct access method to reduce that overhead. Direct access methods usually require direct address pointers to maintain the data interrelationships. If these relationships are highly volatile, then maintaining these pointers can significantly affect overhead. If this be the case, then designers should employ an indexed access method, which usully expresses interrelationships in terms of symbolic pointers, and these are the record keys themselves.

Next, designers must choose a key and must determine whether or not to choose a random access to data through an algorithm (CALC expression in CODASYL) or some type of indexing capability.

The random methods usually require less I/O activity than the indexed methods. Designers can use indexed methods to structure the data sequentially or in the case of inverted list architectures to utilize multiple indexes to satisfy complex queries. Network architectures are particularly weak in indexing and sequential ordered processing of the data base, but very good for random access.

SUMMARY OF OPERATIONS AND PERFORMANCE DESIGN

The final phase in the data base design process, like the previous phases, is one of analyzing and weighing alternatives. The purpose of the techniques outlined is to help you decide just what are your considerations and alternatives. This final phase is the cap, topper, or the ribbon around the package. It is meant to draw the designer's attention to the final details of data base planning.

The process involves two major system functions that are not adequately handled in traditional design methodology: the operational data base function and the data performance function.

The designer evaluates the operational considerations of performance and tuning, application interfacing, archiving, and concurrent processing because it has been demonstrated that they have a significant impact upon a data base design. This likewise holds true for the performance considerations of record grouping, blocking, access method, and most important of all, DBMS architecture.

It is sincerely hoped that these techniques will prove as valuable to you as they have been to others. Succeeding chapters will discuss the data base design methodology evolving from data analysis in the context of four data base management archetypes; hierarchies, networks, inversions, and relational.

DATA DICTIONARY: ESSENTIAL DESIGN TOOL

Throughout the process of data analysis and data base design, designers have been compiling vast amounts of data about data. How do they store it? How do they organize it? The data base design tool that is invaluable during initial data base design and essential during subsequent data enhancement is the *data dictionary*.

The stages of data base design can all be recorded in the dictionary as they evolve. Any subsequent modification to the design can easily be recorded in the data dictionary. Some dictionary products, depending on the DBMS, can automatically generate schema and subschema code.

Dictionary development has paralleled the development of data base technology. Some products developed as an integral part of the DBMS they were associated with, such as integrated data dictionary for IDMS (see Figure 8.8), while others, not integrated into the DBMS software, were developed as separate software packages such as the IBM DB/DC data dictionary, Control-2000 from MRI and the ADABAS data dictionary from Software-AG.

These dictionaries operate under the control of the DBMS they support. As such, however, they tend to support only their own data base software, paying scant attention to conventional files. The aforementioned products, however, are undergoing tremendous development and enhancement to lessen these types of deficiencies. The IBM product, as an example, is now a Class A program product, which has undergone three major changes between 1981 and 1983 (see Figure 8.9).

With the addition of an on-line interactive query and an update function that augments batch processing, most dictionary products are becoming increasingly more usable and more available. Those dictionaries offering an on-line capability are a much more valuable and dynamic data management tool.

Concurrent with the development of the DBMS related dictionary products, several "free-standing" dictionaries also evolved. These products, such as LEXICON, UCC-10 DATAMANAGER, and PRIDE/LOGIC, operate outside any particular DBMS. They support several different DBMS architectures and in general, earlier in their development, paid more attention to their "conventional file" user community. DATAMANAGER is the one stand-alone product now available that supports the widest range of DBMS products and telecommunication monitors. Figure 8.10 illustrates the functional flow of LEXICON, which is typical of free-standing dictionary products.

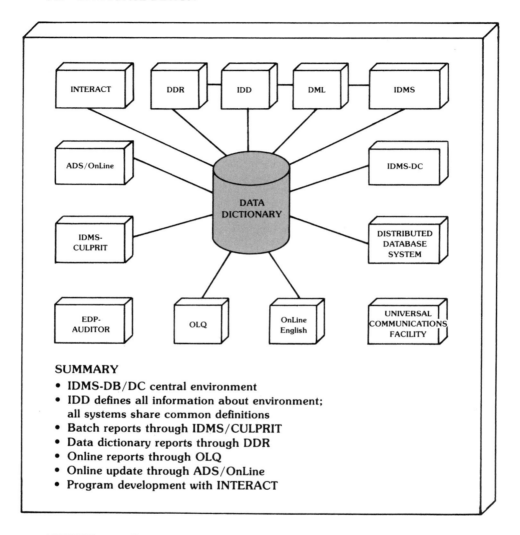

FIGURE 8.8 IDMS Integrated Data Dictionary

The selection of an appropriate dictionary product is as crucial as the selection of a DBMS. In the process of data analysis and data base design, not only must information about an application be uncovered, but also information about the uses of data throughout an organization must be catalogued. This is a monumental task, which in some cases is made much easier through the use of a dictionary. Thus this tool must match the DBMS the organization is using or plans to use. Free-standing dictionaries can alleviate this problem somewhat if users have not chosen a DBMS.

Through the use of a data dictionary, the data base designer can evaluate the various design decisions encountered in the separate phases of design. The dictionar-

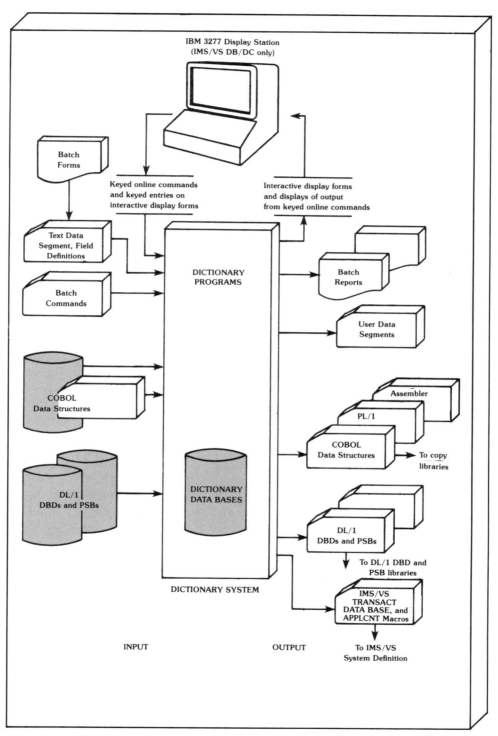

FIGURE 8.9   DB/DC Data Dictionary System of IBM

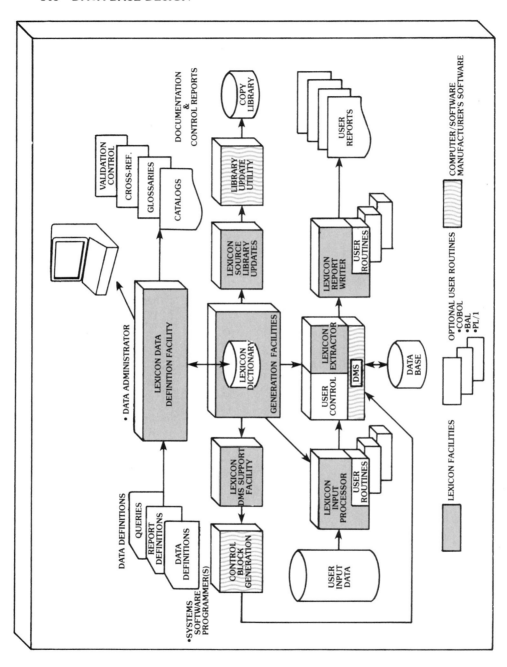

FIGURE 8.10 LEXICON Data Dictionary Product of Arthur Andersen & Company

ies operate by recording information about every data element in the data base, such as its description, use, and structure. Also relationships between elements are included in the dictionary, such as what elements are contained in which records. These relations are then expanded to records within files and files within data bases.

Information about programs and how they relate to one another are sometimes also recorded. The program relationships also include the files and data bases utilized by the program. When this is done for all programs in a system, the system information can be accumulated such as its description and purpose and all its programs, files, and data bases.

The information builds upon itself much the same as a bill of materials type data base. With the kinds of data stored in the dictionary, it is now possible to pose data base questions such as: Which programs use file X? What data bases are affected by system X? In which records is Element A found? If element Z is expanded, which systems and programs are affected by the change?

These types of queries are built in common function reports in most dictionary products. In addition, the dictionaries act as source generators for file copylib members, plus DDL and DML code for the various DBMS products they support.

An effective data dictionary thus becomes an indispensable tool to data base designers, both during the early stages of information gathering and data base design, and the future restructuring and design that accompanies data base maintenance.

As the importance of the dictionary product grows with the increased emphasis by organizations upon data base and data resource management, the dictionary will take an even more active role than today. In the ideal dictionary product of the future (see Figure 8.11) the dictionary will be a primary interface between the users and their data bases. The dictionary will not only be used to query the dictionary data base but also to query the other data bases defined by the dictionary. Additionally, this future free-standing dictionary product should be able to handle serveral separate DBMS products simultaneously.

Dictionaries are setting the stage for the time when users complete their data analysis, and load up their dictionaries with the information they have gathered, and then wait for the dictionary literally to design their data bases for them. Current hardware limitations in storage and access times preclude this happening today, but the pressure is on, and the computer industry has responded brilliantly to this kind of challenge in the past.

As Henry C. Lefkovits states in the summary of his text *Data Dictionary Systems*:

> In summation, the over-all picture which we have presented is one of a gradual change in the architecture of computing systems. One where the data dictionary or data dictionary/directory system moves closer and closer to the core of the computing system, and architecture where more and more other components become dependent on the data dictionary/directory system, and where its data base begins to resemble a model of the enterprise's total system. Such an outcome is not overly surprising, if it is remembered that a substantial component of the activities of an enterprise consists of data and the processes that operate on data.

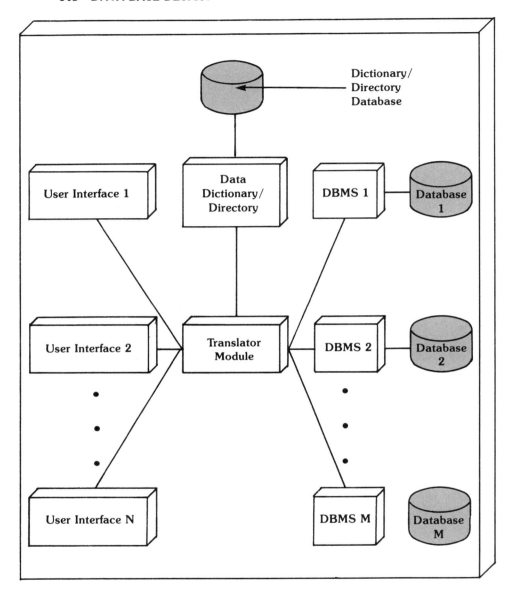

FIGURE 8.11 Data Dictionary System of the Future

The future portends great hope for programmers—less data base software which could make data base design an automatic machine function. One of the most essential cogs in automated data base design is the availability of the programmable data algorithms which are possible with data analysis techniques. The future is not far away.[6]

THE ROLE OF THE DATA BASE ADMINISTRATOR

The dictionary will be the primary tool of the data base designer not only in the future but right now. Who are the designers—the individuals who design and implement the data base and control the data dictionary? The answer is the data base administrator, the DBA.

The DBA is responsible for the design, control and administration of the data resource (data base) of an organization. The DBA is responsible for administering the data resource in behalf of the organization. This person represents functional authority and responsibility for data. This function provides a data service that fulfills user application requirements.

As regards the data dictionary, the DBA

Controls and maintains it
Establishes the contribution methodology for it
Controls the access to it
Records and controls data base authorization in it
And has the ultimate responsibility for it

The data base administration group in an organization must provide and control:

Data base structure
Physical and logical data base descriptions
Program data base specifications
Data element and segment definition call sequences
Data base integrity and security
Data base reorganization and back-up procedures
Data base standards and tools
Design Aids and modeling work
Testing of data base and networks

Additionally, the data base administration group must monitor both the data base's utilization of system resources and the application's use of the data resource. The DBA must always strive to improve the performance of the data base and the programs that access it. The office must also act as a watchdog agency to assure that *designers* adhere to the organization audit requirements.

There are, however, limits to the DBA's role. The job function should not call for the DBA to write application programs. Additionally, the system programming function should be done by a separate branch in the data processing organization. The DBA can recommend that system programming action be taken, but the DBA should not perform it. Unless designated by the responsible function for specific data, the DBA should not have the power to authorize data access. In fact, the job should not call for any data access authority or responsibility. Nor should the job call for any data value responsibility. The only exception to this rule might be the data contained in the data dictionary files. Above all the *DBA is not the Czar of Data!* What good would the security and privacy controls within the organization be if one person could do everything?

Nevertheless, the role of data base administrator despite its limitations, requires a person of above average skills and knowledge. Typically persons seeking the position have either an application analysis background with programming experience or come from the ranks of systems programming profession. Frequently both backgrounds can be found in a single candidate for the job. If one background is preferable over the other, then it is applications analysis, because frequently analysis involves a great deal of experience with data and certainly knowledge of the organization's applications.

The DBA should have had education and experience in batch and teleprocessing programming, on-line networking, and data base software internals.

Creating the DBA Function in an Organization

To expand upon this a bit further let us discuss creating the DBA function in an organization. Primarily we are concerned with four areas when defining the purpose and role of the DBA in an organization; these are as follows:

1.   The potential job functions
2.   The tools of the office
3.   The interfaces to the DBA within and without the organization
4.   The quantity, quality, knowledge, and placement of the staff within the organization

Job Functions of the DBA

The potential job functions can be divided into five different areas of development.

Data Selection and Data Base Structure.   The DBA must know all the user's data requirements. DBAs have to determine the data's location within the organization and its source availability. They must create both the physical and the logical structures for the organizations' data. They must be aware of the physical space available for storage and also the types of media to be used to store it. Data base generation and modification are also the responsibility of the DBA. (The actual task of doing the generation should be a system programming function.)

Performance.   The DBA must recommend changes to the form and structure of the physical data in order to improve performance and response time. To this end the DBA must simulate, model, and monitor the data base and all the systems that access it.

Protection.   The job calls for the DBA to protect the data base by controlling the access to it and manipulation of it. The integrity of the data base is one of the prime functions of the office. Additionally, all aspects of data base recovery and restart are within the province of the DBA. Indeed all aspects of security and privacy violation monitoring are included under the protection function that belongs to the DBA.

Documentation.   In a data base environment documentation is essential. One of the major responsibilities of the job of data base administrator is the creation and maintenance of data documentation. This documentation includes cataloging the physical data base descriptions, creating and maintaining the organizational standards, procedures, and passwords, plus defining the usage measurement procedures and standards.

Support Services.   The final responsibility of the DBA is creating and maintaining adequate date base support services.'The DBA must support the data base training effort up to and including the DBA or members of his staff actually conducting courses. The data base requires a tremendous effort in the area of utilities for maintenance, recovery, integrity and a number of ancillary functions. The DBA and staff must act as a liaison to the rest of the organization on data-base matters. They are in effect an internal consulting team prepared to render expert assistance to others concerning data base function.

Tools of the DBA

As with the job functions having five areas of development there are five tools of the data base administration. To carry out the above job functions, the DBA employs these five tools:

The DBMS.   The data base management system itself is a prime tool of the DBA. It has multiple access techniques to aid in rapid information retrieval. Most also have a capability for structuring some type of logical data base tailored to individual application views of data. The DBMS is a tool that promotes data independence. The DBMS aids the DBA by providing the software to monitor the data base security, integrity, and privacy. It also provides a method, through logging, to recover the data base.

Data Base Utilities.   The utilities provided to the DBA allow for the movement of data from one piece of physical media to another. The utilities provide the DBA with the ability to reorganize, back out, and unload or reload the data base.

Standards.   Even the data base standards are a tool of the DBA. Without naming and documentation standards, no one would be able to control the access and manipulation of the data base.

Simulators and Monitors.   Simulators and monitors are necessary tools for gathering the statistics and data needed in order to have good performance planning. The monitor also allows the DBA to realize when violations of standards or procedures have taken place. These tools allow the DBA to keep a finger on the pulse of the data base.

The Dictionary. The ultimate tool or weapon in the DBA's arsenal is the data dictionary. This item can become the single most important tool of the DBA because it allows for the control of all the other tools. Dictionaries are more than just a cross reference of data definitions. They can be used to control and store the physical data base definitions as well as the logical definitions. They can also control file layouts, copy areas, and record descriptions. The dictionary is the warehouse for the central maintenance of information about data.

Interfaces of the DBA

There are six areas of concern regarding the interfaces to the DBA from within the organization and from outside it.

The User. The first interface to the DBA office is with the ultimate user of the data base. It is with the end user that the DBA determines the ownership of data. It is with the user that the DBA agrees upon access and integrity standards. Documentation and standards are implemented and approved with the advice and consent of the user. Ultimately just what the service level of the data base should be is determined through the interface between the user and the DBA.

Management. The DBA must report to management upon the performance of the data base. The DBA must inspire confidence in data base and in the ability of the data base to perform well in any given situation. The DBA must correlate the management objectives of the organization with the technology of data base.

Applications Areas. The analysts and programmer belong to a third group that must interface with the DBA. To them the DBA must provide information about the form and structure of the data. They in turn must submit specifications for review and approval of change to the DBA. The DBA will provide them with the necessary standards and technical support to do their job.

Operations. The DBA must also work with the operational arm of the data processing department. With them the DBA must work out and recommend procedures for physical media balancing, recovery, security, and integrity procedures, and working out the details for day-to-day monitoring and audit support.

Vendors. The DBA must also interface with the data base software vendors. The purpose of this interface is twofold: first to maintain a technical awareness of what is happening in the industry, and second to correct any problems regarding the data base software or hardware.

Education. The last interface concerns educating members of the organization about data base. The DBA should review and make recommendations on all data base courses and materials both internal and external to the organizations. Ultimately the DBA may present seminars to all the previously mentioned interface groups.

The DBA's Staff

The DBA. The data base administrator is the prime member of this staff. (In fact the DBA may be the only member.) DBAs should be very management oriented and familiar with the goals and objectives of the organization. They must have a generalized knowledge and familiarity with all areas of data processing, not just data base. DBAs should be dynamic individuals capable of doing many things and making adequate transitions from one to the other. The role is a highly visible one, and it is not one for shrinking violets. (Modesty is not an attribute in this job.)

The Staff. Generally the DBA's staff is a small and highly experienced group of synergistic individuals. All should have supervisory skills and should be the prime pool of candidates within the organization to be successors to the DBA's job. Thus they too must also be communicators and diplomats.

Knowledge. The entire staff must know data base technology inside out. They should also know generalized computing technology as well. All should have familiarity with the major aspects of programming and systems design. A knowledge of the industry within which their organization exists is most beneficial. Indeed knowledge of their own corporation, its mission and purpose, along with its products, markets, and channels would be essential to the successful completion of their jobs.

Placement within the Organization. The data base administration function should be separate and distinct from that of programming, operations, and systems programming. As such the DBA should report to the highest DP executive. His or her rank should be equal to that of any other manager in the organization with the same degree of responsibility.

The importance of the data base administration roles cannot be stressed too strongly in an organization that has made the commitment to "go data base." A strong authority within the guidelines stated above is essential to the task of managing and controlling an organization's data resource. Without centralized control, data base methodology will never emerge as anything more than a very expensive access method.

NOTES

1. William C. Mair, Donald R. Wood, and Keagle W. Davis, *Computer Control and Audit* (Wellesley, Mass.: QED Information Sciences, Inc., 1981), p. 390.

2. Ibid.
3. Ibid.
4. T. Jack McElreath, *IMS Design and Implementation Techniques* (Wellesley, Mass.: QED Information Sciences, Inc., 1979) p. 11.1.
5. C. Finkelstein, *Data Analysis and Design of Information Systems* (Australia: Infocom Australia, 1980), p. 404.
6. Henry C. Lefkovits, *Data Dictionary Systems* (Wellesley, Mass.: QED Information Sciences, Inc., 1977), p. 108.

9 Designing for Network Architectures

Total grandeur of a total edifice, chosen by an inquisitor of structures for himself.

Wallace Stevens, "To an old philosopher in Rome"

This is a first of four chapters relating the design process to specific architecture types and in turn to specific DBMS products. In dealing with networks, this chapter uses two such products, TOTAL and IDMS.

TOTAL is the older product of the two and has well over 2,000 licensees worldwide. It runs on virtually any machine and was one of the earliest of the network type products. IDMS is one of the more popular of the CODASYL network products, and due to its popularity and, in particular the widespread use of the CODASYL group of products, it is a natural topic for inclusion here.

The chapters on specific DBMS products will be brief and are not intended for use by DBAs as the ultimate design reference by any means. The goal and direction of these chapters is intended to aide and inform the systems designer or analyst of some of the options available to the DBA doing design and implementation. The view again is intended to be one of the "peeking over the DBA's shoulder."

IDMS SCHEMA (CODASYL ARCHITECTURE)

An IDMS implementation of the physical data base structure appears very similar to the relational map. The designer determines the grouping of data by utilizing the proper LOCATION MODE statement (CALC, VIA, or DIRECT). By specifying "LOCATION MODE IS VIA OWNER-SET" the designer places a member record in a specified set on or near the page containing its owner record. CALC stores records by a direct randomizing algorithm using a data item that is a key. DIRECT lets the user specify a particular page on which to store an item.

In an IDMS structure a one-to-many relationship is implemented as a set relationship between an owner record and one or more member records. Many member records are chained to one owner record by a set relationship chain. The chain is processed by a forward (next) or backward (prior) pointer specified by the design. If an owner must be directly processed from any member (based on usage map), an owner pointer can be specified pointing from every member of that set (see Figure 9.1) to the owner.

TOTAL SCHEMA (NETWORK ARCHITECTURE)

TOTAL is an example of another type of network architecture. The limitations or restrictions of this product are based on the master-file, variable-entry file structures employed. TOTAL permits entry into the data base only through master files. The one-to-many relationships are stored in TOTAL by putting the manys (members) into a variable-entry file. This structure is very similar to the owner-member chains described in IDMS. The chain supports both forward and backward pointers. Support also exists for direct access back to the owner of the set. See Figure 9.2 for sample TOTAL schema. For those situations in which a member is also an owner, designers must construct an intermediate master file to allow direct access to the member record that is stored in a variable-entry record instead of a variable-entry file. In the sample problem, the ORDER and INVOICE entities are both variable-entry files. There is no way to get directly from ORDER to LINEITEM and INVOICE to INVLINE because all are variable-entry files. Because it is necessary to process INVLINE and LINEITEM directly, the designer must define two additional master files.

In TOTAL a variable-entry file may reference another variable entry file only via an intervening master file. Likewise, a requirement to go directly from master file to master file requires an intervening variable-entry file.

TOTAL does offer some control in record grouping by limiting the length to the physical and logical records in the variable-entry files. However, separate I/O accesses are required for variable-entry and master files involved in a set relationship. Excessive lengths in the variable-entry file chain could require additional I/O's to satisfy a particular request for all of a record.

IMPLICATIONS OF DBMS SELECTION

IDMS (CODASYL)

IDMS subschema descriptions require entries for the name of the schema, subschema and the device media control block (DMCL). Copy the AREA section of the subschema from the schema. In the following COBOL example, the PRODUCT region and the BACKORDER region are copied, and the BACKORDER region is prohibited from being updated.

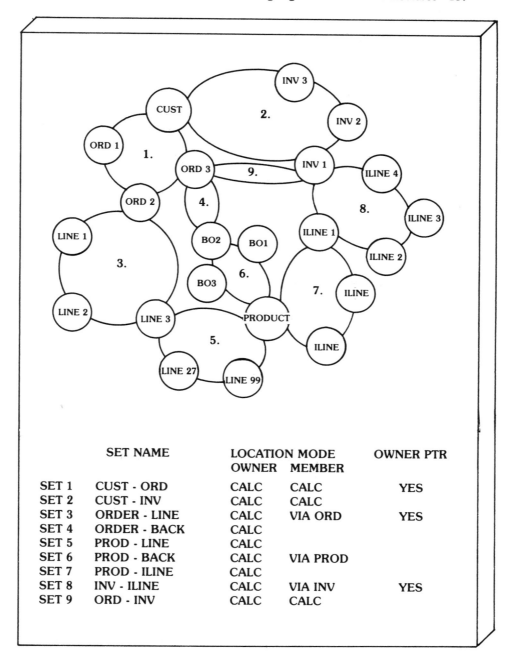

	SET NAME	LOCATION MODE		OWNER PTR
		OWNER	MEMBER	
SET 1	CUST - ORD	CALC	CALC	YES
SET 2	CUST - INV	CALC	CALC	
SET 3	ORDER - LINE	CALC	VIA ORD	YES
SET 4	ORDER - BACK	CALC		
SET 5	PROD - LINE	CALC		
SET 6	PROD - BACK	CALC	VIA PROD	
SET 7	PROD - ILINE	CALC		
SET 8	INV - ILINE	CALC	VIA INV	YES
SET 9	ORD - INV	CALC	CALC	

FIGURE 9.1 Sample E-Z Chair Corporation IDMS Schema

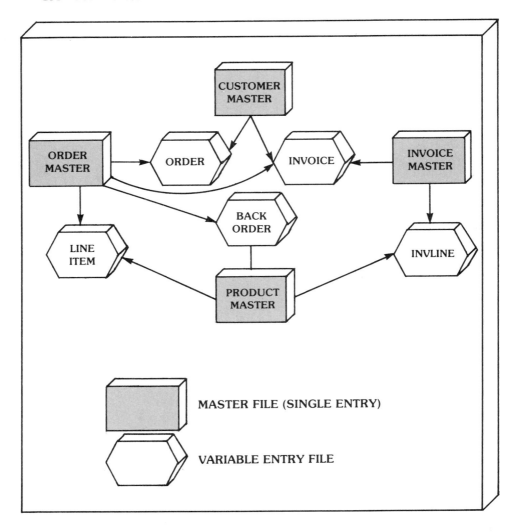

FIGURE 9.2   Sample E-Z Chair TOTAL Schema

AREA SECTION.
    COPY PRODUCT-REGION AREA.
    COPY BACKORDER-REGION AREA PRIVACY LOCK FOR UPDATE IS "NO."

Information in the records to be included in a subschema is contained in the Record Section of the subschema description. In this section privacy locks are optionally specified for all the access verbs (STORE, CONNECT, FIND, GET, ERASE, DISCONNECT, and MODIFY). Additionally, field-level sensitivity can be specified by coding only certain fields in the record. In the following example, the product invoice and customer records are specified and only the invoiced amount field of customer can be accessed. The product record is marked nonerasable.

    RECORD SECTION.
        COPY PRODUCT-RECORD PRIVACY LOCK FOR ERASE IS "NO."
        COPY INVOICE-RECORD.
        01 CUSTOMER-RECORD
            02 CUSTOMER INVOICED-AMOUNT   PIC 9(5)V99.

A SET SECTION specifies information about sets to the subschema. Privacy locks can be specified for the verbs FIND, CONNECT, and DISCONNECT.

    SET SECTION.
        COPY ORDER-LINERTEM SET.
        COPY INVOICE-INVLINE SET.
        COPY PRODUCT-BACKORDER SET PRIVACY LOCK FOR
            DISCONNECT IS
            "NO."

TOTAL Subschema

TOTAL does not supply the versatility to set access security that CODASYL type data bases do. TOTAL permits access to the data base according to whether or not security logic was built into the application program. Once initial entry has been obtained by a program into a TOTAL data base, the only security controls available are those imposed by the DBA when he examines the program code. The system imposes security of read or update only during "sign on" program initialization. The restrictions placed on the user view accessed are those imposed by the Schema (master file, variable-entry file) structure. Figure 9.3 illustrates the subschema paths in the sample problem. The path from master to variable to master, and so on, is called the *linkage path*.

   There are no subschema provisions as such in TOTAL. Different linkage paths within the TOTAL schema, however, could be designed. This would perform a similar function to the subschema in terms of entry and direction of flow. The task of the designers is to try and determine the shortest linkage paths to accomplish any transaction objectives.

SECURITY AND AUDIT DESIGN

CODASYL Data Integrity

Backup and recovery are generally available as described earlier. In most CODASYL DBMS products this involves restoration back to the AREA level.

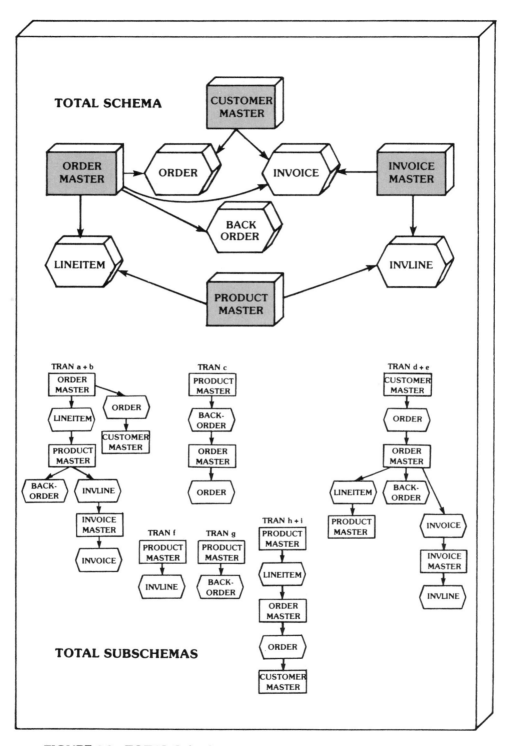

FIGURE 9.3   TOTAL Subschemas

160

'As an example, Cullinane's (now Cullinet) IDMS provides two utility programs entitled IDMSDUMP and IDMSRSTR with which to copy and restore the data base. Additionally, IDMS also supplies three utilities: IDMSRBCK, IDMSRFWD, and IDMSJFIX, which utilize a journal (log) file to back out and restore the data base.

IDMSDUMP transfers selected areas or the entire data base to another file on a medium (disk or tape) or the user's choice.

IDMSRSTR transfers the contents of a dump file back to the data base.

IDMSRBCK reads a journal file backward and restores before images to the data base.

IDMSFRWD reads a journal file forward and restores after images to the data base. Prints journal file also.

IDMSJFIX copies and fixes a journal file that has been abnormally terminated because of a system failure.

Figure 9.4 illustrates data base recovery methodology for IDMS resulting from program, system, or disk failure.

TOTAL Data Integrity

TOTAL provides backup and recovery facilities similar to the CODASYL type DBMS products, with separate utilities that can back out and restore the data base from a log file. TOTAL provides reasonably adequate recovery procedures since the package includes a means for recording the data necessary to restart the system from the last known point. This point could include the last checkpoint, initiation of task that abended, or initiation of the log. A series of CNTL macros provides a variety of system functions for this purpose.

Data integrity is considered to consist of two separate levels: the data set level and the internal data item format level. At the data item format level it is the user's responsibility that mixed data not be placed in an improperly formatted field. For example, TOTAL cannot perform internal checks on data format to see that decimal data is not placed in a binary field. At the level of the logical data structure and the linkage chains, the data set level, TOTAL assumes full responsibility.

TOTAL provides privacy and security at the element (field) level. Users may assign a password of up to eight characters to each field. For each retrieval call, only those elements or fields specified in the password list are returned to the user. Users must make additional security provisions either by using the operating system or by coding user exit routines that employ the TOTAL exit interface routine DATBSXT.

The final exercise will be to examine TOTAL and IDMS in the context of operations and performance design.

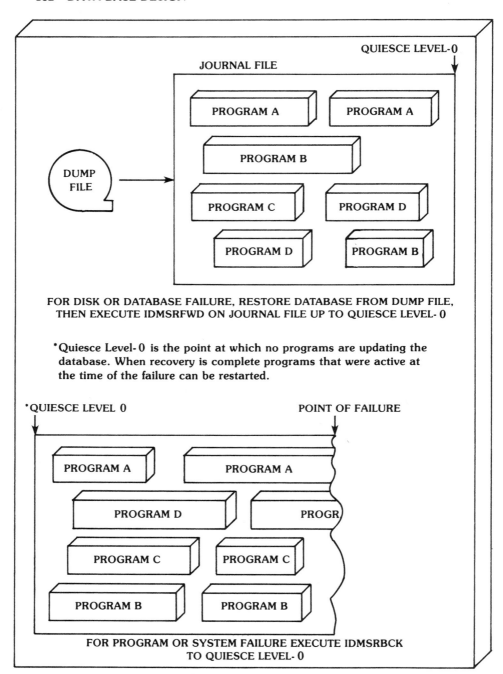

FIGURE 9.4 IDMS Recovery

IDMS AND CODASYL OPERATIONS AND PERFORMANCE DESIGN CONSIDERATIONS

The CODASYL type architectures can use a design tool called the *Bachman diagram* for documenting detailed design decisions. Figure 9.5 is an illustration of a Bachman diagram. An explanation of the terms used is as follows:

RECORD NAME	Name of the record type or entity
IDENTIFICATION	Unique identification number of record type
LENGTH MODE	Fixed (F); variable (V); fixed compressed (FC); or variable compressed (VC)
LOCATION MODE	CALC (random by key); VIA (near to owner); DIRECT (store key sequential-indexed)
LENGTH	Actual record length for fixed or maximum length for variable.
CALC KEY or VIA SET	For CALC records, name of key field; for VIA records, name of set record will be near; for DIRECT, blank

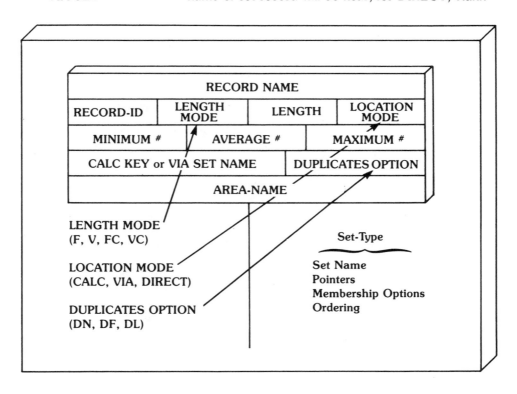

FIGURE 9.5 Bachman Diagram

DUPLICATES OPTION	For CALC records, disposition of records with duplicate control keys: DN (duplicates not allowed); DF (duplicates first); DL (duplicates last)
AREA	Area name where stored

The following are a list of the set-type options:

SET-NAME	Name of the set
POINTERS	Set linkage options: N (next pointer); NP (next prior pointers); NO (next owner pointers); NPO (next prior and owner pointers)
MEMBERSHIP OPTIONS	Disconnect and connect options: MA (mandatory automatic); MM (mandatory manual); OA (optional automatic); OM (optional manual)
ORDERING	Position of new records in the set: FIRST, LAST, NEXT, PRIOR, or SORTED

The disconnect and connect options are explained thus:

When using STORE and CONNECT verbs:

AUTOMATIC	A record occurrence is implicity connected to the set upon being stored.
MANUAL	A record occurrence is not connected on storage but only by explicitly using the CONNECT verb.

When using ERASE and DISCONNECT verbs:

MANDATORY	Disconnection can be accomplished only by the ERASE verb.
OPTIONAL	Records can be disconnected without being erased from the data base.

Figure 9.6 refers to a portion of the sample E-Z Chair Corporation problem to illustrate the uses to which the Bachman diagram must be put. The device can be very helpful when designers create the schema code in order to indicate at a glance the data base structure. Designers could utilize the Bachman diagram for drawing a relational map useful not only for design but also for documentation.

The choice of access method of CALC, VIA, or DIRECT has very important effects on the performance of the data base. In Figure 9.6 CALC designations were chosen for CUSTOMER and ORDER because both are primary entry points to the data base. The VIA option was selected for the LINEITEM entity in order to keep it near its ORDER owner entity and minimize I/O activity. The VIA option is one way to group records in a CODASYL DBMS. The DIRECT option is not used too often. The data base key is used to store the data directly to a user specified area. It can be

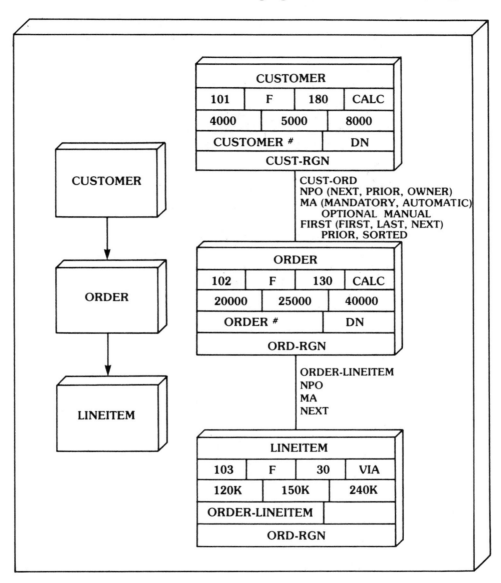

FIGURE 9.6   Example of Bachman Diagram

utilized to store data serially in an indexed fashion. The Sequential Processing Facility (SPF) of IDMS uses the DIRECT location mode to store records in physically sequential order.

TOTAL OPERATIONS AND PERFORMANCE CONSIDERATIONS

The TOTAL data base architecture is not too flexible in record grouping, and it does not have many built-in options for access method variation. Because TOTAL dictates that MASTER records and variable-entry records must reside in separate files, record grouping to minimize I/O is restricted.

However, different record types may coincide on the variable-entry file. The only problem with mixing record types on the variable-entry file is that it may result in the wasting of disk space. Variable-entry files are in fixed-length blocks. If the different record types to be contained in the same file are of widely varying size, there can be a problem. The record size of the largest record type determines the blocking; therefore, smaller record types would contain wasted pad space.

TOTAL attempts to improve its operating efficiency on the basis of designating certain access paths as primary linkage paths. When this is done, new records added along this path are kept as close as possible to the prior record in the path in order to minimize the path distance being covered in a retrieval operation. The problem occurs when a record occurs simultaneously in a number of linkage paths; only one can be designated as primary.

As Cohen says in *Data Base Management Systems*,

> Performance in the manipulation and retrieval of records from a TOTAL data base relies heavily on the (DBA's) knowledge of the utilization of the data base, and therefore on his choices for primary linkage path designation. This means that a situation may easily arise in which records are arranged most efficiently for one or two linkage paths and extremely inefficiently for other linkage paths through the same file.[1]

Master, or single-entry files, are randomly distributed over their data space via the algorithm built into TOTAL. Designers can resolve conflicts in placement by placing the duplicate or synonym record as close as possible to its home location (the position in the data base to which it originally tried to randomize). At various times, in order to keep all records as close to the home location as possible, movement occurs within the data space. This is very helpful when users retrieve a record, but the constant reorganization of the data space can raise overhead during insertion. TOTAL determines where a record is placed. Therefore the only performance option available to the designer is changing the blocking factor.

As Cohen puts it

> ...efficiencies in manipulation and retrieval are literally up to the programmer. TOTAL does not confront the user with mysteries of operation,

but rather makes all of its techniques directly available for his employment. The effectiveness of the entire system depends upon the designer and the implementor.[2]

Each record in a variable-entry data set lies in one or more chains whose owner or head is a randomly addressable record in a single-entry or master file data set. These chains are called linkage paths. Within the variable-entry files the effect of a variable type record format can be created if designers carefully choose the record types and place related records of the same or different types along the same linkage path. In Figure 9.7, the order file from the sample problem could be expressed as a combination master header file and variable-entry order file with the body of the order being in the order variable-entry file along with trailer items for each lineitem in the order. This process might appear to be inefficient, but TOTAL generally attempts to place the logical records on the same linkage path as close as possible to each other, so that all the related records are near each other. Often they reside on the same physical block and will usually be stored at least in the same cylinder of disk storage.

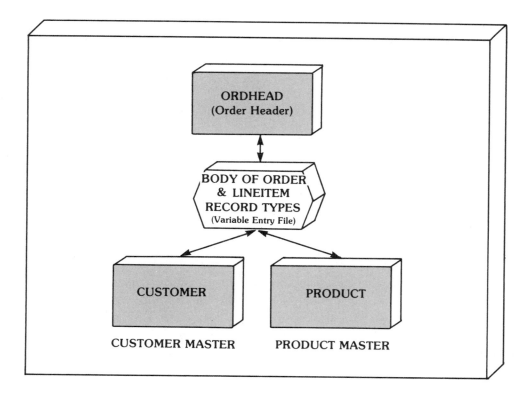

FIGURE 9.7 TOTAL Order File Example

NOTES

1. Leo J. Cohen, *Data Base Management Systems*, 6th ed. (Wellesley, Mass.: QED Information Sciences, Inc., 1979), pp. 4–71.
2. Ibid.

10 Designing for Hierarchical Architectures

In a hierarchy, every employee tends to rise to his level of incompetence.

Laurence Johnston Peter,
The Peter Principle

This chapter will follow the design process for hierarchical data base management systems, specifically IBM's Information Management System (IMS). These structures were constructed out of efforts to better process variable length records and more specifically bill of materials or explosion-implosion files. The IBM product is by far the most popular of the breed and has one of the largest user bases of any DBMS being sold today—hence the use of the product as an example here.

The design and, more important, the implementation of this product are not trivial exercises. The variety of options, access methods, bells, and whistles are among the greatest offered by any DBMS. Unfortunately for the user, using them properly requires extensive training. IMS has the reputation in the industry of being very slow because of the overhead burden of its many options. Most of this bad press relates to a fundamental misunderstanding on the part of the user of just how the product works.

Poor design is only part of the story. Operations and performance are very closely linked to the program and call structure. For this reason a brief discussion on the importance of the DML is included in the operation and performance section of this chapter.

IMS SCHEMA (HIERARCHICAL ARCHITECTURE)

IBM's Information Management System can ideally express the one-to-many relationship through the (inverted) tree structure. The many-to-many relationships require

169

the establishment of logically related data bases. Keyed entry to an IMS structure is through the root. The root can be in a physical or logical structure. An alternative keyed entry can be made via secondary index. Secondary indexes do not provide the full capabilities that logical relationships do in IMS; however, maintaining secondary indexes requires much less overhead.

The schema design (see Figure 10.1) incorporates three separate physical data base structures—an order data base, a product data base, and a customer data base. Designers can develop liaisons between the two by using the root keys that are contained as foreign keys in each data base's dependent segments. The schema is coded in a control block called the DBD (data base description). See sample code in Figure 10.2.

Users can gain entry to all the data base using order number through the use of a secondary index. Processing via the secondary index would not allow access to the INVOICE and INVLINE entities (segments). Only the path to the root segment (CUSTOMER), referred to as the target segment, and those segments dependent on the segment (ORDER), referred to as the *source segment*, are available. Inserting and deleting orders through the secondary index would be quite costly. This customer-to-order relationship could also be created via a logical relationship that would allow full access to all dependents of the ORDER segment. There is a logical relationship between the customer data base and the product data base. The BACKORDER segment of the product data base is said to be the *logical child* of the ORDER segment, which is then termed the *logical parent*.

In this instance the physical parent of BACKORDER, the PRODUCT segment, is attached (concatenated) with the logical child when it is viewed from the logical parent.

Direct access to segments in IMS can be done only to the root segment. All dependent segments are retrieved by either a direct address or relative block address pointer. The type of pointer depends on the IMS access method chosen. The only exception to this is the use of a secondary index. But they sometimes have limited processing capabilities, and update logic can be very costly.

Creating the DBD from the loaded data model is easy if the designer recognizes the significance of the ROOT with the entity point and associating dependent segments in physical data bases based on the load numbers in the data model. A high number of accesses between segments indicates a need to associate that segment (entity) under the root in the same data base record. When there is a choice of where to place an entity, such as whether LINEITEM should be placed physically under ORDER or under PRODUCT, choose the insert-delete path. In this instance LINE-ITEM is inserted and deleted most often through the ORDER.

One aspect of weighting the numbers generated through transaction path analysis is to consider the type of access. In an IMS system, for instance, a read access would have a weight of 1. An update access however could have a weight of from 3 to 4, because updates require 2 I/Os, one to read and one to write back. The additional weight is for logging before and after images. Likewise inserts and deletes would have weights between 1 and 2. Multiply the total accesses by this weight factor, and see what it has on the path totals.

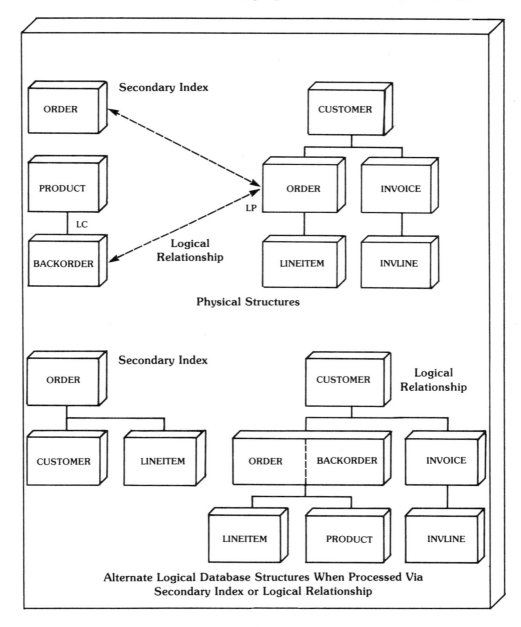

FIGURE 10.1   Sample E-Z Chair IMS Schema

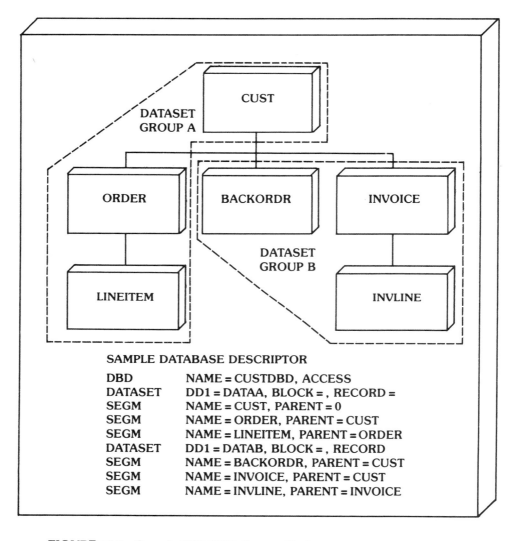

FIGURE 10.2   Sample IMS DBD Source Code

IMS SUBSCHEMA

Subschema specification in IMS is done through a separate control block called the Program Specification Block or PSB. The PSB describes the program's view of the data base. This control block works in conjunction with one or more Data Base Descriptions (DBDs) which describe the *physical* or *logical* data base (See Figure 10.3 on IMS program-data independence.) Within each PSB are pointers that describe the access path IMS will take between segments. In effect these pointers, called Program

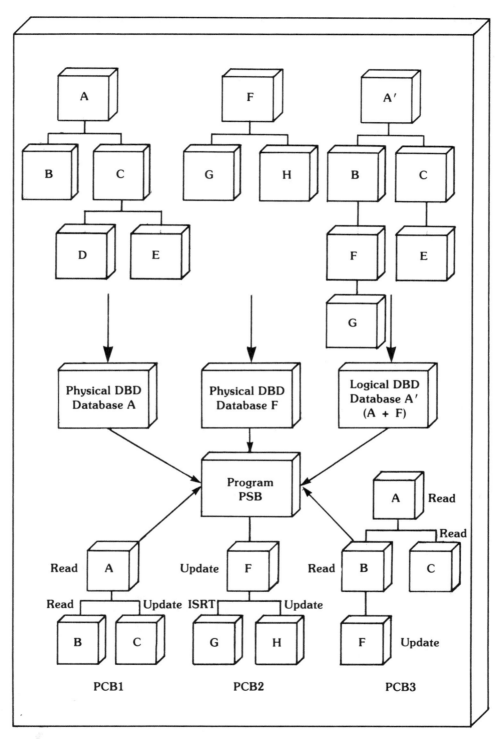

FIGURE 10.3   IMS Program Data Independence

Communication Blocks or PCBs, are separate user-views of a subset of the data base. One PSB can have many PCBs, and one PCB can relate back to a particular physical DBD or a particular logical DBD, which inturn describes a logical structure that may embody one or more physical data bases.

In the example described in Figure 10.3, two physical data bases, data base A and data base F, are described in separate physical DBDs. A third data base A^1 is a logical structure combining data base A and F together. In the *logical* DBD describing this structure, data base F root segment is a logical parent of segment B in data base A. Notice also that the designer did not have to describe all of the segments in data bases A and F. This is a discretionary decision for the designer.

The Program Specification Block has three separate PCBs. PCB1 describes a subset of data base A. PCB2 describes a subset of data base F, and PCB3 describes a subset of data base A.

The designer can specify access control at the segment or field level in IMS. The designer has a choice of read, insert, delete, replace, or load in combinations of one or more sensitivity options. These are coded in the PSB as part of the *processing option parameter*.

IMS has the additional advantage (drawback?) that the subschema is coded outside the program in a separate assembler macro language format. This relieves the program of having absolute knowledge of the data base being accessed in order to "navigate" around the data base. IMS keeps track of positions automatically. The choice of PCB determines the path used, the order of segment presentation to the program, and what the program can do to or with the segment after it is retrieved.

Also, by maintaining the access controls to a data base outside the program, the DBA can control access and security of the data bases using separate libraries and utilities. In fact, the entire responsibility for control block generation can be and usually is in the DBA's department and not in the programming department.

Figure 10.4 shows sample PSB coding.

SUMMARY OF SUBSCHEMA DESIGN

The usage map developed from data analysis determines all the separate user-views from the application being designed. From the usage map the designer is able to create subsets of the physical records and segments needed to satisfy the various application requests for data (transactions).

From these subsets of data and the various user views, the designer then proceeds through a process of logical synthesis. *Logical synthesis* combines the similar user-views into one view or subschema, taking into account the security and audit controls that might necessitate keeping two otherwise similar views separate.

The security and audit evaluation requires that the designer compare the various user-paths with each user view and the types of access activity being done (read-only, update, add, and delete). When designers have completed this evaluation, they can then design various controls for each subschema.

```
PCB        TYPE = DB, DBDNAME = ORDERED
SENSEG     NAME = ORDER, PARENT = 0, PROCOPT = A UPDATE
SENSEG     NAME = LINEITEM, PARENT = ORDER, PROCOPT = A
           UPDATE
SENSEG     NAME = CUSTOMER, PARENT = ORDER, PROCOPT = G
           READ ONLY
SENSEG     NAME = INVOICE, PARENT = ORDER, PROCOPT = IR
           INSERT, REPLACE
SENSEG     NAME = INVLINE, PARENT = INVOICE, PROCOPT = ID
           INSERT, DELETE
PCB        TYPE = DB, DBDNAME = PRODDBD, PROCOPT = A*
           UPDATE
SENSEG     NAME = PRODUCT, PARENT = 0
SENSEG     NAME = BACKORDER, PARENT = PRODUCT
PSBGEN
END
```

LEGEND

PROCOPT =	PARENT =
G = GET (READ)	0 = NO PARENT (ROOT)
I = INSERT	ELSE SEGMENT NAME
R = REPLACE	
D = DELETE	DBDNAME = NAME OF PHYSICAL OR LOGICAL DBD
A = ALL (GIRD)	
L = LOAD	

*NOTICE PROCOPT CAN BE CODED AT THE SEGMENT LEVEL OR AT THE PCB LEVEL.

FIGURE 10.4   Sample IMS Program Specification Block Coding

The specific implementation of subschemas and their security controls varies greatly from DBMS to DBMS. However, each DBMS does have some way of implementing a subschema and providing security for it.

It seems that those systems that remove the security and subschema design from the program and implement it through outside logical file utilities (such as the IMS Program Specification Block (PSB) and the ADABAS utility control feature ADA-

MINT) offer the greatest flexibility and data independence for the programmer along with simplicity and ease of control for the DBA.

IMS is perhaps the single best example of any DBMS on the market that illustrates the variety of subschema processing control options. IMS has some of the most extensive data base tailoring options available.

Ideally expressed, subschema support in a DBMS should allow for a high degree of data independence with a minimal amount of programmer interaction. The DBMS should do the "navigation" through the data base, not the program. The DBMS of choice is one that can provide a logical structure, suitable for the application and yet independent of the physical structure of the data base. In addition, this DBMS is one that does not require serious system overhead. Additionally, the maintenance of the logical structure should be a separate, distinct, and controllable process by the data base administrator or the DBA's staff.

IMS DATA INTEGRITY

Critics of the IMS DBMS product usually complain of its excessive overhead and complexity. Some of the reasons for this overhead are the rather involved options available to the user for maintaining data base integrity. The support provided for IMS recovery and restart is rather significant. There is plenty of rope out there with which a user can fool. Unfortunately one tends to hang oneself when given too much rope. IMS is a sophisticated product and is not for the unsophisticated user.

The logging function is one of the most complete available in the industry, not only providing before and after image copying, but also providing information on lines, data bases, inquiries, transaction response times as well as numerous other statistical information. The array of utilities to help utilize and manage this effort are also significant. Figure 10.5 illustrates the IMS recovery and restart options.

In the on-line environment, restart/recovery is automatic, and backout of abended transactions is dynamic. The system provides ample facilities for warm start or emergency restart in the event of normal or abnormal system termination. The user sets checkpoint frequency.

For batch applications a conditionally executed step within the program JCL (Job Control Language) stream controls applications backout. Checkpoint frequency is set by the programmer and executed via a checkpoint called IMS. Programmers should use batch checkpoint restart only on extremely long-running jobs when it would be desirable to rerun data only partially.

Significant audit trail information is available from analysis of the log tape. Automatic validity and consistency routines, which are user coded, are available through the edit compression routine exits.

One of the unique log management utilities available with IMS is *change accumulation*. This provides the ability to combine several log tapes into one composite log tape. This utility sorts and merges the log tapes and saves only the oldest before image and the newest after image affecting a particular transaction or segment of data. Thus, transactions that go against the same data 7 or 8 times would have 7 or 8 corresponding before and after images per log. A total of 7 or 8 logs will generate 128 before and

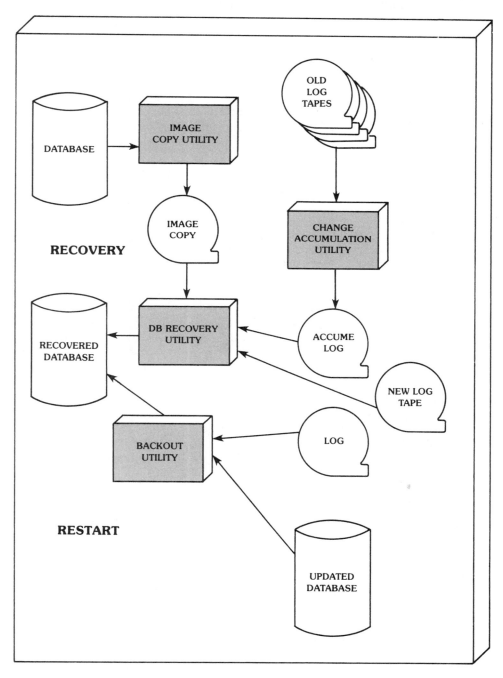

FIGURE 10.5 IMS Integrity Utilities

after images. Change accumulation would take the first before image and the last after image and write only those two to the change accumulation log.

IMS OPERATIONS AND PERFORMANCE DESIGN

IMS is one DBMS product that provides a great deal of choice and flexibility to the designer for access methods, indexing, and record grouping. Unlike TOTAL and to a lesser degree CODASYL type DBMS products, IMS removes many of the performance considerations from the application program and leaves it in the control blocks that define the schema and subschemas.

Generally speaking, active records in an IMS hierarchy should be kept near the top (root) and to the left. Hierarchically speaking, these records (segments) are nearer the front of the file. Since in IMS the only direct access is to the root segment, the shorter the path to the chained dependent (child) segments under the root, the quicker users can access those segments.

This is not to say that there are not suitable ways of rapidly accessing dependent segments. The variety of pointer options is formidable, and their respective effects on the access performance is profound. For a better understanding of these IMS details an excellent book has been written by T.J. MacElreath (see Bibliography).

IMS structures generally work better in terms of space allocation and free space for new segments if the segments are kept uniform in length. In the case of extreme differences in segment size or access activity, designers can arrange separate data set grouping which does not alter the hierarchy. See Figure 10.2, which illustrates data set grouping. The drawback to record grouping is that it will take at least two physical I/O operations to fetch the entire data base record (a root and all its dependents). The implementation is merely the defining of two or more DATASET macros in the DBD generation. Notice that the DATASET macro sets up a separate JCL ddname for each data set for Job Control Language purposes. Also, designers can specify separate record and block size information for economical space allocation by IMS.

IMS also has a variety of access methods which dictate how the segments are physically stored on the data base. The choices are as follows:

GSAM
(Generalize Sequential Access Method)
Standard sequential file that is defined to IMS for checkpoint restart capabilities.
SHSAM
(Simple Hierarchical Sequential Access Method)
Root-only sequential file compatible with OS and DLI processing. Inserts and deletes are accomplished by recopying the file.
HSAM
(Hierarchical Sequential Access Method)
Not compatible with OS; dependents physically adjacent; limited provisions for random access to data.

SHISAM

(Simple Hierarchical Indexed Sequential Access Method)
Root-only file; stored in physically adjacent sequential order; compatible with VSAM and DLI.

HISAM

(Hierarchical Indexed Sequential Access Method)
Segment grouping by physical adjacency, with all segments of a single data base record residing in the same logical record. Data base has an indexed data set and an overflow data set. The entire data base record will be attempted to be stored in the index data set. Overflow is chained to by relative record number and not direct address pointers.

HDAM

(Hierarchical Direct Access Method)
Root is randomly stored via a user-written or IBM-supplied randomizer module—similar to CALC in CODASYL. Dependent segments are chained via direct address pointers off the root.

HIDAM

(Hierarchical Indexed Direct Access Method)
Access to root segment is via an index with a direct address pointer. Data base records are stored in physical sequential order. Dependent segments are treated identically to HDAM.

In actual practice three access methods, HISAM, HDAM, and HIDAM, are used in 99% of all implementations. The direct access methods, HDAM and HIDAM, are the most popular of the three. The HISAM sequential physical adjacency is not very practical for most applications because if the application is too dynamic and the data too volatile, maintaining the structure will require constant reorganization. This frequent reorganization is likely to substantially raise overhead. In the HDAM-HIDAM access methods, the designer weighs rapid access, less disk I/O (usually 1.1 I/Os per request) found in HDAM against the benefits of physical sequential data base record order found in HIDAM.

IMS also has performance efficiencies based on the number and types of pointer options available. This particular aspect of IMS design is too detailed to discuss adequately in this text. Pointer option selecting, however, means trying to balance the benefits of increased direct address pointers (to speed access to individual dependent segments) and the increased space costs and maintenance overhead of those pointers. Users should know the logical access needs of the application and select the pointer options accordingly.

The designer must also weigh the benefits of logical data bases as opposed to physical data bases. IMS is very capable of rearranging single or multiple physical data base structures into a single logical structure that more appropriately accommodate an application's view of the data. The amount of logical pointer overhead incurred depends on the choice of symbolic or direct address pointers. While direct address pointers require less space than symbolic pointers, they do require synchronous processing and reorganization of the data bases involved in the logical relationship. On the other hand symbolic pointers dispense with the need for synchronous processing but incur substantial space overhead. Symbolic pointers require enough additional space to maintain the fully concatenated key of the logical dependent. The designer must determine if the program data independence and flexibility gained via the logical relation is worth the cost.

Earlier it was stated that a lot of the performance considerations for the application were removed from the program. This does not mean that the program has no effect on the data base's performance. Considerable performance benefit can be derived if designers choose the appropriate call structure or call option.

Users employ techniques such as the IMS PATH CALL to fetch multiple segment types along the same logical path in a data base call. Even the choice of call function such as GET UNIQE (GU) versus a GET NEXT (GN) can severely affect program performance.

GN calls require *100 times less* processing by IMS as do GU calls. GN processing in the right circumstances, as when transactions are sorted in data base order, can have a full hundredfold benefit in program performance over the same processing using GU calls.

There are numerous techniques using options in the call such as command codes, multiple positioning, Boolean arguments and the aforementioned path call, which when used properly can have up to a thousandfold elapsed time performance improvement. More specific information on these techniques can be obtained in the specific text listed in the Bibliography.

The work of the data base designer or DBA does not end when the schema is done.

11 Designing for Relational Architectures

The best laid schemes o'mice and men gang aft aglay

Robert Burns,
"Man Was Made to Mourn," 1786

The most fundamental property of relational data bases is that the data is viewed in terms of tables instead of networks or hierarchies. Tables can be described in columns and rows. The rows correspond to records or segments and the columns represent fields within records. Rows are sometimes referred to as *tuples*, or as *n*-tuples, where the *n* signifies the number of columns in the row. The columns likewise are often referred to as *domains*. The entire relation or table is called the *entity*.

The thing that makes tables different from the standard flat files is strict adherence to the following rules:

1. Each relation on entity represents a single record type.
2. There are a specific number of attributes on fields in each entity.
3. Attributes are normalized (no repeating or naming groups).
4. No duplicate tuples.
5. The order of tuples is immaterial.
6. Domains or columns can be shared between entities and are in fact the basis by which new relations can be created between two or more different tables.

It is in fact this last quality of new table formation that is the key to relational data base systems.

The operation and manipulation of tables can be expressed algebraically in terms of three basic functions: *selection, projection,* and *join.* Selections create subsets of all table records. Projections create subsets of all the columns in a table. Joins allow combining of tables. Because of the mathematical nature of these operations, it is possible to create very powerful and concise data-manipulation languages for relational data base management systems. These three operations—selection on key, projection of new relations, and joins based on data coupling—were explained earlier in Chapter 3. In order to make the relations or tables truly data-independent, the tuples should be in third normal form.

It is the terminology of relational theory that makes the subject seem overly complex. Because these systems are still being worked on theoretically, the usage naming and definition of terms is still evolving. A rough equivalency table of the current terminology in reference to a table would be as follows:

Relation	=	table, entity on record type
Tuple	=	row, record, or segment occurrence
Attribute	=	column name or field type
Element	=	data item or field; coded attribute
Cardinality	=	number of rows in a table
Degree	=	number of columns in a table
n-tuple	=	a row from a table with n columns
n-any relations =		table with n columns

The *domain*, though roughly equivalent to a column, has the following meaning: all values that may occur for a specific field type come from a domain of all the possible values of this type. It is possible therefore to have many different field types with the same domain. For example, weight is a domain; weight of package and weight of person are two different field types within the same domain.

In addition to the algebraic constructs of selection, projection, and join other operations emerge from classical set theory, such as *union*, *intersection*, and *difference*. The classic definition, in strictest set theory, of a relation is (according to Codd):

> Given sets S1, S2, Sn, R is a relation of these n sets if it is a set of n-tuples, each of which has as its first element from S1, its second from S2, and so forth. R is the subset of the CARTESIAN PRODUCT S1 $\times$ S2 $\times$ Sn. Sj is the jth domain of R. R is said to have degree n.[1]

Is it any wonder given this definition that most of us tend to shrug our shoulders, close our eyes, and hold our nose while wading through set theory and papers on relational data base?

As confusing as some of this all is, the commercial products that have emerged are rather straightforward and simple to use. Their flexibility and degree of "user friendliness" definitely put them in the forefront of products to be considered in the move to data base.

This chapter will talk about two current IBM products in the relational data base category, system/38 and QBE. There is a third IBM product system and its commercially available version, called SQL/DS, which was announced by IBM in 1983. It will be referenced less specifically. I do not mean to imply that other software vendors do not market "relational DBMS" products. However, I am familiar with only these three personally. Users of the MAGNUM, ORACLE, INGRES, and NOMAD products will not, it is hoped, be offended by their exclusion here.

As these products mature along with the hardware on which they operate, it is expected that their large file performance aspects will improve dramatically. The reason I focus on system/38 and QBE is that within the framework of this type of architecture these two products exemplify the general characteristics of the group as a whole quite nicely.

The pattern of review as with previous chapters is to follow the four stages of data base design and touch on the specific of each system as it pertains to the current stage. Again the process is intended as informational and not as a complete technical explanation of the product.

SYSTEM/38 SCHEMA (RELATIONAL ARCHITECTURE)

No good example of a true relational data base that performs well with large files is available on the market today. In a true relational data base the relational map would be the data base schema produced via data analysis. According to Thomas F. Meurer, president of Eastern Technical Associates, Inc., "We'll need trillion-byte memory and content addressable storage to implement a relational DBMS."[2]

Currently most relational-type systems in order to perform better provide relational views from a structured type data base. System/38 is such a relational structured system.

Under System/38 the data base is implemented as two-dimensional table relations. Each relation contains a key made up of one or several concatenated fields, plus the attributes of the key (see Figure 11.1). The implementation of this DBMS is tied directly to the System/38 hardware because portions of the hardware microcode are devoted to the DBMS (see Figure 11.2).

Records are stored in System/38 in an area called the *data space*, which is an arrival sequence file containing records in of the same format. Record lengths up to 32 kilobytes and files up to 256 megabytes can currently be supported.

Another area, called the *data space index*, is used to provide access paths to data other than in arrival sequence. This index allows for logical reordering of the records in one or more data spaces based on "fork characters," which are constants, and keys, which are field values within the records. The key fields allow for the logical ordering of the data with attributes for absolute values, alternative collating sequences, as well as ascending and descending sequence. In addition, the fork characters, which are 1-byte constants, allow for the ordering of data duplicate keys. The data space index provides capabilities similar to inverted list structures. In this manner the various physical files contained in the data spaces to be processed are different-looking logical files.

System/38 is not a true relational DBMS. A physical file in the data space is similar

Product

Number	Name	Price	Cost
0115	Chair	100.00	42.00
0320	Sofa	800.00	375.00

Order

Order #	Customer #	Date
593813	04135	06/29/84
604032	00933	07/25/84

Lineitem

Order #	Product #	Quantity
593813	0320	2
435310	9320	6

Customer

Customer #	Name	Address
02501	A.J. Smith Inc.	
02502	Paine Furniture	
02510	Issac's Inc.	

Invoice

Invoice #	Order #	Customer #	Date	Amount
006718	593813	04135	07/06/84	9345.29
13254	945690	01010	10/10/83	7523.50

Invline

Invoice #	Product #	Qty Shipped	Discount	Qty Back Ordered
006718	0320	5	.05	1
009814	0023	2	.06	0

FIGURE 11.1   System/38 Table Arrays

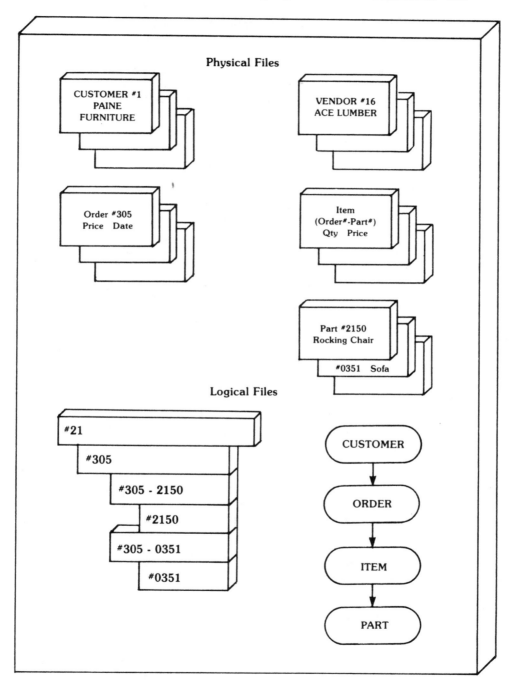

FIGURE 11.2 System/38 Physical and Logical Files

to a true relational file; however, the key values of each record are stored with the record. This requirement matches that of the inverted list structure as well as the relational architecture.

The logical file constructed by System/38 is a hierarchical file that allows multiple logical structures. Having multiple logical views and being able to combine them or jump from one to the other provides users with many of the functions found in network type architectures.

QBE: QUERY-BY-EXAMPLE-SCHEMA

"QBE is a high level data base management language that provides a convenient and unified style to query, update, define and control relational data base."[3] Essentially QBE is a piece of software used to manipulate data that is contained in one or more tables or relations. The physical implementation of the files is in the same manner as System/38.

The designer of the schema in the relational data base environment has small work to do indeed. Once the work of creating the entities is done, virtually 90% of the design task is completed. The remaining 10% is to figure which attributes, specifically those that maintain redundant keys, are to be kept or deleted. The foreign key specification is extremely important. The communication between files, which are merely groups of similar entities, is remarkably similar to the inverted list architectures. The relationships between files are maintained through the process of *data coupling*.

The uniqueness of QBE is the manner in which those files are manipulated by the user. QBE is geared to the on-line user, and its approach to data retreival and update uses a "fill in the blanks" methodology. The user's perception of the information is that of a table containing columns and rows of attributes or data elements. All the tables grouped together constitute the data base.

When performing an operation against the data base, the user fills in an example of a solution to that operation in skeleton tables that can be dynamically coupled to actual tables in the data base. Programming is done within these two-dimensional skeleton tables. See Figure 11.3 for an example of the table skeleton.

The user fills in the name of the table such as EMP in the table name field. This points the query at the EMP on employee table. The user may then fill in or let the system fill other data item headings such as NAME, DEPT, SKILL, and SALARY. If the query was to print all the employees in Department 36, the 36 would be put under the DEPT heading, and "P" under the NAME heading ("P" is for print); then the enter key would be depressed. See Figure 11.4.

SYSTEM/38—SUBSCHEMA

In System/38 the subschema is implied through the creation of the logical file structure. In this manner a designer can reorganize and restructure the two-dimensional table files to provide an alternate format and access path geared to the requirements of the various applications.

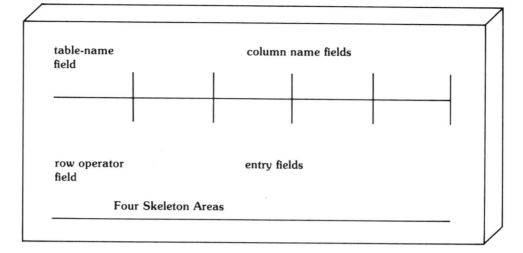

FIGURE 11.3   QBE Table Skeleton

With qualified retrieval, you request only a partial list of the data elements available in one or more columns. You qualify the acceptable data elements by means of constant elements. You may, if you wish, also define comparison to be performed with the constant element.

QUERY: Print the names of the employees in the EMP table for DEPT 36

EMP	NAME	SALARY	MGR	DEPT
	P			F.36

An example element is used primarily to associate or link data in different tables or in the same table. In cases where such a link is not required, you can either enter an example element or omit it without affecting the result.

FIGURE 11.4   QBE Query Example

The logical files constructed from the physical file entity tables are in a hierarchical format for System/38 (see Figure 11.5). In a true relational architecture there would have to be some file structure for the subschema to be mapped upon in order for security and access controls to exist. System/38 uses this pseudo-hierarchical structure.

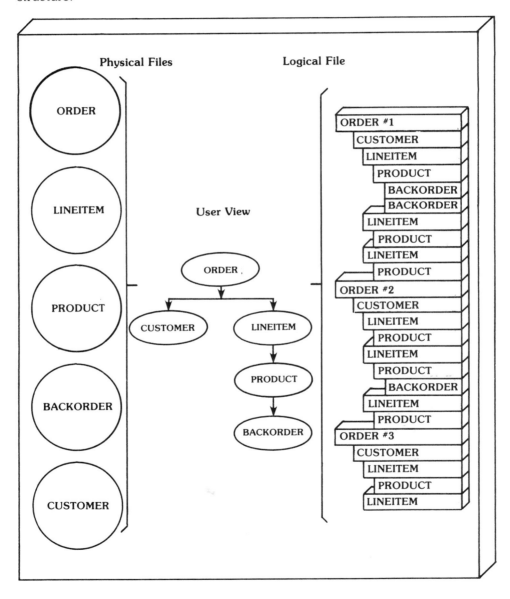

FIGURE 11.5 System/38 Pseudo-hierarchy

Security considerations in System/38 are related directly to the hardware. Microcode within the hardware is necessary to read or write to the files. All operations are made through microcode instruction interfaces that enforce a machine code object level authorization. For this reason IBM feels that items such as keyword locks and data encryption are not necessary for the System/38 data base facility.

The access paths define the ordering of records within the logical files. The order can be key sequenced or entry sequenced. A user who creates a file becomes the "owner" of the file and must specify "Public," "Private," or "Normal" authorization. "Public" allows any other user to read and update the file. "Private" means only the owner can use the data file. "Normal" implies a set of authorized users specified by system default may access the file. Creation of a logical file requires the creator (owner) to have authorization to use those physical files that make up the logical file.

QBE—Subschema

Logical files or user tables called snapshots can be created by QBE. Figure 11.6 illustrates the dynamic coupling of two entity tables, SALES and SUPPLY. The user can elect to make this SAL-SUP combination a permanent file structure called a snapshot. Security in QBE is at the file level, and authorization and processing option for each user are kept in a system maintained authority table. The authority table contains the names of tables and of users authorized to access them, as well as the conditions under which access is permitted.

The subschema as it exists in the more structured architectures is used to map out application-specific paths of access intent and extent. In the relational data base architecture, because of the inherent lack of a rigid physical structure, the security is reduced to that of the file or table.

System/38 Data Integrity

The System/38 hardware depends on microcode and data encryption to provide data security and integrity. The integrity features of this data base management system are based on microcode. All operation against the data is done in MOVE MODE: the data base user never has access to the actual physical data or even the address of that data. Thus only through using the appropriate data base commands can programmers access the data. Individual records are locked so that problems with concurrent update cannot occur.

Dynamic backout of individual transactions and data base copy features are also provided. Because of the rather unique structure of this particular DBMS, most integrity design considerations are complete by the end of the subschema design process. Also the dedicated hardware feature does not offer the same problems of backout and restart/recovery found in a large-scale system.

QBE Data Integrity

Data integrity at the file level is similar to other DBMS products with the user of logging and recovery utilities. At the logical level QBE uses four tables to maintain

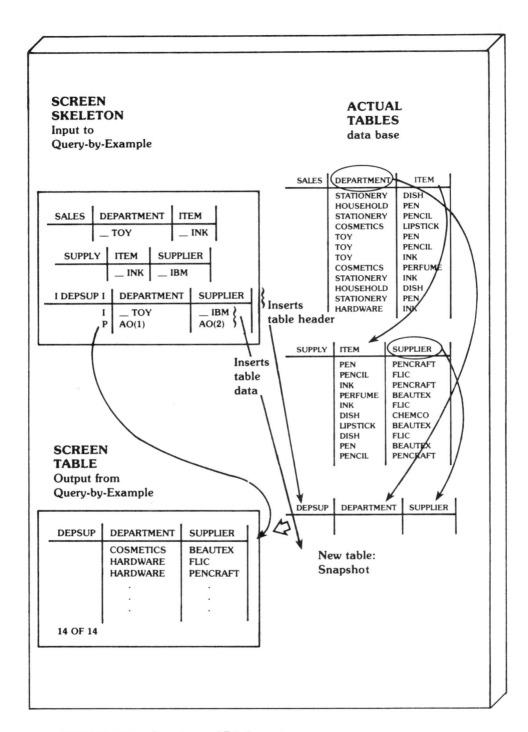

FIGURE 11.6   Creating a QBE Snapshot

system data integrity. The AUTHORITY table has already been explained. There are three others: TABLE, DOMAIN, and PROGRAM.

The TABLE table consists of a list of the table names in the entire system. Additionally the name of the owner of the table is maintained also.

The DOMAIN table contains a list of the valid domains in the system. The table has all the previously defined domains in the system along with their attributes such as NAME, OWNER, DATA TYPE, IMAGE, plus the minimum input column width and maximum output column width, called the MIN ICW and MAX OCW, respectively.

Last is the PROGRAM table, which contains all the prestored queries or programs. The data contained in this table is the name grower and comments information. Once inserted only the comments field can be updated.

SYSTEM/38 and QBE—Performance

Performance options for System/38 and QBE are severely limited because of the current level of hardware implementation. Data coupling on the current generation of computers is not very efficient nor all that practical for large dynamic files.

The characteristics for structured and unstructured (relational) data base systems are different. Structured systems, which are the current generation of major data base management systems, have form and structure inherent in their storage. They can represent the most commonly accepted data relationships, the one to ones, one to many's, and the many to many's. They can produce and control, through the subschema, the needs for and context of alternative views or substructures.

On the other hand relational unstructured systems, which are the probable direction of future data base management system have limited or no inherent structure in their storage. All the relationships between data entities are produced and controlled by the system. There are many alternatives for data definition either through structure binding or data coupling.

System R/SQL is a new full function DBMS announced by IBM in early 1980. The product had been under development at the San Jose research laboratory since 1974. The objective of this product was to build a complete product that could be used to solve real data base problems. The difference in System R has been the inclusion of expanded capabilities for data independence, automatic concurrency control, a more flexible security authorization system, dynamic logical structure definition, a full gamut of data base recovery options, and finally greater controls for tuning and usability.

Products such as System R and INGRES are among the new breed of relational systems and as such incorporate more of the functions and options of the older, more structured systems. For more detailed information on this "new breed," see C.J. Dates's *An Introduction to Database Systems*," 3rd edition, and specific references found in the Bibliography.

This push to relational structures is motivated by increased data independence. With data independence the application user need not be concerned about the physical structure or storage technique of the real data. The ideal is that data will be produced in any form requested regardless of when the form is specified.

The reality of the situation however is this: Data will always have some form even if derives only from the fact that two things are stored next to each other. Additionally, in the real world, users are sensitive to the time and cost of producing data for processing. Finally, the ultimate reality is that physical storage media, schema addressing, and access methods influence the usability of data. The realities must be reduced to a realistic performance scale by the hardware before true relational data bases are a fait accompli.

NOTES

1. E.F. Codd, "Normalized Data Base Structure: A Brief Tutorial," p. 163. *Proceedings of ACM Sigfidet Workshop on Data Description and Access*, 1971.
2. "The Future of Relational DBMS," *Computerworld* (July 12, 1980): p. 5.
3. M.M. Zloof, "Query-By-Example: A Data Base Language," *IBM Systems Journal* 16, no. 4 (1977): 324.

12 Designing for the Inverted List Structure

While memory holds a seat in this distracted globe. Remember thee! Yea from the table of my memory I'll wipe away all trivial fond records.

Shakespeare, *Hamlet*

This final chapter will relate the implementation problems encountered in designing inverted file structures. Inverted file systems are the closest structures to relational files without actually being relational. The physical files generally are flat structures in which a great deal of inversion or indexing has taken place to link otherwise unattached files together. The flat structures are roughly equivalent to the tables found in relational schemes.

There are a number of inverted list products on the market today such as DATACOM/DB, FOCUS, Model-204, ADABAS, and System 2000. In this chapter I will specifically discuss ADABAS and System 2000. For more details, see Cohen's *Data Base Management Systems* and Atre's *Data Base Management Systems for the Eighties*.

ADABAS Schema (Inverted List Structure)

The ADABAS DBMS software product is quite similar in structure to relational architectures. It has none of the direct pointers or chains found in the network or hierarchical architectures. The common keys within the records themselves establish relationships among the various records (entities). This is a familiar technique; users gain entry into this data complex through external index files or index data bases (see Figure 12.1). The data files themselves are typically just variable-length recor of records but to a relative address in an address table, or address converter, which then

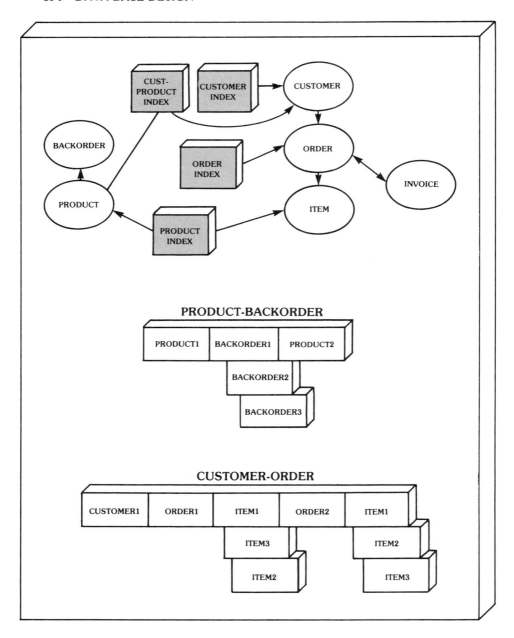

FIGURE 12.1   Sample ADABAS Schema

points directly to the physical data record. The lists of keys and attributes (descriptors) are determined by the third-normal-form entities resulting from normalization. The flexibility of the schema is geared to the multiplicity of index structures that can be defined.

ADABAS is particularly suited for those organizations whose data base applications require rapid response to highly complex query-type transactions. The physical data base record is accessed only after all the appropriate indexes relating to the query request are searched and the specified fields along with the records containing them are located.

Most other data base architectures might require entire scans of the physical data base(s) to satisfy a complex query request. The drawback to ADABAS, as with any other inverted list DBMS, is that multiple high-level indexes containing fields of a highly dynamic content require a considerable amount of index maintenance.

All the fields of a single logical record occupy physically adjacent storage positions within the same physical block. The individual field values are variable-length strings, preceded by a length code. Data is retrieved at the field level, not by the record or segment; ADABAS automatically formats the fields desired in the desired structure. ADABAS provides a very general capability for random retrieval of data and for efficient sequential access to data. Each physical file may be coupled with up to 80 other files, and each record may be coupled with any number of records from another file. Up to five coupled files can be searched on a single query. Because of the flexibility of the data coupling features of ADABAS, it does not seem necessary to construct special "logical file structures" in the application program.

The actual ADABAS physical schema is a single physical file broken up into mini-file segments. The first segment in this single physical data set contains the ADABAS index structure. The remaining segments correspond to the flat data files representing the other "data bases."

System 2000 Schema—Fully Inverted List Structure

Whereas ADABAS is not dependent on a pointer, System 2000 is very pointer dependent. Rather than groups of indexes tied to a flat-file data record with little or limited structure, System 2000 utilizes a hierarchical physical file implementation. Six data sets are used to implement the physical file location. (See Figure 12.2.) Every record in the data file is pointed to from a hierarchical location table (HLT). Entrance into the HLT can come either directly from the unique values table (UVT) for unique value indexed fields or indirectly from the multiple occurrence table (MOT) for a nonunique data item via the UVT.

Additionally there is the definition directory file (DDF) and a general overflow file, which handles overflow from the UVT the DDF and the data files.

The schema or view resulting from this type of structure is not unlike that of the IMS hierarchical architecture. The physical structure and parent-child and repeating group structures are defined in the definition directory. System 2000 refers to the parent-child structures as ancestor-sibling.

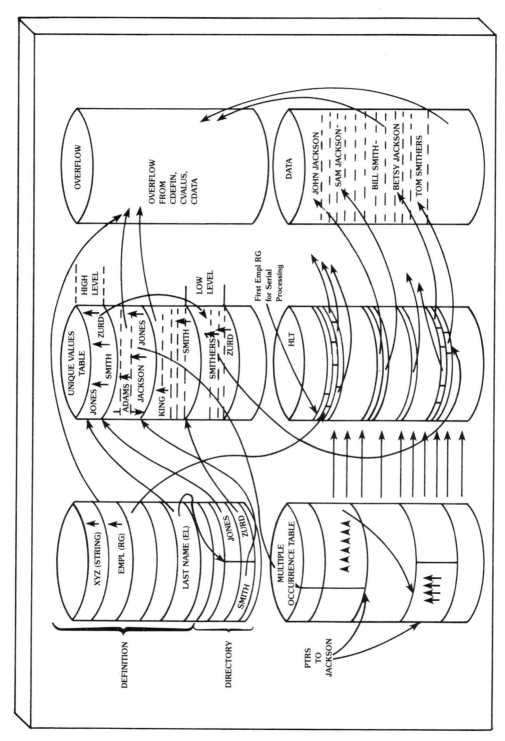

FIGURE 12.2 Overview of System 2000 Physical File Organization

ADABAS SUBSCHEMA

In ADABAS the programmer describes the data needs of the application and the function desired to the DBA. From the list of commands found in Figure 12.3, the DBA then creates a customer version module for that application, using these ADAMINT commands and the appropriate parameter statements.

Although ADABAS provides greater data independence than most systems, the application is still tied to a file structure. The user must specify in which file a field resides prior to the retrieval of that field. This prevents data from moving around freely. ADAMINT delivers the fields required by an application in a flat-file logical record. In this manner the ADAMINT macrolike code creates a logical file that is

xxxxxxxxx functions—	Meaning
FINDSET	Find a set of records based on particular search arguments.
READSET	Read data from the set of records previously found.
LOKATE	Establish a position in a file for sequential processing to begin.
SEQREAD	Sequentially access records that have been located.
REREAD	Read the same record again.
UPDATE	Update one or more data fields within a record.
ADDNEW	Establish a new record.
DELETER	Delete a record from a file.
RELEASE	Release a record that was to be updated.
SIGNON	Start a data base session.
SIGNOFF	Start a data base session.
CHEKPNT	Establish a checkpoint on the ADABAS log.
SNAPINT	Dump the user's view of his communication area.
ERRANAL	Analyze the response code.

FIGURE 12.3   ADAMINT DML

independent of the application program. Thus the user can manipulate the data without recoding the application. Figure 12.4 illustrates this logical file concept.

The identification of a user-view requiring keyed entry into the data base, using a field other than the primary key of the ADABAS record, required the definition of that field as an index descriptor. If users detect this requirement for additional index descriptors during subschema design, it means it is necessary to redesign the earlier schema design.

SYSTEM 2000 SUBSCHEMA

System 2000 relies heavily on physical rather than logical relationships for its operation. However, logical views can be constructed by defining the appropriate structures in the HLT. As Cohen points out in *Data Base Management Systems*,

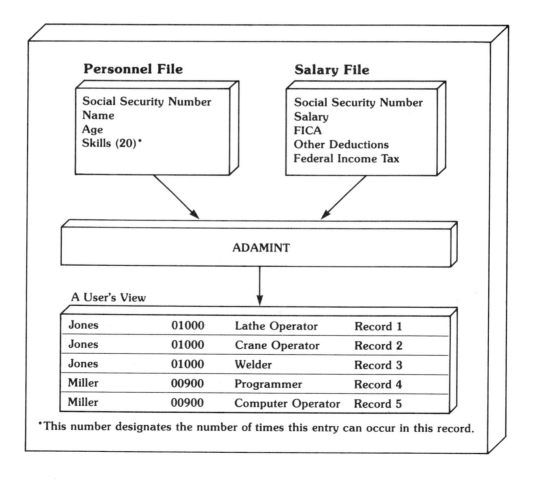

FIGURE 12.4   ADAMINT Logical Record

In S2000 it is somewhat redundant to speak of construction of logical file organizations because the data base description itself describes a logical as opposed to a physical file organization. The system constructs its physical file in a somewhat serial organization and uses the data in the data base description to construct various kinds of reference tables.[2]

The data base description is made up of four component types, called strings, user functions, elements, and repeating groups. The basic unit of data definition is the last component type, the *repeating group* (RG). These are defined to occupy various levels of a hierarchical tree structure related to other RGs as an ancestor or descendant.

RGs are composed of elements and other RGs. The hierarchical paths are indicated by nesting the RG and linking them by defining relationships to their parents. A single definition can contain up to 32 nested levels of RGs, and more than one RG can be at each level within the 32.

INVERTED LIST DATA INTEGRITY

Inverted list DBMS products follow a similar pattern with regard to data integrity as the other noninverted list products. Software-AG's DBMS product, ADABAS, does offer some unique security and data integrity options. Password security is available at the file and field level. A security code from 0 to 15 can be assigned by ADABAS for read, update, and write access to data.

One of the unique security devices available at the option of the ADABAS user is the data enciphering/deciphering capability. To employ this capability, the user supplies an eight-digit cipher key of any arbitrary value. When data is entered or loaded, ADABAS uses the cipher key to encipher the data before it is stored. In order to retrieve deciphered data, the user must supply the same cipher key with which the data was enciphered and stored. Without the cipher key, only garbage data will be returned to the program.

The usual logging and checkpoint type facilities available to other DBMS users are available to ADABAS users. ADABAS maintains a status file of all incomplete transactions such that if ADABAS itself went down, a simple warm start would complete the unfinished transaction without necessitating a total data base recovery.

ADABAS also has some rather nice integrity features. ADABAS automatically checks for format errors. If a field has a packed decimal format, only packed data with a valid sign can be stored in it. Any attempt to modify a field with data in the wrong format will result in an error status code from ADABAS and no update will take place.

There are no pointers or structure linking one record to another in ADABAS; therefore, it is unlikely that an application could inadvertently destroy structure data or pointers.

System 2000 uses a series of user commands to set up security features. A master password and up to 20 additional passwords can be assigned by the holder of the master password. Processing options on the data files can be restricted by the use of the ASSIGN command to limit access to retrieval, update or use only as a qualifier in a query. The passwords and assignments may be at the data base, repeating group, or element level.

Integrity is maintained by System 2000 using an update file, which may be tape or disk to record the update command, start and terminate logging, or to unload the data base from a backup file.

ADABAS OPERATIONS AND PERFORMANCE DESIGN

Because ADABAS supports conventional or flat-file record formats, users can directly implement the entities derived from third normal form, in the form of conventional files used in ADABAS record formats. There are physical limits to ADABAS data bases. The Internal Sequence Number (ISN) is unique for each record. An ISN occupies 3 bytes of storage; this limits the file size to around 17 million records (2^{24}). Up to 200 descriptors are permitted per file and up to 12 phonetic descriptors are allowed per line. However, inserting a record with more than 15 to 20 indexes results in severe I/O overhead because every index requires an index block entry. ADABAS is unique among DBMS products in that it can retrieve data phonetically. Through the use of a phonetic descriptor, the user can retrieve all records that have a key that *sounds* like another key ("bored" for "board," "made" for "maid," "Zonka" for "Csonka").

Users may couple a single file to 80 other files and may reference up to 5 coupled files in a single query. The data base itself may be composed of up to 255 different files. A physical record, after going through the ADABAS compression routines, can reduce the data storage space required with a 20 to 80% efficiency according to Software-AG.

Figure 12.5 describes the operation of the ADABAS indexing chain. As can be surmised from the illustration, the only thing that really affects performance on ADABAS, or for that matter any inverted list architecture DBMS, is the complexity and volatility of the index. Complex Boolean searches involving multicoupled files with numerous descriptors naturally are going to be poorer performers than less involved application requests.

For single description fields or descriptors with unique keys (such as order number or customer number), an average of 1.5 accesses per retrieval can be achieved even with files consisting of several million records. For more complex queries there can be a number of accesses to the ADABAS work file as well as the associator, where Boolean logic is performed on fabricated bit strings. ADABAS does, however, in the case of complex queries, select the index value with the smallest set of records. This number can be obtained from the count field in the index that contains the number of ISNs associated with each key value.

Record blocking can also affect the number of physical I/O operations the DBMS requires to satisfy the application request for data. As one can see from the illustration, the actual data contained within the ADABAS data file is stored and retrieved in blocks.

SYSTEM 2000's OPERATION AND PERFORMANCE DESIGN

System 2000 is relatively easy to understand and use because there is only one basic file organization from which the system constructs a variety of tables. The user is not

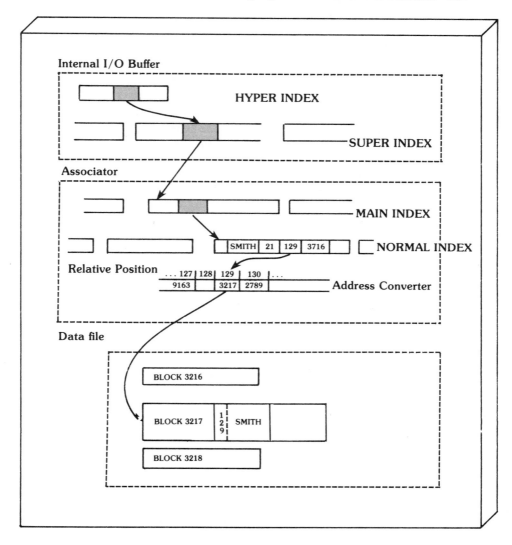

FIGURE 12.5 ADABAS Indexing Search for Descriptor "Smith"

concerned with a variety of pointers, chains, or access method choices. Within the constraints of the system, there are few techniques available to get around the system.

The tables are built from elements designated as keys. There are no limits on the number of keys in a data base. However, in System 2000 the inverted index list tables can get quite large and if the given occurrence on a particular table exceeds the block size, block chaining can result, which will affect performance. Index "padding" can forestall the need of reorganizing the index to avoid block I/O chaining.

In System 2000, reorganization is required when either the inverted lists have become fragmented so that the most common key values are spread over many blocks. (System 2000 calls blocks *pages*) or because deletes exceed additions and the freed up space is not being reused.

Review

Inverted file systems are known and used for their multikey access methods, which make them among the best query products. Little skill is needed to install and use them effectively. They are user friendly and can be used readily by nontechnical personnel. Design and conversion problems are minimal because of the flat-file nature of the physical files.

However, these systems can have heavy costs associated with file and index maintenance, CPU utilization, and very large-scale file processing. Selection of any architecture really relates back to what is the ultimate goal or demands placed upon your system. The perfect data base management system for all occasions does not yet exist.

REFERENCES

1. Leo J. Cohen, *Data Base Management Systems*, 6th ed. (Wellesley, Mass.: QED Information Sciences, Inc., 1979).
2. Ibid., pp. 4–116.

APPENDIXES

Appendix A

Usage Maps for the Sample Problem

Transaction Path Analysis Form

Transaction ID A   **Description** Create An Order   **Peak Load** 60

Unique ID	From Entity	Num	To Entity	Access	Avg	Mult	During One Tran	Acc Wt	Adj. I/O	During Stress Period
0-2	·	1	ORDER	U	1	1	1	3	3	180
2-1	ORDER	1	CUSTOMER	R	1	1	1	1	1	60
2-3	ORDER	1	LINEITEM	I	6	1	6	2	12	720
3-4	LINEITEM	6	PRODUCT	U	1	1	6	3	18	1080
2-5	ORDER	1	BACKORDER	I	.1	1	.1	2	.2	12
									34.2	2052

Column group headers: Path Description | Number Times Path Occurs | Number Times Path Used

Transaction Path Analysis Form

Transaction ID B   **Description** Create An Invoice   **Peak Load** 60

Unique ID	From Entity	Num	To Entity	Access	Avg	Mult	During One Tran	Acc Wt	Adj. I/O	During Stress Period
	Path Description				Number Times Path Occurs		Number Times Path Used			
0-2	•	1	ORDER	R	1	1	1	1	1	60
2-1	ORDER	1	CUSTOMER	U	1	1	1	3	3	180
2-3	ORDER	1	LINEITEM	R	6	1	6	1	6	360
3-4	LINEITEM	6	PRODUCT	R	1	1	6	1	6	360
2-5	ORDER	1	BACKORDER	R	.1	1	.1	1	.1	6
4-7	PRODUCT	6	INVLINE	I	60	1/60	6	2	12	720
7-6	INVLINE	6	INVOICE	I	1	1/6	1	2	2	120
									30.1	1806

Transaction Path Analysis Form

Transaction ID C   **Description** Update a Backorder   **Peak Load** 3

Unique ID	From Entity	Num	To Entity	Access	Avg	Mult	During One Tran	Acc Wt	Adj. I/O	During Stress Period
	Path Description				Number Times Path Occurs		Number Times Path Used			
0-4	•	1	PRODUCT	U	1	1	1	3	3	9
4-5	PRODUCT	1	BACKORDER	U	.5	1	.5	3	1.5	4.5
5-2	BACKORDER	.5	ORDER	U	1	1	.5	3	1.5	4.5
									6	18

Transaction Path Analysis Form

Transaction ID D **Description** Customer Order Query **Peak Load** 10

Unique ID	From Entity	Num	To Entity	Access	Avg	Mult	During One Tran	Acc Wt	Adj. I/O	During Stress Period
0-1	•	1	CUSTOMER	R	1	1	1	1	1	10
1-2	CUSTOMER	1	ORDER	R	5	1	5	1	5	50
2-3	ORDER	5	LINEITEM	R	6	1	30	1	30	300
3-4	LINEITEM	30	PRODUCT	R'	1	1	30	1	30	300
2-5	ORDER	5	BACKORDER	R	.1	1	.5	1	.5	5
1-6	CUSTOMER	1	INVOICE	R	10	1	10	1	10	100
6-7	INVOICE	10	INVLINE	R	6	1	60	1	60	600
									136.5	1365

Column groups: Path Description | Number Times Path Occurs | Number Times Path Used

Transaction Path Analysis Form

Transaction ID E **Description** Customer Backorder Query **Peak Load** 6

Unique ID	From Entity	Num	To Entity	Access	Avg	Mult	During One Tran	Acc Wt	Adj. I/O	During Stress Period
0-1	•	1	CUSTOMER	R	1	1	1	1	1	6
1-2	CUSTOMER	1	ORDER	R	5	1	5	1	5	30
2-5	ORDER	5	BACKORDER	R	.1	1	.5	1	.5	3
5-4	BACKORDER	.5	PRODUCT	R	1	1	.5	1	.5	3
									7	42

Transaction Path Analysis Form

Transaction ID F   **Description**   Product Invoice Query   **Peak Load** 2

Unique ID	Path Description			Access	Number Times Path Occurs		Number Times Path Used			
	From Entity	Num	To Entity		Avg	Mult	During One Tran	Acc Wt	Adj. I/O	During Stress Period
0-4	•	1	PRODUCT	R	1	1	1	1	1	2
4-7	PRODUCT	1	INVLINE	R	60	1	60	1	60	120
									61	122

Transaction Path Analysis Form

Transaction ID G   **Description**   Product Backorder Query   **Peak Load** 5

Unique ID	Path Description			Access	Number Times Path Occurs		Number Times Path Used			
	From Entity	Num	To Entity		Avg	Mult	During One Tran	Acc Wt	Adj. I/O	During Stress Period
0-4	•	1	PRODUCT	R	1	1	1	1	1	.5
4-5	PRODUCT	1	BACKORDER	R	.5	1	.5	1	.5	2.5
									1.5	7.5

Transaction Path Analysis Form

Transaction ID H   **Description** Product Customer Query   **Peak Load** 5

Unique ID	From Entity	Num	To Entity	Access	Number Times Path Occurs Avg	Mult	During One Tran	Acc Wt	Adj. I/O	During Stress Period
0-4	•	1	PRODUCT	R	1	1	1	1	1	· 5
4-3	PRODUCT	1	LINEITEM	R	30	1	30	1	30	150
3-2	LINEITEM	30	ORDER	R	1	1	30	1	30	150
2-1	ORDER	30	CUSTOMER	R´	1	1	30	1	30	150
									91	455

Transaction Path Analysis Form

Transaction ID I   **Description** Product Order Query   **Peak Load** 10

Unique ID	From Entity	Num	To Entity	Access	Number Times Path Occurs Avg	Mult	During One Tran	Acc Wt	Adj. I/O	During Stress Period
0-4	•	1	PRODUCT	R	1	1	1	1	1	10
4-3	PRODUCT	1	LINEITEM	R	30	1	30	1	30	300
3-2	LINEITEM	30	ORDER	R	1	1	30	1	30	300
									61	610

Appendix B

Glossary of Terms

access method   The algorithm by which an item of physical data is identified and located by the operating system and the routines; external to the application program, which stores and retrieves that item.

access path   The route taken through the logical structure of the data base in terms of the data relationships used by the system in order to locate a logical data unit or units.

access time   The time interval between the instant the application calls for a unit of data to or from its work area and the instant the operation is completed.

address   The location of a unit of data within a physical record either relative to the beginning of a data set or an exact device address.

after image   A duplicate copy of a record made after it has been modified.

alternate entry point
A data element whose occurrences have been indexed so that users can gain entry to the data base if the user knows the value of some occurrence of that element.

area
A named logical subdivision of the addressable storage space in the data base; it may contain occurrences of records, sets, and parts of sets of various types that can be mapped onto storage media.

array
An n-dimensional collection of data items, all of which have identified characteristics.

attribute
The values associated with an entity or domain. A characteristic or description of an entity. Different entities may have common attributes such as color, size, or cost.

attribute migration
Replacement of a relation by two or more of its projections such that it may be recovered by taking the natural join of these projections.

Bachman diagram
A design tool for documenting detailed design decisions.

before image
A duplicate copy of a record made before it has been modified.

binary search
The procedure for finding an element of an order table by successively halving the interval and then evaluate the remaining half where that element is known to exist (dichotomizing search).

block
A physical grouping of physical records serving as a primary unit of transfer between an external storage device and the main memory of a computer.

candidate key
An attribute or combination of attributes of a relation such that for each tuple of that relation, the value of the key uniquely identifies that tuple, and no attribute in the key can be discarded without destroying the uniqueness.

chain
A continuous series of linked records in which each record contains a pointer forward and/or backward to another record in the chain. Thus from any point on the chain, it is possible to process all records by sequentially following the chain.

checkpoint	A position in a routine or program where information or data is stored for the purpose of reconstructing the data in the event of recovery or restart.
compression	The shortening of data so that it will require less room for storage (for example by eliminating blank or repeated characters).
concatenation	The aggregation of separately stored units of data into one contiguous unit.
(CAS) content addressable storage	A secondary storage device designed for the rapid retrieval of data by a sequential scan of the values stored, rather than by the use of hardware addressing techniques.
contention	The situation where two application programs attempt to access the same unit of data simultaneously.
data aggregate	A named collection of data items within a record.
data analysis	The detailed four-stage analysis of the total data within an application to identify the data elements and the relationships between them with a view to rationalizing the control of data within the application and to minimizing data redundancy.
data base	A common pool of shared data. All record and set occurrences and areas controlled by a specific schema. A generalized, common, integrated collection of company or installation-owned data which fulfills the data requirements of all applications which access it, and which it structured to model the natural data relationships which exist in an enterprise.
(DBA) data base administrator	A person or persons given the responsibility for the definition, organization, protection, and efficiency of the data base for an enterprise.
data base dictionary or directory	A repository for data about data, containing definitions, purposes, controls, formats and relationships about elements, records, files, programs, systems and data bases.
(DBMS) data base management system	The data processing system providing the means to access, organize, and control all information stored in the data base.

(DDL) data description language	The language used to describe the data base, or that part of the data base known to a program.
data item	The smallest unit of named data, an occurrence that is a representation of a value.
data dependence	The concept of separating the definitions of logical and physical data, such that application programs need not be dependent on where or how physical units of data are stored.
(DML) data manipulation language	The language used to cause data to be transferred between the application program and the data base.
data model	A conceptual representation of data aggregates and their interrelationships.
data set	A collection of stored records.
data structure	The relationships between units of data.
(DMCL) device media control language	The language used to specify the storage of data at a physical level, including control of space on each device, overflow, buffering and paging.
direct access	A way of retrieving data whereby a disk address can be reached immediately without sequential reading.
distributed data base	A data base under the overall control of a central DBMS, but where the devices on which it is stored are not all attached to the same processor.
distributed processing	A hardware configuration where several computers at different locations are communicating with one another, and possibly with a large computer.
domains	The groups of like data by which a relation is defined.
end user	A person who uses data to meet organizational responsibilities but who typically has no data processing skills.
entity	A person, place, thing or event of interest to the organization and about which data may be recorded. Something requiring

identification either through names or description. It can be conceptual or physical.

entity name
The symbol by which a person, place, thing, class, or any object of thought is known.

entry point
A data element whose occurrences are used as primary access to a data base. The coded form of an attribute.

field
A position or range of positions in a record that contain a data element.

file
That physical portion of the data base, which is managed as one unit by the operating system of the computer. A set of entities composed of one or more fields for each entity.

first normal form
The type of relation that has the property that none of its domains have elements that are themselves relations. First normal form can be obtained by removing repeating groups from unnormalized data and making them separate entities.

flat file
A single-level file having only one record type.

foreign key
A segment of a record that is not its primary key but whose elements are values of the primary key of some other record.

full inversion
The inversion of all record fields so that the record as such does not have to be stored. Now considered impractical in commercial DBMSs.

function dependence
An attribute or collection of attributes of a relation is functionally dependent on a second attribute of that relation if at every instant, each value of the first attribute is associated with no more than one value of the second attribute under the relation

$$\text{Rel A} \rightarrow \text{Rel B}$$

functional analysis
A top-down approach to gathering information.

hierarchy
One or more sets of directed relationships between two or more units of data, such that some units of data are considered owners, while others are considered members, and such that one unit has no owner and all the other data units have one owner.

host language The programming language used to write the application program in which the data manipulation language commands are embedded.

identifier A unit of data that gives a name to an entity and that is frequently used as a key for access to a data record. One or more fields with pointers to the records they index.

index A collection of copies of the keys in a group of records with pointers to the records they index.

indexed sequential A type of access method in which one field in the record is designated as the prime key. An index of prime key values is automatically kept and is used to gain direct access to the indexed records.

intersection data Data describing the relationship between two units of data.

inverted file A storage organization in which an index is provided for the values of each type of data item.

join The operation of combining two relations with some domain in common, such that all original information is preserved.

key A field used to access records directly or to sequence them based on the contents of the field.

linkage A mechanism for connecting one unit of data to another.

list A series of linked records of which each contains a pointer to its successor in the list.

location mode The method by which the DBMS controls the assignment of a unique identifier to records.

log A journal of before and after images of records used in conjunction with checkpoint data to recover a system of its data sets.

logical data The data the application program presents to or receives from the data base.

logical record A collection of data items independent of their physical record. Portions of the same logical record may be part of different physical records.

logical structure	The set of relationships between two or more units of data.
logical synthesis	The combining of similar user-views into one view or sub-schema.
member record	A record within a set where that record has a dependent relationship with the owner of the set.
Network	One or more collections of directed relationships among three or more units of data; some units of data are considered owners, while others are considered members. Each member may have more than one owner.
normalization	A process of data element grouping around a key. See: **first normal form**; **second normal form**; **third normal form**.
optimal third normal form	A collection of relations is in optimal third normal form, when the number of relations used to define a given collection of data is at a minimum, and there are no pairs of attributes within a relation. One member of the pair transitively dependent on the other in some relation.
owner record	A record that determines the existence of a set, and with which any records of that set have a dependent relationship.
physical data	The data the DBMS presents to the operating system for storage or receives from it for processing.
pointer	A link to a data area in external storage either through a physical address or through the key of the destination data.
pointer array	A collection of pointers associated with an owner record and used to link it with the member records contained in its set.
position	The place in the data base that the DBMS remembers as the current position of activity for an application program.
primary key	The domain or combination of domains of a given relation that uniquely define each tuple of that relation.
prime attribute	Any attribute of a relation that participates in at least one candidate key of that relation.

projection   The operation of selection from a relation-specified domain and then removing any tuples that are now duplicated, thereby producing a second, more limited relation.

query language Any high-level user-oriented language, frequently used on line and interactive, that supports data base access without special application coding.

randomizing   A method of storing and accessing data that uses an algorithm to manipulate one of the data elements in each unit to produce an address in a predetermined area of space. The unit is either stored at that address or a pointer left there tells where to find it.

realm   A logical subdivision of the data base into which records of specified types may be stored.

recovery   The method for restoring a data base to its correct condition following some type of error.

redundancy   A situation where there are multiple occurrences of a particular unit of data in a data base.

relation   A relation exists between a group of sets if each element in each set has a logical connection with the corresponding elements in other sets. A tabular representation of records within a file.

relational model A logical view of data in which all data elements are grouped in relations of the third form.

relationship   A meaningful association between units of data in which the ordering of data is of no significance. Examples are the one to one, one to many, and many to many.

reorganization A process of arranging or rearranging the relative physical placement of data units in a data base.

repeating group A collection of data that occurs an arbitrary number of times within a record occurrence. It may consist of data items, vectors, and repeating groups.

restructure   The process of adding to or deleting from the types of data units and data relationship represented in a data base, of rearranging data units that are components of larger data units, and of making the corresponding changes to the data base schema.

ring structure A way of relating units of data so that a pointer in each record leads to the next record, and the last record leads back to the first.

roll-back process of reversing the recent activities of a system to restore some or all of the data base to its state at a previous point in time.

schema A complete description of the data base in terms of the characteristics of the data and the implicit and explicit relationship between data units.

secondary key An alternate key that may or may not be unique and that represents an entity.

second normal form A relation is in second normal form if it is in first normal form and every nonprime attribute of the relation is fully dependent on each of its candidate keys. This can be attained by removing those attributes from a first normal form relation that are only partially dependent on the primary key of that relation.

segment A unit of data in a logical structure. In IMS, also the physical unit of data that supports the logical unit.

sequential processing A way of storing or retrieving data by starting at the first unit in a collection and getting the remaining units in sequence one by one.

set A named collection of related records representing a one-to-many relationship between the owner and member records.

set selection The process by which a DBMS uses a specified algorithm to determine the appropriate occurrence of set type for the purpose of accessing or inserting a member record.

seven dwarfs Doc, Happy, Sneezy, Grumpy, Bashful, Sleepy, Dopey.

subschema A description of those data units and relationships from a data base of interest to a particular application program.

symbolic pointer   The storing of a key field as a way of pointing to the record whose key is stored.

third normal form   When data is in second normal form and its non-key domains (if any) are mutually independent and fully dependent on the primary key.

transitive dependence   A dependence among attributes which is indirectly implied, because of direct functional dependence with other attributes.

$$Rel\ A \rightarrow Rel\ B \quad Rel\ B \rightarrow Rel\ C$$
$$Rel\ A \rightarrow Rel\ C$$

relation A implies relation B; relation B implies relation C; therefore, relation C is transitively dependent upon relation A.

tuple   An ordered collection of one or more data elements which make up a record. A row within a table.

union   The operation of combining two relations with all domain in common, together with the elimination of any identical tuples.

unit of data   A collection of one or more data elements. Units of data may be data aggregates or records or single data elements.

vector   A one-dimensional, ordered collection of data items, all of which have identical characteristics.

Appendix C
Solution to Normalization Sample Problem

UN-NORMALIZED DATA ATTRIBUTES

INVOICE   (**Invoice #**, shipment #, invoice date, order #, customer name, order date, delivery date, customer #, customer bill-to, customer ship-to, special instructions, total amount, discount *product #, description, quantity ordered, quantity shipped, back-ordered, unit price, total price*, discount amount, billed amount)

FIRST NORMAL FORM

INVOICE   (**Invoice #**, shipment #, invoice date, order #, customer name, order date, delivery date, customer #, customer bill-to, customer ship-to, special instructions, total amount, discount, discount amount, billed amount)

INVLINE   (**Invoice #-product #**, description, quantity ordered, quantity shipped, quantity back-ordered, unit price, total price)

SECOND NORMAL FORM

INVOICE   (**Invoice #**, shipment #, invoice date, order #, customer name, order date, delivery date, customer #, customer bill-to, customer ship-to, special instructions, total amount, discount, discount amount, billed amount)

INVLINE	(**Invoice #-product #,** quantity shipped, total price)
PRODUCT	(**Product #,** description, unit price)
BACK ORDER	(**Backorder #,** product #, invoice #, order #, quantity back-ordered)
LINE ITEM	(**Order #-product #,** quantity ordered)

NORMALIZED DATA ATTRIBUTES

INVOICE	(**Invoice #,** shipment #, invoice date, order #, customer #, delivery date, total amount, discount amount, billed amount, special instructions)
INVLINE	(**Invoice #-product #,** quantity shipped, total price)
CUSTOMER	(**Customer #,** customer name, customer bill-to, discount, customer ship-to)
PRODUCT	(**Product #,** description, unit price)
ORDER	(**Order #,** order date)
BACKORDER	(**Backorder #,** product #, invoice #, order #, quantity back-ordered)
LINE ITEM	(**Order #-product #,** quantity ordered)

Appendix D

Solution to Functional Analysis Sample Problem

UNNORMALIZED ENTITIES:

CUSTOMER	customer number, name, shipping address, bill-to address, discount rate.
SALESMAN	salesman number, name, salary, commission rate, monthly quota, territory number.
PRODUCT	product number, description, sale price, manufacturing cost, quantity on hand, quantity on order, product discount.
VENDOR	vendor number, name, address (part number, part name, part price)
ORDER	order number, date, delivery address, customer number, (product number, name, quantity, price)
INVOICE	invoice number, date, order number, customer number (product number, name, quantity shipped, backordered, price discount)
PART	part number, name, quantity on hand, quantity on order, vendor number, cost.
WAREHOUSE	warehouse number, address, capacity, (product number, name, quantity on hand, warehouse location)

STOCKHOLDER	stockholder number, name, address, shares
VENDOR-PERFORMANCE	performance record number, vendor number (part number, actual delivery time, actual price) supplier contact name, contact phone number
PRODUCT-PERFORMANCE	performance record number, product number (order number, actual delivery time, actual price), shipping contact name, phone ext
SALES-RECORD	Sale number, customer number, order number, salesman number, current YTD sales, last year YTD sales, current profit YTD, last year profit YTD.

FULLY NORMALIZED ENTITIES:

CUSTOMER	customer number, name, shipping address, bill-to-address, discount rate
SALESMAN	salesman number, name, salary, commission rate, monthly quota, territory number
PRODUCT	product number, description, sale price, manufacturing cost, quantity on hand, quantity on order, product discount
VENDOR	vendor number, name, address
VENDOR-PART	vendor number–part number, part price, quantity on hand, quantity on order
VENDOR-PERFORMANCE	performance record number, vendor number, contact name, contact phone
VENDOR-PERF-PART	performance record number–part number, actual delivery date, actual price
PART	part number, name, quantity on hand, quantity on order
ORDER	Order number, date, customer number
ORDERED-PRODUCT	order number–product number, quantity, price
INVOICE	invoice number, customer number, order number, date
INVOICED-PRODUCT	invoice number–product number, quantity shipped, price, discount
BACKORDER	backorder number, product number, invoice number, quantity
WAREHOUSE	warehouse number, address, capacity
WAREHOUSE-PRODUCT	warehouse number–product number, quantity on hand, location
STOCKHOLDER	stockholder number, name, address, shares
PRODUCT-PERFORMANCE	performance record number, product number, shipper contact name, contact phone

| PRODUCT-PERF-ORDER | performance record number–order, actual delivery date, actual price |
| SALES-RECORD | sale number, customer number, order number, invoice number, salesman number, current YTD, sales, last YTD sales, current profit YTD, last year profit YTD |

As you can see, there are a number of fields that have the same name but are in fact different values. DISCOUNT applies to product and to customer differently. Quantity (QTY) fields are dependent on the key of the entity in which it is contained. PART QTY ON HAND could be a different value from VENDOR-PART QTY ON HAND if there is more than one vendor for that part. PRICE could differ depending on order, customer, or vendor. Functional analysis helps point out to the designer the need for understanding how the end-user utilizes the data.

The sample problem is also full of holes, particularly in the performance records. ACTUAL is compared to promised, but where is promised? Somehow the order or the invoice must be tied back to performance. Also some provision must be made for differentiating orders FROM customers as opposed to orders TO vendors for parts.

The real purpose of the problem was to give you a chance to polish up on normalization skills. However even the normalization solution provided is subject to further interpretation. If the fields that have the same name are in fact the same value they should not be projected out into separate entities. Also there are attributes such as TERRITORY that may be interpreted as a separate entity.

Appendix E

The Nine Deliverables

The following material is offered as a Data Analysis "cookbook." These are the steps one would follow in order to do data analysis.

DELIVERABLES

1. Third NORMAL FORM ENTITY LIST
    A. Collect data
    B. First NORMAL FORM
    C. Second NORMAL FORM
    D. Third NORMAL FORM
2. Volume Table
3. Entity Relationship Map
4. Usage map of Each Transaction
5. Initial composite map
6. Revised composite map
7. Transaction path analysis form(s)
8. Load matrix
9. Loaded data model

Deliverable 1: Third NORMAL FORM Entity List

A. COLLECT DATA (for EACH DOCUMENT)

1. List all attributes (in no particular order).
2. Underline repeating attributes.
3. Identify the key (verify with user)
   a. Write it down (if necessary)
   b. Circle it.
4. Name entity
   a. Anglicize the key (or)
   b. Ask "This key identifies ... ?" (or)
   c. Use a common or user-oriented name (Invoice-line vs. Invoiced Product).

B. First NORMAL FORM (REPEATING GROUPS)

1. Remove repeating groups (attribute[s]) to a new entity.
2. Identify the key of the new entity
   a. The key will always be nonatomic
   b. First part—original entity's primary key
   c. Rest—attribute(s) which ID's repeating attributes (IDENTIFIER)
   d. Write it down (IF NECESSARY)
   e. Circle it.
3. Name the new entity
   a. Anglicize the key (or)
   b. Ask "This key identifies ... ?" (or)
   c. Use a common or user-oriented name (Invoice-line vs. Invoiced Product).

Determining Dependency

Ask one, some or all of the following questions. If the answer is 'yes' you've determined dependency.

1. If part of the nonatomic key changes, will this attribute value change? (Example; If Order number changes, will Quantity Ordered change?)
2. Where (in what entity) is this attribute one-on-one with what key?
   2a. Make sure you've placed it as high up in the logical hierarchical structure possible (where it's still one-on-one with the key—down, out, and up).
3. Could this attribute exist prior (historically) to the existence of the entity it is in?
4. Does only one occurrence of the value of this attribute exist in the entity?
5. Can you determine the attribute's value only after a certain entity is created? (Example; Shipping Instructions only when there is something to ship.)

C. Second NORMAL FORM (Partial Dependency)

1. Search the entities until you indentify an entity with a nonatomic key. Proceed to step 2 with that entity.

2. Remove attributes that are dependent on only part of the nonatomic key into new entity (IES).
3. Identify the key (it will be the identifier portion of the original nonatomic key).
    a. Write it down (if necessary)
    b. Circle it.
4. Name the new entity
    a. Anglicize the key (or)
    b. Ask "This key identifies . . . ?" (or)
    c. Use a common or user-oriented name (Invoice-line vs. Invoiced Product).

Determine Dependency

As one, some or all of the following questions. If the answer is 'yes' you've determined dependency.

1. If part of the nonatomic key changes, will this attribute value change? (Example: If order number changes, will quantity ordered change?)
2. Where (in what entity) is this attribute one-on-one with what key?
    2a. Make sure you've placed it as high up in the logical hierarchical structure possible (where it's still one-on-one with they key—Down, out and up).
3. Could this attribute exist prior (historically) to the existence of the entity it is in?
4. Does only one occurrence of the value of this attribute exist in the entity?
5. Can you determine the attribute's value only after a certain entity is created? (Example: Shipping Instructions only when there is something to ship.)

D. Third NORMAL FORM (Nondependency)

(Looking for attributes in the "wrong" entity)

1. Determine if attribute is not directly dependent on the primary key (does it relate better to some other attribute other than the key?).
2. Remove nondependent attribute to a new entity.
3. Identify the key—it is the attribute that the nondependent attribute does relate to
    a. Write it down (if necessary)
    b. Circle it.
4. Name the new entity
    a. Anglicize the key (or)
    b. Ask "this key identifies . . . ?" (or)
    c. Use a common or user-oriented name (Invoice-line vs. Invoiced Product).
5. The key attribute *stays* in the original entity (becomes a FOREIGN KEY, the "MANY" end of a one-to-many relationship).
6. Combine your "Ducks" (Different entities with the same primary key).

See rules for DETERMINING DEPENDENCY on prior normalization pages.

Deliverable 2: Volume Table

1. Draw empty (volume) table
    a. Label the Entity Name column on the left hand side

    b. Label the Volume column in the center

    c. Label the Frequency column on the right-hand side.

2. Fill in the "GIVEN" volumes (in volume column) from the specifications.
3. Fill in the frequencies (in frequency column) from the specifications, for entities whose volumes were not "GIVEN."
4. Compute the remaining (NOT GIVEN) volumes, using the frequencies from the table.
5. Fill in the calculated volumes in volume column.

Deliverable 3: Entity Relationship Map

1. Draw an entity at tahe top center of the page that contains no foreign keys. This becomes the "current" entity.
2. Going from the top of the entity list, find other entity(ies) that contain the "current" entity's primary key.
3. When one is found, go to step 5.
4. If none (or no more) found, use next entity from top of list that has not had its primary key used in a foreign-key search. Draw it, if necessary, and go to step 2 with this new "current" entity.
5. Draw the found entity near the "current" entity.
6. Draw a "MANY" box on the entity with the foreign key.
7. Connect the two entities with a relationship line.
8. Verify the relationship.
9. Fill in the volumes, if necessary.
10. Divide the volume of the "one" entity into the volume of the "many" entity. Put this "Average Path Occurrence" (the answer) in the box connected to the foreign entity.
11. Go to step 2

(*Don't use volumes* to determine relationship(s) (1:M)
"*Don't think*," *use the foreign key rule*):

THE ENTITY THE FOREIGN KEY IS IN INDICATES THE "MANY" END OF A "ONE-TO-MANY" RELATIONSHIP.

Deliverable 4: Usage Map of Each Transaction (one for each transaction)

1. Decide entry point
    Start from "what we know," e.g., Order Entry Clerk (what does Order Entry Clerk know?) Order Number (what entities key on Order Number?)
2. Decide what attributes are needed?
    a. What entity (ies) contain this attribute?
    b. When faced with choices always go to the place that gives you the fewest number of accesses (entities).
3. Determine the ideal direction of flow (NO TRANSPORTATION PROBLEMS). Look at the system as if this were the only transaction. "I have my druthers"

1. How would you design it?
2. How would it flow?
4. Decide type of access
   What are you going to do with entity when you get it?
   Read,   Update,   Delete, Store
   Fetch,   Update,   Delete, Store
   Read,   Update,   Delete, Add
   Fetch,   Update,   Delete, Add
   Get,   Replace, Delete, Insert.

Deliverable 5: Initial Composite Map

1. Draw logical requirements (each transaction usage map) on top of the entity-relationship map (from E-R Mapping)

   The resulting deliverable yields:
   a. Relationship paths that exist that we do not presently use
   b. Relationship paths that exist that we do use by one or more of our transactions
   c. Relationship paths that do not exist (no logical relationship), but that we do use for one or more of our defined transactions. These are transportation problems that we must resolve in the next step.

Deliverable 6: Revised Composite Map

Solve the transportations problems...

Indirectly—By using existing paths between entities for transportation only. Ask yourself (in this same transaction's logical flow) what is the closest entity to my problem entity(ies) that I've already reached?

Directly—Add a foreign key to the entity on the "many" end of the path you wish to use. Remember, if you decide to go this route, you have introduced a new field and should go back through all the steps to handle this new field (Normalization, Volume Table, E-R Mapping, and so forth).

Consider the expense/ramifications/advantages of the Indirect or Direct Method.

Deliverable 7: Transaction Path Analysis Form

TRANSACTION-ID   Transactions are usually named or identified by a code. Put that value in TRANSACTION-ID.

DESCRIPTION   The transaction does something. In a simple way state what that something is, in English, and place it in DESCRIPTION.

PEAK LOAD	A transaction can occur many times a day. There are times during the day when the system is working hard. This stress period may last for minutes or hours. Determine the number of times this transaction would be executed during this stress period. Place that number in PEAK LOAD.
UNIQUE-ID	A transaction can access many different records or entities. In order to access an entity you use a path to that entity. A path is described as going FROM one place TO another place. Assign a code for each placed involved in your system. The code for the place outside your system will be 0. Thus a path from place 3 to place 9 could be coded as 3-9 (FROM-TO). A Path entering your system at place 7 would be coded 0-7. Put these values in UNIQUE-ID.
FROM ENTITY	Each transaction path starts from one place and goes to another. Record the name of the starting place of the path in the FROM ENTITY.
NUM	This is a number. It is the number of "FROM ENTITIES" being used by this transaction for this path. The value of NUM is determined by finding the "FROM ENTITY" name in the "TO ENTITY" column. Once you have found it, record the value of DURING ONE TRAN for that TO ENTITY in every NUM that uses that entity.
TO ENTITY	Record the name of the place the path LEADS in the TO ENTITY. (See FROM ENTITY)
ACCESS	Each path accesses a TO ENTITY. If the access is for the purpose of reading the TO ENTITY, the ACCESS is R. If the purpose of the access is to insert, delete, or update the TO ENTITY, then the ACCESS will be I, D, or U, respectively.
AVG	This is a number. If the path you are using is coming from a "many" entity to a "one" entity, then the number will be 1. If the path is going from a "one" to a "many," then the number will be the value in the box, along that path, from the relationship map. On entry this value will always be a one.

MULT

This is a number having a range of values from 0 to 1. It is called MULT because you will multiply other numbers with it. MULT is a probability. It is the probability that this transaction will take this path some, all, or some percentage of time. The value of MULT is determined by creating a fraction. The denominator of this fraction will be AVG. The numerator can take on several values.

1. The value of the numerator will be equal to AVG if you always take all the path(s). Thus MULT equals one. (AVG over AVG)

2. The value of the numerator can also be obtained by knowing a percentage. The value in the numerator is the product of the known percentage and the AVG. Example: You take a path(s) 20% of the time, put the product of .2 and the AVG in the numerator. (Since percent times AVG, divided by AVG, equals percent; the value of MULT will always be equal to the known percent.)

3. The value of the numerator can be a number less than AVG. This occurs when a specific number of accesses can be determined. Example: AVG = 20, there are 20 different TO ENTITIES on average to go along this path. You wish to go to only a specific 2. Therefore put a 2 in the numerator.

DURING ONE TRAN

This is a number, a product really. The product obtained by multiplying NUM * AVG * MULT. Place that product in DURING-ONE-TRAN. On entry DURING-ONE-TRAN always equals 1.

ACCT WT.

Is the access weighting factor. This factor is a number used to adjust and inflate the cost of accessing an entity. One kind of access costs more than another kind of access. The cost of reading a record is not as great as the cost of reading and writing a record (update). For different systems the cost in I/O activity for each kind of record access can be determined. The examples in this book used R = 1, and D = 2 and U = 3. This is but a guideline; each DBMS will be different.

ADJ. I/O

The adjusted I/O is another number that is a product of multiplication. The ADJ. I/O is the inflated I/O cost. The value of ADJ. I/O is determined by multiplying DURING ONE TRAN by ACC WT. and recording that product in ADJ. I/O.

DURING STRESS   Is also a product. The product if ADJ. I/O times PEAK
PERIOD   LOAD. Record the result of this multiplication in DURING
   STRESS PERIOD.

By adding all the ADJ. I/O numbers you can determine the total adjusted I/O for the entire transaction. If you could determine the average cost of an I/O on your system, then a rough estimate of transaction response time could be determined by multiplying the two.

Totaling the DURING STRESS PERIOD column would give the total I/O activity for the transaction during the stress period.

Deliverable 8: Load Matrix

Transfer the values from the Transaction Path Analysis Forms.

1.   *Left section*—Transaction ID and Peak Load (both from header section of The Transaction Path Analysis Form.
2.   *Top section*—Enter each Unique ID (only once for all Path Analysis Forms) in the Path ID section.
3.   *Right section*—Transfer the transaction totals for ADJ I/O and During Stress Period to Per Tran and Stress Period columns respectively (in the correct Tran ID row).
4.   *Center section*—Transfer the During Stress Period for each path on every Path Analysis Form to the box located at the intersection of the correct path and correct transaction.
5.   *Bottom section*—Add up all the values in any one column (path) and put the total in the Individual Path Totals under the correct Path -ID. These totals will be needed in the last step, which will create the Loaded Data Model.

Deliverable 9: Loaded Data Model

1.   Draw a new, clean Entity-Relationship Map reflecting:
     a. Entities
     b. Entity volumes
     c. Entity numbers assigned during the Usage Mapping
     d. "Many" boxes
     e. Relationship lines
     f. Average Path Occurrences calculated during E-R Mapping

2.   Draw a path line between the "from" and "to" entities for that transaction path. Include the arrowhead to show directionality.
3.   Transfer Individual Path Totals calculated on the Load Matrix Form to their corresponding paths. Place the transferred total near the "to" end of each transaction path.

APPENDIX F

Two Sample Case Studies

PREFACE

Each of the two sample specification documents that follow contains the following components:

1. a simple narrative or application description;
2. a list of sample system outputs;
3. a list of some of the transactions to be processed by the system in order to produce the outputs.

The first case deals with a banking application, while the other concerns an order-processing system similar to the E-Z Chair problem.

Each case is provided with a solution illustrating all nine deliverables from the data analysis method. The solutions are merely guidelines to the possible configurations for the loaded data model. Solutions will vary, based on the interpretation of *how* the business is to be conducted. Remember, data analysis only tells you *what* data is used. It is up to the analyst to discover how the data is being used. Remember, also, when designing physical files, that "form ever follows function."

INTRODUCTION TO BANKING CASE STUDY

The following is a sample of a typical banking application subsystem. We obtain the entity lists by normalizing the sample documents; we determine the volumes and frequencies by reading the narrative. A step-by-step de-composition into third normal form has been included for one of the documents. The other documents are shown only in their final normalized format.

The sample solutions for all nine deliverables were obtained by following strictly the how-to list in the preceding appendix. Good luck!

CASE STUDY

The Zamboni Bank & Trust Company is conducting business in Berkshire County, Massachusetts, a unit banking state. The bank currently has assets of $386 million and liabilities of $346 million. In order to improve and increase the services to their accountholders and to maintain their competitive edge the bank has decided to implement an automatic teller system for their depositors.

Currently the bank is processing 162,000 checking and 90,000 savings accounts using a combination of manual procedures, accounting machines, and a small third-generation computer. It has been verified that approximately 98 percent of the bank's customers have a checking account and 50 percent have a savings account. On the average, each customer makes 6 deposits, 8 withdrawals (not including checks) and 2 transfers a month. The customers with checking accounts write, on average, 22 checks per month. The bank is anticipating a heavily used automatic teller function. In fact, each customer is expected to use this function 15 times per month, on average, for deposits, withdrawals, transfers, and account balance inquiries. The auto teller deposits and manual deposits will allow customers to deposit many "foreign" checks on one deposit slip. Each slip averages 8 foreign checks per deposit. The bank will have a total of 24 locations, including home office, branch offices, and auto tellers. One-half of 1 percent of checking transactions are expected to be overdrafts and the system should have the facility to create an installment loan entry if the customer has overdraft protection. If the customer does not have overdraft protection, the check creating the overdraft is returned for "insufficient funds" and the account is assessed a $10 penalty.

The new system should have the capability to perform at least the following functions:

1. Deposits may be in the form of cash or check. These will be received by mail, employer direct-deposit, at the teller window, or at the new automatic teller machine.

2. Deposits may be made to checking, savings, or a combination of both.

3. Withdrawals may be in the form of account holder checks or cash advances.

4. A transfer facility will be made available which should be bi-directional, that is, savings to checking or checking to savings. A transfer may not create a negative balance.

5. Mail processing will generate debit/credit memos for the appropriate account, based on the transaction type. Cash deposits will be posted on the day of deposit and check deposits will be posted to a credit suspense until cleared and then posted to the account on that day. Returned checks will be assessed a $10 penalty (this amount should be easy to update) against the account balance, but cannot make the account go negative. If a penalty is assessed against an account and causes a minus balance, the penalty amount will be carried to the next statement date. The check causing the overdraft will be mailed to the account holder with a copy of the debit memo and the notation "insufficient funds."

6. Employer direct deposit checks will be treated as "cash."

7. Withdrawals will be posted to the account on the day of receipt and may take two forms.

8. Cash advance at the teller machine or by check. The account balance will be reduced by the amount of the withdrawal. Account balances will not be allowed when the withdrawal would cause the account to have a negative balance, except when the account has overdraft protection, which would then create a debit memo affecting the Installment Loan Accounting System. When a check is returned for insufficient funds, a $10 penalty will be assessed. If the account shows a balance less than the amount of the check but also shows an uncollected amount (suspense) which together are greater than the amount of the check, the check will be returned, with the legend "uncollected funds" and no penalty will be assessed.

9. Account holders should be able to verify their account balances from either the teller window or from the automatic teller machines. Inquiry balances will reflect the current balances only and any historical or special inquiries would be handled by one of the bank's customer representatives using the most current daily journals.

10. Statements will be staggered throughout the month and will have all account activity since the date of last statement (inquiries excepted). Statements will be triggered by the account's anniversary date. That is, if the account was opened on May 12, statements would be printed on the twelfth day of every month. When the twelfth falls on a legal holiday or over the weekend, the statements will be printed with an as-of date of the next legal day of business. Cancelled checks, statements, and promotional material will be routed to the mail center for automated stuffing and distribution. The statement mailings at the mail center are not to be considered as part of the automatic teller system.

CUSTOMER STATEMENT

ZAMBONI BANK

John and Mary Customer
5 Main Street
Anywhere, MA 99999

Ending Date
Starting Date
Account Number

	Checking	Savings
Beginning balance	1137.96	2008.05
Deposits, payments, credits	1100.00	300.00
Checks, withdrawals, debits	1200.00	—0—
Interest paid	8.38	14.20
Monthly charges	3.96	1.00
Ending balance		

ACCOUNT ACTIVITY

Checking

ACTIVITY	LOCATION	DATE	AMOUNT
41	014	0209	192.13
•	•	•	
•	•	•	
•	•	•	
•	•	•	

Monthly charges 3.96
Interest 8.38

Savings

ACTIVITY	LOCATION	DATE	AMOUNT
21	003	0204	51.80
•	•	•	•
•	•	•	•
•	•	•	•
•	•	•	•

Monthly charges 1.00
Interest 14.20

CHECK ACTIVITY

CHECKNUM	DATE	AMOUNT
0173	0205	11.57
0175*	0205	6.15
•	•	•
•	•	•
•	•	•
•	•	•

CHECKNUM	DATE	AMOUNT
0203	0209	100.08
•	•	•
•	•	•
•	•	•
•	•	•

Total   1191.18

STATEMENTS

Depositor's account number
Depositor's name
Depositor's address
    Street
    City
    State
    Zip
Date last statement
Date this statement
Checking account data
    Beginning balance
    Deposits/payments and credits total
    Checks/withdrawals and debits total
    Interest paid
    Monthly charges
    Ending balance
Savings account data
    Beginning balance
    Deposits/payments and credits total
    Checks/withdrawals and debits total
    Interest paid
    Monthly charges
    Ending balance

Checking account activity
    Deposits/credits
        Deposit type
        Location of deposit
            Location description
            Location number
        Date of deposit
        Amount of deposit
    Withdrawals/debits
        Withdrawal type
        Location of withdrawal
            Location description
            Location number
        Date of withdrawal
        Amount of withdrawal
    Checks
        Check number
        Check date
        Check amount
    Monthly charges
    Interest this year

AUTOMATIC TELLER RECEIPT

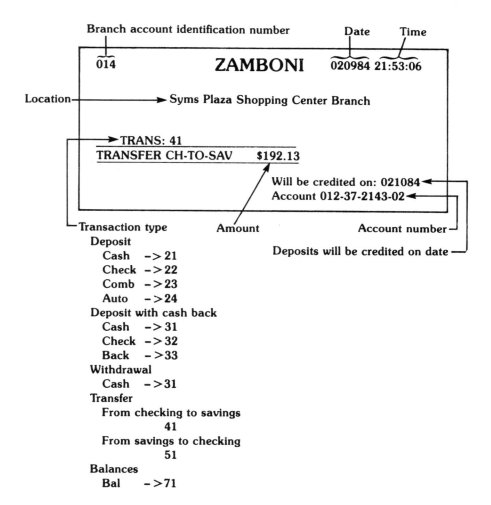

Branch account identification number   Date   Time

014   **ZAMBONI**   020984 21:53:06

Location ──────────► Syms Plaza Shopping Center Branch

────► TRANS: 41
TRANSFER CH-TO-SAV $192.13

Will be credited on: 021084 ◄────
Account 012-37-2143-02 ◄────

Transaction type   Amount   Account number ──┘
  Deposit   Deposits will be credited on date ──┘
    Cash   -> 21
    Check -> 22
    Comb   -> 23
    Auto   -> 24
  Deposit with cash back
    Cash   -> 31
    Check -> 32
    Back   -> 33
  Withdrawal
    Cash   -> 31
  Transfer
    From checking to savings
                41
    From savings to checking
                51
  Balances
    Bal   -> 71

CHECK

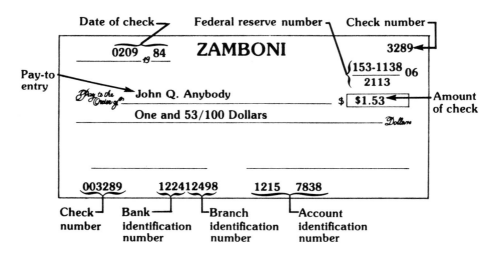

DEPOSIT SLIP

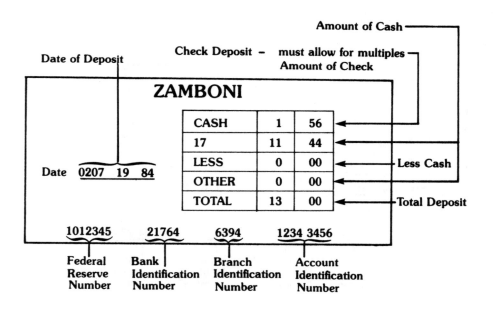

SAVINGS ACCOUNT DEPOSIT SLIP

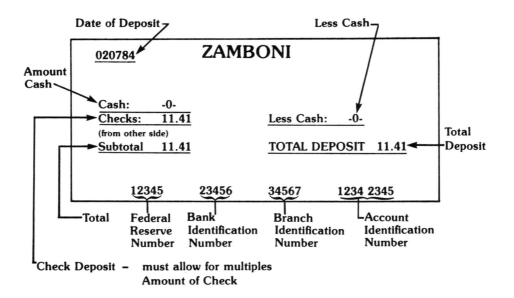

TRANSFER SLIP

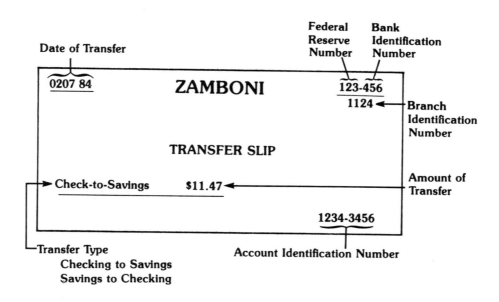

DEBIT/CREDIT MEMO

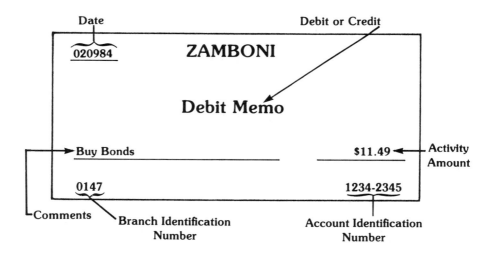

INTRODUCTION TO ORDER CASE STUDY

The following case, featuring the Nosnikrep Corporation, is one that expands upon the order type system introduced in the E-Z Chair Company example used throughout this book. The Nosnikrep case is slightly larger and gives a better sense of the internal data organization in such a system. As in the preceding bank case problem, a sample solution with all nine deliverables of the data analysis method is provided.

---

1. APPLICATION DESCRIPTION

This division of Nosnikrep Corporation is a manufacturer and wholesale distributor of paint and painting supplies. The company purchases components from various suppliers, assembles some components into products, and repackages others into new products. The organization then sells them to customers who have their own retail outlets.

Customer retailers are spread across the United States, which is categorized into twelve geographic regions. Each customer home office is classed by region, although the customer may have retail outlets in a number of different regions. Thus, the outlets may have a different region code than the home office.

Nosnikrep has one hundred sales men and women who sell on a full-time and part-time basis to customers. Full-time salespersons are paid by salary plus commission, and part timers are paid at a higher commission rate, but without a salary.

Each salesperson has a defined geographic territory, and the territories may overlap regional boundaries. No salesperson shares the same territory with another salesperson. The sales staff reports to a group of ten area managers. The managers are on a salary and commission basis.

Orders are placed through the sales staff by the customers' buyers in the retail outlets. There is an average of eight ordered products on each outlet's order, with an average unit quantity ordered of twelve for each product.

Sales are made only to customers with preestablished credit. Invoices are sent to the home offices of customers, and a copy of the invoice accompanies the goods shipped to the retail outlet by whom they were ordered. Incomplete orders may be shipped; in fact, there is an average of 1.2 shipments (and associated invoices) per order. Each of the 6,000 customers places an average of five orders per week, and there is an average of five retail outlets per customer. Back-order processing is completed so that there are never more than two shipments for any product on a customer's order (one extra shipment for each backorder).

A product consists of one or more components. Backordered product will cause a separate one line item invoice to be created. There are no products that are combined with other products to produce a third group of products. The inventory consists of "generic product" and "retail product." Generic products, such as "blue paint," may have several retail product codes based on container size. Generic products have from one to thirty retail product codes, with an average of five, associated with each. Nosnikrep currently manufactures 3,200 generic products using some 16,000 components. A generic product is composed of ten components on average. Resupply of components, complete customer billing, payables, and receivables processing have not been included in this exercise.

2. REPORTS AND DOCUMENTS

Picking Slip

Customer#	**Delivery Address**	**Date Required**
Retail Outlet#	**Date of Order**	**Order#**

Product#	**Generic Code**	**Quantity**	**Bin Location**

The following legend is used to resolve alias names on the above document, with names on the finalized third normal form entity list.

LEGEND:

Delivery Address	OUTLET-ADDRESS
Quantity	QTY-SHIPPED
Generic Code	GEN #

```
┌─────────────────────────────────────────────────────────────────┐
│ Invoice                                                           │
├─────────────────────────────────────────────────────────────────┤
│ Customer Name      Delivery Address        Date of Invoice        │
│                                                                   │
│ Customer#          Retail Outlet#          Date Required          │
│                                                                   │
│ Invoice#           Shipment#               Date of Order          │
│                                                                   │
│ Order#                                                            │
│                                                                   │
├─────────────────────────────────────────────────────────────────┤
│ Product#   Description          Qty. Ordered   Unit Price   Total │
│                                                                   │
│                                                                   │
│                                                                   │
│                                                                   │
│                                                        ─────────  │
│                              Total Amt. Due $ ─────────────       │
└─────────────────────────────────────────────────────────────────┘
```

The following legend is used to resolve alias names on the above document, with names on the finalized third normal form entity list.

LEGEND:

Delivery Address	OUTLET ADDRESS
Total	TOTAL-PRICE
Total Amt Due $	INVOICE-TOTAL-AMOUNT

Statement

Customer#	Customer Name	Address	Statement Date

Invoice#	Retail Outlet#	Date of Invoice	Invoice Amt.

Total Invoiced Amt. $ _____

The following legend is used to resolve alias names on the above document, with names on the finalized third normal form entity list.

LEGEND:

Address	CUST ADDRESS
Statement Date	CURRENT DATE from Computer
Total Invoiced Amt $	Sum of INVOICE-TOTAL-AMT

Manufacturing Process Worksheet

Product Code _____   Reorder Level _____

                                      Production Level _____

Description

_____

Generic Code _____   Mixing Cost $_____

                                      Manufacture Time_____hrs.
Description

_____

Comp.#	Qty.	Description	Unit Cost	Total

Component Cost $_____

Latest Total Cost $_____

The following legend is used to resolve alias names on the above document, with names on the finalized third normal form entity list.

LEGEND:

Product Code	PROD #
Generic Code	GEN #
Qty.	COMP QTY/GEN
Component Cost $	Sum of UNIT-COSTS
Latest Total Cost $	Sum of COMPONENT-COST and MIX - COST

Weekly Sales Analysis by Territory

Manager#	Territory Manager	Date
Territory#	Territory Name	
Salesman#	Salesman Name	Commission

Total Sales

The following legend is used to resolve alias names on the above document, with names on the finalized third normal form entity list.

LEGEND:

Territory Manager	MANAGER NAME
Date	Current Date from Computer
Total Sales	Sum of All INVOICE-TOTAL AMOUNTS

Monthly Sales Analysis by Region

Customer#	Customer Outlet Name	Total Sales

The following legend is used to resolve alias names on the above document, with names on the finalized third normal form entity list.

LEGEND:

Total Sales	Sum of All INVOICE-TOTAL- AMOUNTS by Outlet

3. BATCH AND ONLINE TRANSACTIONS TO BE PROCESSED

a. A picking slip is generated for the selection and dispatch of ordered goods. The amount shipped is also determined at this time.

b. When all retail product for an order has been selected and packed, an invoice and copy for those products is produced. Should the invoiced amount cause a customer's account balance to exceed his credit limit, the sales manager responsible for that customer must approve the shipment of goods (credit is exceeded on 5 percent of all orders). A running total of the salesperson's YTD commission amount is also calculated.

c. When back-ordered products are assembled, the outstanding orders for those products are met, with invoices generated as in the procedure from transaction *b* above.

d. When the quantity in stock of any product reaches a reorder level, instructions for its assembly are automatically generated. On average, each product is designated for an assembly run at least once a week. This transaction produces the manufacturing process work sheet.

e. Commission for salespeople and sales managers is calculated weekly on the basis of invoiced goods, and a weekly sales analysis by territory in manager territory order is produced, with one sheet for each territory under a manager.

f. Monthly statements to customers are produced, together with monthly sales reports by customers within region.

g. When the initial shipment of a part-shipped order is received at the customer outlet, in 10 percent of the cases there is an inquiry from the customer about the expected delivery date of the back-ordered product. This requires the examination of the expected resupply date of those components that make up the generic product and matching that information to a run date for the retail product. The invoice data is available to the inquiry operator. Determine if BO has already been shipped; if not, will the run date be met. Is the component on hand and, if so, is there enough. (The back order will have been shipped half the time.)

Sample Solution to Banking Case Study

STATEMENT FOLLOWING DATA COLLECTION

STATEMENT (**ACCOUNT NUMBER-ENDING DATE,** CUSTOMER NAME, CUSTOMER ADDRESS, PRIOR ENDING DATE, MONTHLY ANNIVERSARY DATE, ANNUAL INTEREST AMOUNT, *BEGINNING BALANCE, CREDITS, DEBITS, INTEREST, CHARGES, CURRENT BALANCE, ACCOUNT TYPE, ACTIVITY TYPE, AMOUNT, LOCATION NUMBER, LOCATION DESCRIPTION, CHECK NUMBER, CHECK DATE*)

FIRST NORMAL FORM

STATEMENT (**ACCOUNT NUMBER-ENDING DATE,** CUSTOMER NAME, CUSTOMER ADDRESS, PRIOR ENDING DATE, MONTHLY ANNIVERSARY DATE, ANNUAL INTEREST AMOUNT)

CUSTOMER-ACCOUNT (**ACCOUNT NUMBER-ENDING DATE-ACCOUNT TYPE,** BEGINNING BALANCE, CREDITS, DEBITS, INTEREST, CHARGES, CURRENT BALANCE)

ACTIVITY (**ACCOUNT NUMBER-ENDING DATE-ACCOUNT TYPE-ACTIVITY DATE-ACTIVITY TYPE,** AMOUNT, LOCATION NUMBER, LOCATION DESCRIPTION, CHECK NUMBER, CHECK DATE)

SECOND NORMAL FORM

STATEMENT (**ACCOUNT NUMBER-ENDING DATE,** PRIOR ENDING DATE, ANNUAL INTEREST AMOUNT)

CUSTOMER (**ACCOUNT NUMBER,** CUSTOMER NAME, CUSTOMER ADDRESS, MONTHLY ANNIVERSARY DATE)

CUSTOMER-ACCOUNT (**ACCOUNT NUMBER-ENDING DATE-ACCOUNT TYPE,** BEGINNING BALANCE, CREDITS, DEBITS, INTEREST, CHARGES, CURRENT BALANCE)

ACTIVITY (**ACCOUNT NUMBER-ENDING DATE-ACCOUNT TYPE-ACTIVITY DATE-ACTIVITY TYPE,** AMOUNT, LOCATION NUMBER, LOCATION DESCRIPTION, CHECK NUMBER, CHECK DATE)

NORMALIZED ENTITY LIST

STATEMENT (**ACCOUNT NUMBER-ENDING DATE,** PRIOR ENDING DATE, ANNUAL INTEREST AMOUNT)

CUSTOMER	(**ACCOUNT NUMBER,** CUSTOMER NAME, CUSTOMER ADDRESS, MONTHLY ANNIVERSARY DATE)
CUSTOMER-ACCOUNT	(**ACCOUNT NUMBER-ENDING DATE-ACCOUNT TYPE,** BEGINNING BALANCE, CREDITS, DEBITS, INTEREST, CHARGES, CURRENT BALANCE)
ACTIVITY	(**ACCOUNT NUMBER-ENDING DATE-ACCOUNT TYPE-ACTIVITY DATE-ACTIVITY TYPE,** AMOUNT, LOCATION NUMBER, CHECK NUMBER, CHECK DATE)
BRANCH-LOCATION	(**LOCATION NUMBER,** LOCATION DESCRIPTION)

FULLY NORMALIZED

CUSTOMER	(**ACCOUNT NUMBER,** CUSTOMER NAME, CUSTOMER ADDRESS, MONTHLY ANNIVERSARY DATE)
STATEMENT	(**ACCOUNT NUMBER-ENDING DATE,** PRIOR ENDING DATE, ANNUAL INTEREST AMOUNT)
CUSTOMER-ACCOUNT	(**ACCOUNT NUMBER-ENDING DATE-ACCOUNT TYPE,** BEGINNING BALANCE, CREDITS, DEBITS, INTEREST, CHARGES, CURRENT BALANCE)
ACTIVITY	(**ACCOUNT NUMBER-ENDING DATE-ACCOUNT TYPE-ACTIVITY DATE-ACTIVITY TYPE,** AMOUNT, LOCATION NUMBER, CHECK NUMBER, FEDERAL RESERVE NUMBER, BANK ID NUMBER, CASH RETURNED, CREDITED ON DATE, AUTOTELLER TRANSACTION TYPE, TIME)
BRANCH-LOCATION	(**LOCATION NUMBER,** LOCATION DESCRIPTION)
CHECK	(**ACCOUNT NUMBER-DATE-CHECK NUMBER,** PAY-TO ENTRY, AMOUNT, FEDERAL RESERVE NUMBER, BANK ID NUMBER, BANK LOCATION NUMBER)
FOREIGN-CHECK-DEPOSIT	(**ACCOUNT NUMBER-ENDING DATE-ACCOUNT TYPE-ACTIVITY DATE-ACTIVITY TYPE-DEPOSIT NUMBER,** AMOUNT DEPOSITED)
AUTOMATIC-TRANS.	(**ACCOUNT NUMBER-DATE-TIME,** LOCATION NUMBER, LOCATION DESCRIPTION, CREDITED-ON DATE, TRANSACTION TYPE)

VOLUME TABLE

ENTITY	VOLUME	FREQUENCY
CUSTOMER	180,000	GIVEN
STATEMENT	180,000	1/cust/month
CUSTOMER-ACCOUNT	252,000	(98% × 180,000) + (50% × 180,000)
ACTIVITY	2,880,000	(6 + 8 + 2) × 180,000
BRANCH-LOCATION	24	GIVEN
CHECK	3,960,000	22/cust/month
FOREIGN-CHECK-DEPOSIT	8,640,000	8/deposit/cust/month
AUTOMATIC TRANSACTIONS	900,000	5/cust/month

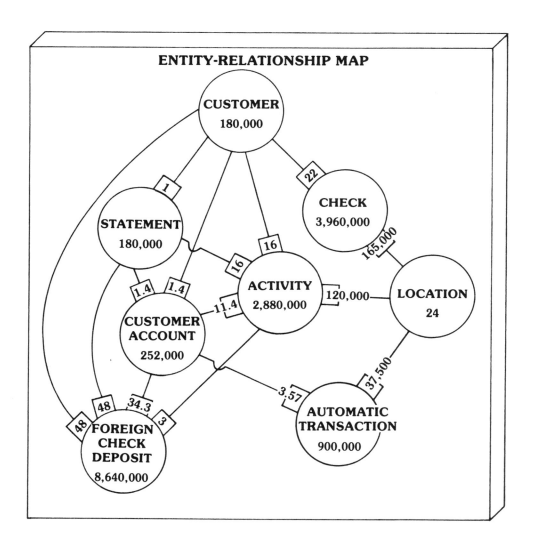

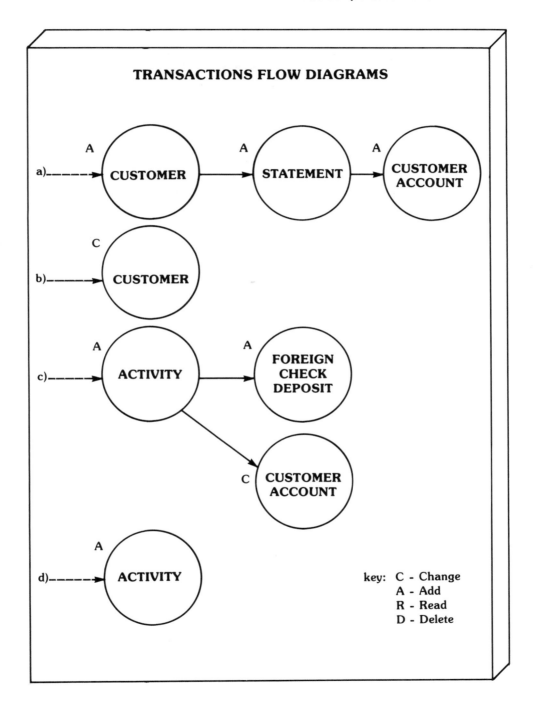

TRANSACTIONS FLOW DIAGRAMS

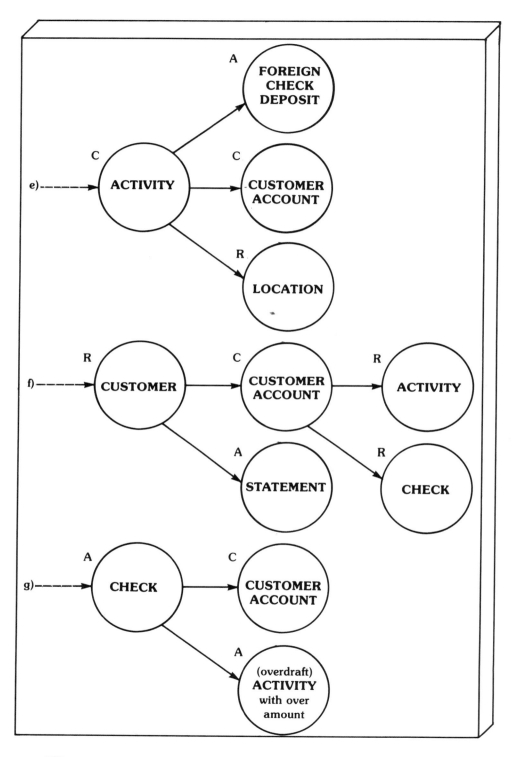

260

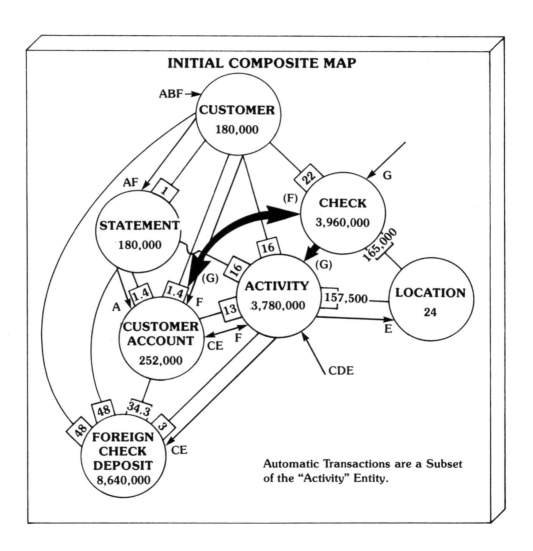

INITIAL COMPOSITE MAP

Automatic Transactions are a Subset
of the "Activity" Entity.

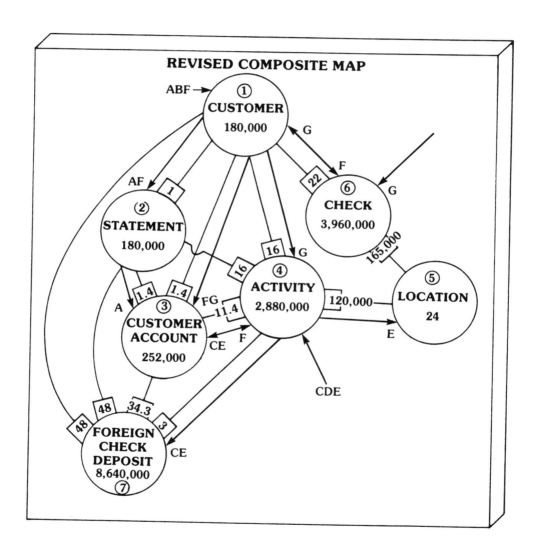

TRANSACTION LIST

**Peak
Load**

10/day	a. Add a customer to the customer file
100/day	b. Change a customer's master record
20,000/ hour	c. Accept and process over-the-counter activities, deposits, withdrawals and transfers
100k/day	d. Accept Autoteller activities
100k/day	e. Process Autoteller activities
180,000	f. Generate monthly customer statements
200k/day	g. Process checks on account (handle overdrafts)

Transaction Path Analysis Form

Transaction ID A **Description** Add a Customer **Peak Load** 10

Unique ID	From Entity	Num	To Entity	Access	Avg	Mult	During One Tran	Acc Wt	Adj. I/O	During Stress Period
			Path Description		Number Times Path Occurs		Number Times Path Used			
0-1	•	1	CUST	A	1	1	1	2	2	20
1-2	CUST	1	STATEMENT	A	1	1	1	2	2	20
2-3	STATE	1	CUST-ACCT	A	1.4	1/1.4	1	2	2	20
									6	60

Transaction Path Analysis Form

Transaction ID B **Description** Change a Customer's File **Peak Load** 100

Unique ID	From Entity	Num	To Entity	Access	Avg	Mult	During One Tran	Acc Wt	Adj. I/O	During Stress Period
0-1	•	1	CUST	C	1	1	1	3	3	300
									3	300

Transaction Path Analysis Form

Transaction ID C **Description** Teller Activities (except checks) **Peak Load** 20,000

Unique ID	From Entity	Num	To Entity	Access	Avg	Mult	During One Tran	Acc Wt	Adj. I/O	During Stress Period
0.4		1	ACTIVITY	A	1	1	1	2	2	40,000
4-7	ACT'TY	1	FOR CH DEP	A	34.3	3/34.3	3	2	6	120,000
4-3	ACT'TY	1	CUST-ACCT	C	1	1	1	3	3	60,000
									11	220,000

Transaction Path Analysis Form

Transaction ID D   **Description** Auto Teller Activities (except checks) **Peak Load** 100,000

Path Description					Number Times Path Occurs		Number Times Path Used			
Unique ID	From Entity	Num	To Entity	Access	Avg	Mult	During One Tran	Acc Wt	Adj. I/O	During Stress Period
0-4	•	1	ACTIVITY	A	1	1	1	2	2	200,000
									2	200,000

Transaction Path Analysis Form

Transaction ID E   **Description** Process Auto Tellers Activities   **Peak Load** 100,000

Path Description					Number Times Path Occurs		Number Times Path Used			
Unique ID	From Entity	Num	To Entity	Access	Avg	Mult	During One Tran	Acc Wt	Adj. I/O	During Stress Period
0-4	•	1	ACTIVITY	C	1	1	1	3	3	300,000
4-7	ACTTY	1	FOR CH DEP	A	34.3	3/34.3	3	2	6	600,000
4-3	ACTTY	1	CUST-ACCT	C	1	1	1	3	3	300,000
4-5	ACTTY	1	LOCATION	R	1	1	1	1	1	100,000
									13	1,300,000

Transaction Path Analysis Form

Transaction ID F   **Description** Gen Monthly Statements   **Peak Load** 180,000

Path Description					Number Times Path Occurs		Number Times Path Used			
Unique ID	From Entity	Num	To Entity	Access	Avg	Mult	During One Tran	Acc Wt	Adj. I/O	During Stress Period
0-1	•	1	CUSTOMER	R	1	1	1	1	1	180,000
1-2	CUST	1	STATEMENT	A	1	1	1	2	2	360,000
1-3	CUST	1	CUST-ACCT	C	1.4	1.4/1.4	1.4	3	4.2	776,000
1-6	CUST	1	CHECK	R	22	1	22	1	22	3,960,000
3-4	CUST-ACT	1.4	ACTIVITY	R	11.4	1	11.4	1	11.4	2,052,000
									40.6	7,328,000

Transaction Path Analysis Form

Transaction ID G   **Description** Process Checks   **Peak Load**   200,000

Path Description					Number Times Path Occurs		Number Times Path Used			
Unique ID	From Entity	Num	To Entity	Access	Avg	Mult	During One Tran	Acc Wt	Adj. I/O	During Stress Period
0-6	•	1	CHECK	A	1	1	1	2	2	400K
6-1	CHECK	1	CUSTOMER	R	1	1	1	1	1	200K
0-3	CUST	1	CUST-AC CT	C	1.4	1/1.4	1	3	3	200K
1-4	CUST	1	ACTIVITY	A	16	(½%)	.08	2	.16	32K
									6.16	832K

Path-ID   **Path Use**

Tran ID	Stress Load	0-1	0-4	0-6	1-2	1-3	1-4	1-6	2-3	3-4	4-5	4-7	6-1	4-3	Per Tran	Stress Period
A	10	20			20				20						6	60
B	100	300													3	300
C	20K		40K									120K		60K	11	220K
D	100K		200K												2	200K
E	100K		300K								100K	600K		300K	13	1300K
F	180K	180K			360K	776K		3960K		2052K					40.6	7328K
G	200K			400K		200K	32K						200K			
Individual Path Totals		180,320	900,000	400,000	360,020	976,000	32,000	3,960,000	2,052,000	100,000	720,000	200,000	300,060			

Composite Transaction Path Load Matrix Form

267

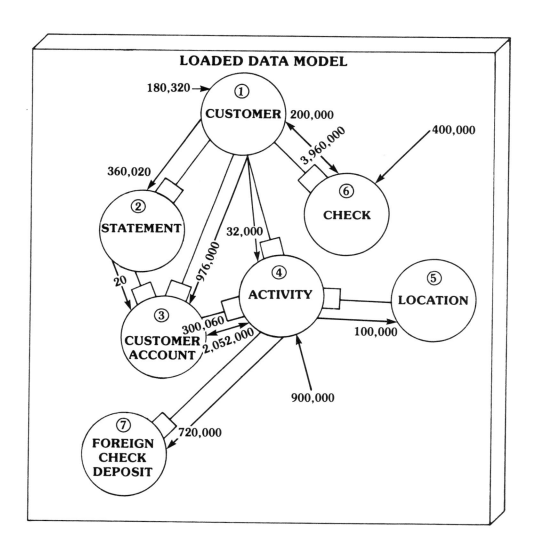

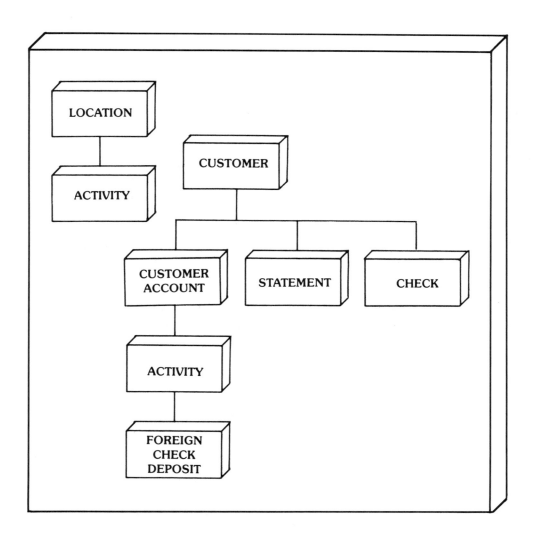

Sample Solution to Order Case Study

THIRD NORMAL FORM ENTITY LIST

CUSTOMER (*CUST#*, CUST. NAME, ADDRESS, REGION#, ACCOUNT BALANCE, CREDIT LIMIT)

OUTLET (*CUST#-OUTLET#*, NAME, ADDRESS, SALESPERSON#, REGION#)

ORDER (*ORDER#*, CUST#, OUTLET#, SALESPERSON#, DATE-OF-ORDER, DATE-REQUIRED)

INVOICE (*INVOICE#*, ORDER#, SHIPMENTS#, DATE-OF-INVOICE, INVOICE-TOTAL-AMOUNT, SHIP-DATE)

LINEITEM (*ORDER#-PROD#*, QTY-ORDERED, QTY BACK-ORDERED, QTY-SHIPPED, TOTAL PRICE)

RET. PRODUCT (*PROD#*, PRODUCT-DESCR, UNIT-PRICE, PROD-LEVEL, QTY-ON-HAND, GEN#, RE-ORDER LEVEL, NEXT-RUN-DATE, BIN LOCATION)

GEN. PRODUCT (*GEN#*, DESCRIPTION, COST, QTY-ON-HAND, RE-ORDER LEVEL, MIX-COST, MANF-TIME)

GEN. COMPONENT (*GEN#-COMP#*, COMP QTY PER GEN, COMP COST PER GEN)

COMPONENT (*COMP#*, COMP-DESCR, QTY-ON-HAND, RE-ORDER-LEVEL, EXPECTED-RESUPPLY-DATE, UNIT-COST)

SALESPERSON (*SALESPERSON#*, NAME, TERRITORY#, RETAINER, MONTHLY-QUOTA, COMMISSION-FACTOR, YTD-COMM-AMT)

TERRITORY (*TERRITORY#*, MANAGER#, SALESPERSON#, YTD-SALES, TERRITORY NAME)

MANAGER (*MANAGER#*, NAME, PHONE EXT., RETAINER, QUOTA, COMMISSION FACTOR)

VOLUME TABLE

ENTITY	VOLUME	FREQUENCY
CUSTOMER	6,000	stated
OUTLET	30,000	5/customer
ORDER	30,000	5/customer/wk
INVOICE	36,000	1.2/order
LINEITEM	240,000	8/order
RET PRODUCT	16,000	5/generic
GENERIC PRODUCT	3,200	stated
GENERIC COMPONENT	32,000	10/generic
COMPONENT	16,000	stated
SALESPERSON	100	stated
TERRITORY	100	1/salesperson
MANAGER	10	stated

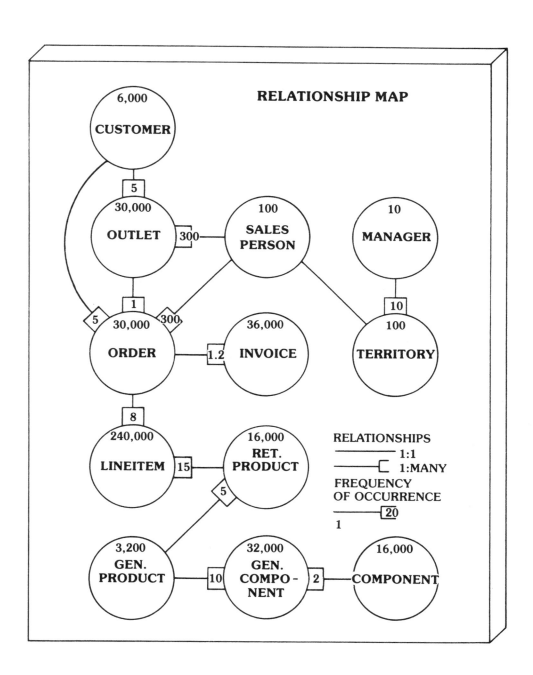

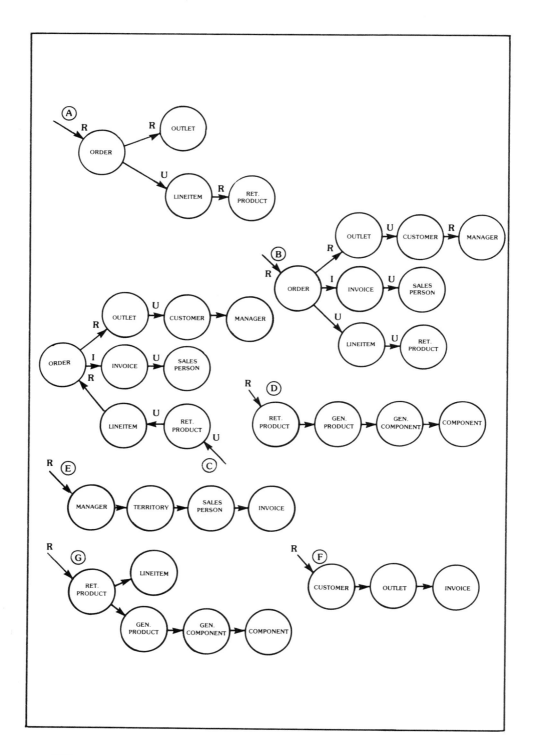

274

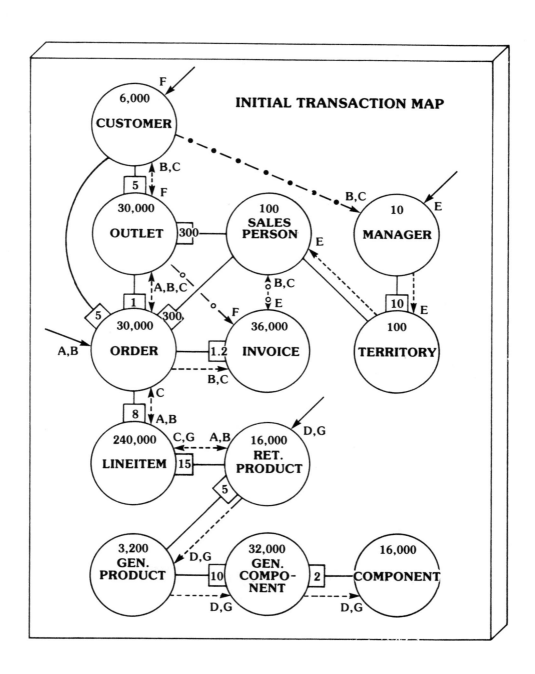

INITIAL TRANSACTION MAP

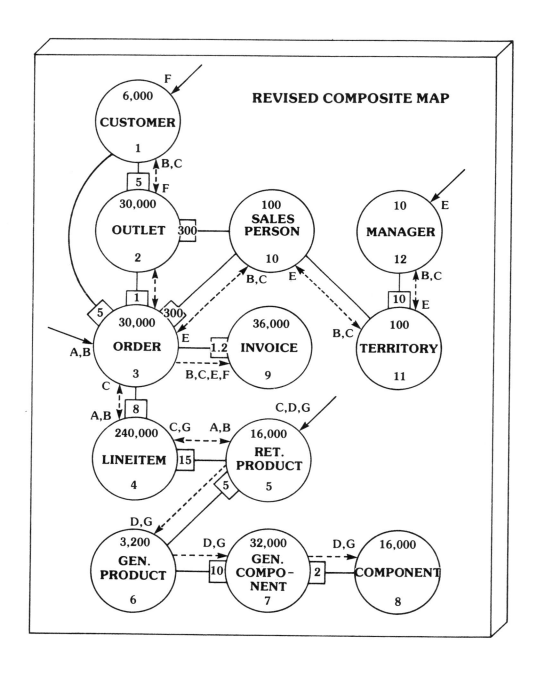

REVISED COMPOSITE MAP

Transaction Path Analysis Form

Transaction ID A   **Description** Picking Slip   **Peak Load** 1000

Unique ID	From Entity	Num	To Entity	Access	Avg	Mult	During One Tran	Acc Wt	Adj. I/O	During Stress Period
					Number Times Path Occurs		**Number Times Path Used**			
0 - 3	*	1	ORDER	R / G	1	1	1	1	1	1000
3 - 2	ORDER	1	OUTLET	R / G	1	1	1	1	1	1000
3 - 4	ORDER	1	LINE	U / R	8	8/8	8	3	24	24000
4 - 5	LINE	8	RET. PROD.	R / G	1	1	8	1	8	8000
									34	34000

Transaction Path Analysis Form

Transaction ID B   **Description** 1st Invoice   **Peak Load** 1000

Unique ID	From Entity	Num	To Entity	Access	Avg	Mult	During One Tran	Acc Wt	Adj. I/O	During Stress Period
					Number Times Path Occurs		**Number Times Path Used**			
0 - 3	*	1	ORDER	R / G	1	1	1	1	1	1000
3 - 2	ORDER	1	OUTLET	R / G	1	1	1	1	1	1000
2 - 1	OUTLET	1	CUSTOMER	U / R	1	1	1	3	3	3000
3 - 9	ORDER	1	INVOICE	I / I	1.2	1/1.2	1	2	2	2000
3 - 10	ORDER	1	SALES	U / R	1	1	1	3	3	3000
3 - 4	ORDER	1	LINEITEM	U / R	8	8/8	8	3	24	24000
4 - 5	LINEITEM	8	RET. PROD.	U / R	1	1	8	3	24	24000
10 - 11	SALES	1	TERRITORY	R / G	1	.05/1	.05	1	.05	50
11 - 12	TERR.	.05	MANAGER	R / G	1	1	.05	1	.05	50
									58.1	58,100

Transaction Path Analysis Form

Transaction ID C   **Description** 2nd Invoice   **Peak Load** 200

Unique ID	From Entity	Num	To Entity	Access	Avg	Mult	During One Tran	Acc Wt	Adj. I/O	During Stress Period
	Path Description				Number Times Path Occurs		Number Times Path Used			
0 - 5	*	1	RET. PROD	U / R	1	1	1	3	3	600
5 - 4	RET.	1	LINEITEM	R / G	15	12/15	12	1	12	2400
5 - 4	RET.	1	LINEITEM	U / R	15	3/15	3	3	9	1800
4 - 3	LINE	15	ORDER	R / G	1	.2/1	3	1	3	600
				OR						or
4 - 3	LINE	3	ORDER	R / G	1	1/1	3	1	3	600
3 - 9	ORDER	3	INVOICE	I / I	1.2	1/1.2	3	2	6	1200
3 - 10	ORDER	3	SALES	U / R	1	1	3	3	9	1800
3 - 2	ORDER	3	OUTLET	R / G	1	1	3	1	3	600
2 - 1	OUTLET	3	CUSTOMER	U / R	1	1	3	3	9	1800
10 - 11	SALES	3	TERRITORY	R / G	1	.05/1	.15	1	.15	30
11 - 12	TERR	.15	MANAGER	R / G	1	1	.15	1	.15	30
									54.3	10,860

Transaction Path Analysis Form

Transaction ID D   **Description** Mfg. Process Worksheet   **Peak Load** 250

Path Description					Number Times Path Occurs		Number Times Path Used			
Unique ID	From Entity	Num	To Entity	Access	Avg	Mult	During One Tran	Acc Wt	Adj. I/O	During Stress Period
0 - 5	•	1	RET. PROD.	R / G	1	1	1	1	1	250
5 - 6	RET. PROD.	1	GEN. PROD.	R / G	1	1	1	1	1	250
6 - 7	GEN. PROD.	1	GEN-COMP	R / G	10	10/10	10	1	10	2500
7 - 8	GEN-COMP	10	COMP.	R / G	1	1	10	1	10	2500
									22	5500

Transaction Path Analysis Form

Transaction ID E   **Description** Weekly Sales by Terr in Mgr Order   **Peak Load** 10

Path Description					Number Times Path Occurs		Number Times Path Used			
Unique ID	From Entity	Num	To Entity	Access	Avg	Mult	During One Tran	Acc Wt	Adj. I/O	During Stress Period
0 - 12	•	1	MANAGER	R / G	1	1	1	1	1	10
12 - 11	MANAGER	1	TERRITORY	R / G	10	10/10	10	1	10	100
11 - 10	TERR.	10	SALES	R / G	1	1	10	1	10	100
10 - 3	SALES	10	ORDER	R / G	300	300/300	3000	1	3000	30,000
3 - 9	ORDER	3000	INVOICE	R / G	1.2	1.2/1.2	3600	1	3600	36,000
									6621	66,210

Transaction Path Analysis Form

Transaction ID F
Description Monthly Sales Reports by Customer & Customer's Monthly Statements   **Peak Load** 100

	Path Description				Number Times Path Occurs		Number Times Path Used			
Unique ID	From Entity	Num	To Entity	Access	Avg	Mult	During One Tran	Acc Wt	Adj. I/O	During Stress Period
0 - 1	•	1	CUSTOMER	R / G	1	1	1	1	1	100
1 - 2	CUSTOMER	1	OUTLET	R / G	5	5/5	5	1	5	500
2 - 3	OUTLET	5	ORDER	R / G	1	1	5	1	5	500
3 - 9	ORDER	5	INVOICE	R / G	1.2	1.2/1.2	6	1	6	600
									17	1700

Transaction Path Analysis Form

Transaction ID G   **Description** Telephone Inquiry   **Peak Load** 50

	Path Description				Number Times Path Occurs		Number Times Path Used			
Unique ID	From Entity	Num	To Entity	Access	Avg	Mult	During One Tran	Acc Wt	Adj. I/O	During Stress Period
0 - 5	•	J	RET. PROD.	R / G	1	1	1	1	1	50
5 - 4	RET. PROD.	1	LINEITEM	R / G	15	8/15	8	1	8	400
5 - 6	RET. PROD.	1		R / G	1	.5/1	.5	1	.5	25
6 - 7	GEN. PROD.	.5		R / G	10	10/10	5	1	5	250
7 - 8	GEN. COMP.	5		R / G	1	1	5	1	5	250
									19.5	975

COMPOSITE TRANSACTION PATH LOAD MATRIX FORM

TRAN ID	STRESS LOAD	0/3	3/4	4/5	3/2	2/1	3/9	3/10	10/11	11/12	0/5	5/4	4/3	5/6	6/7	7/8	0/12	12/11	11/10	10/3	0/1	1/2	2/3	PER TRAN	STRESS PERIOD
A	1000	1000	24000	8000	1000																			34	34000
B	1000	1000	24000	24000	1000	1800	1000	1000	50	50														58.1	58100
C	200				600	1800	1200	1800	30	30	600	4200	600											54.3	10860
D	250										250			250	2500	2500								22	5500
E	10						36000										10	100	100	30000				6621	66210
F	100						600					400		25	250	250					100	500	500	17	1700
G	50										50													19.5	975
INDIVIDUAL PATH TOTALS		2000	48000	32000	2600	2800	39400	2800	80	80	900	4600	600	275	2750	2750	10	100	100	30000	100	500	500		

281

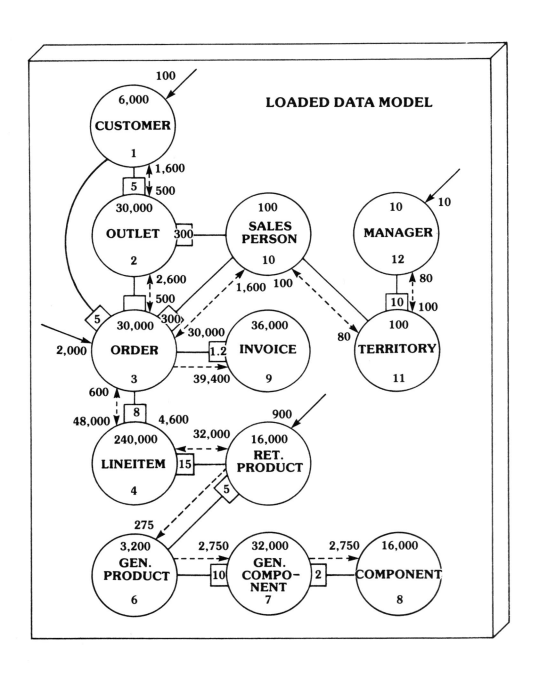

LOADED DATA MODEL

Bibliography

Atre, S. *Data Base, Structured Techniques for Design, Performance and Management.* New York: J. Wiley and Sons, 1980.

———. *Data Base Management Systems for the Eighties.* Wellesley, Mass.: QED Information Sciences, Inc., 1983.

Bachman, C. W. "The Evolution of Storage Structure." *Communications of the ACM.* (July 1972): 628–634.

BIS Applied Systems, Ltd. *Data Base Techniques: Software Selection and Systems Development.* Wellesley, Mass.: QED Information Sciences, Inc., 1980.

Carrol, J.M. *Data Base and Computer Security.* Wellesley, Mass.: QED Information Sciences, Inc., Data Base Management Monograph Series, No. 4, 1976.

Chen, P. *The Entity-Relationship Approach to Logical Data Base Design,* Data Base Management Monograph Series, No. 6 Wellesley, Mass.: QED Information Sciences, Inc., 1977.

Clark, J., and J.A. Hoffer. *Physical Data Base Record Design,* Data Base Management Monograph Series, No. 7. Wellesley, Mass.: QED Information Sciences, Inc.,1979.

CODASYL *Data Base Task Group April '71 Report,* New York: Association for Computing Machinery, ACM, 1977.

———. *Data Description Language Committee Journal of Development,* January 1978. Secretary of the Canadian Government. 1980.

Codd, E.F. "Normalized Data Base Structure: A Brief Tutorial, "*Proceedings of ACM Sigfidet Workshop on Data Description and Access, 1971.*

Cohen, L.J. *Data Base Management Systems: A Critical and Comparative Analysis.* Wellesley, Mass.: QED Information Sciences, Inc., 1979.

———. *Creating and Planning the Corporate Data Base System Project.* Wellesley, Mass.: QED Information Sciences, Inc., 1982.

Cramer, H. *The Elements of Probability Theory and Some of Its Applications.* New York: J. Wiley, 1958.

Curtice, R.M. *Access Mechanisms and Data Structure Support in Data Base Management Systems.* Data Base Management Monograph Series, No. 1, Wellesley, Mass.: QED Information Sciences, Inc., 1975.

———. *Planning for Data Base Systems.* Data Base Management Monograph Series, No. 2. Wellesley, Mass.: QED Information Sciences, Inc., 1978.

Date, C.J. *Introduction to Data Base Management Systems,* 3rd ed., Reading, Mass.: Addison-Wesley, 1976.

DeMarco, T. *Structured Analysis and System Specification.* New York: Yourdan, Inc., 1978–79.

Drucker, P.F. *Management, Task, Responsibilities, Practices.* New York: Harper & Row, 1974.

Finkelstein, C. *Information System for Users and Management.* Infocom Australia. 1980.

———. *Data Analysis and Design of Information Systems.* Infocom Australia. 1980.

Gane, C., and Sarson, T. *Structured Systems Analysis: Tools and Techniques.* New York: IST Data Books, 1977.

Gillenson, M.L. "Back to Data Bas(e)ics," *Computerworld,* December 8, 1980, Indepth.

Gregory, L.A. *A Study of Data Base Processor Technology,* Data Base Management Monograph Series, No. 8. Wellesley, Mass.: QED Information Sciences, Inc., 1979.

Guide International. "Data Base Administration Project: The Data Base Administrator." November 1972.

Hoffer, J.A. *Methods for Primary and Secondary Key Selection,* Data Base Management Monograph Series, No. 9. Wellesley, Mass.: QED Information Sciences, Inc., 1980.

Hutt, A.T.F. *A Relational Data Base Management System.* New York: John Wiley and Sons, 1979.

IBM. *Query-By-Example Terminal Users Guide.* SH20-2078-0. IBM Corporation, 1978.

Janko, J.J. "Relational Design of an IMS Data Base." *On-line 1977* Data Base—London, On-line Conference Ltd. 1977.

Jones, P.E. *Data Base Design Methodology: A Logical Framework.* Data Base Monograph Series, No. 3. Wellesley, Mass.: QED Information Sciences, Inc., 1976.

Katzen, H. *Computer Data Management and Data Base Technology.* New York: Van Nostrand Rheinhold, 1975.

King, P.J.H. "Information Analysis for Data Base Design," *On-line 1977,* Data Base—London, On-line Conferences Ltd., 1977.

Lefkovits, H.C. *Data Dictionary Systems.* Wellesley, Mass.: QED Information Sciences, Inc., 1977.

———. *Information Resource/Data Dictionary Systems.* Wellesley, Mass.: QED Information Sciences, Inc., 1983.

Lewis, T.G., and M.Z. Smith *Applying Data Structures.* Boston: Houghton Mifflin, 1976.

Mair, W.G., D.R. Wood, and K.W. Davis. *Computer Control and Audit,* 2nd ed. Wellesley, Mass.: QED Information Sciences, Inc., 1978.

Martin, J.L. *Computer Data Base Organization.* Englewood Cliffs, N.J.: Prentice-Hall, 1975.

McElreath, T.J. *IMS Design of Implementation Techniques.* Wellesley, Mass.: QED Information Sciences, Inc., 1979.

Nolan, R.L. "Computer Data Bases: The Future Is Now." *Harvard Business Review* September 1973.

———."Managing the Crisis in Data Processing." *Harvard Business Review* March-April 1979).

Palmer, I.R. *Data Base Systems: A Practical Reference.* Wellesley, Mass.: QED Information Sciences, Inc., 1975.

Perron, R. *Design Guide for CODASYL Data Base Management Systems.* Wellesley, Mass.: QED Information Sciences, Inc., 1980.

———. *IDMS. Concepts and Facilities.* Wellesley: Cullinane Corporation, 1977.

Perry, W.E. *Control in a Data Base Environment.* Data Base Management Monograph Series, No. 10, Wellesley, Mass.: QED Information Sciences, Inc., 1980.

Ross, R.G. *An Assessment of Current Data Base Trends.* Data Base Management Monograph Series, No. 5, Wellesley, Mass.: QED Information Sciences, Inc., 1977.

Rubin, M.L. *Documentation Standards and Procedures for On-line Systems.* New York: Van Nostrand Rheinhold, 1979.

Waghorn, W.J. "Data Base," *On-line 1977,* Data Base—London, On-line Conferences Ltd., 1977.

Zloof, M.M. *"Query-By-Example: A Data Base Language." IBM Systems Journal* 16, no. 4 (1977): 324–343.